P9-AOZ-487

*José Vasconcelos and
the Writing of the
Mexican Revolution*

Twayne's Hispanic Americas Series

JOSÉ VASCONCELOS
CORBIS/Bettmann

José Vasconcelos and the Writing of the Mexican Revolution

Luis A. Marentes

University of Massachusetts Amherst

Twayne Publishers
New York

Twayne's Hispanic Americas Series

José Vasconcelos and the Writing of the Mexican Revolution
Luis A. Marentes

Copyright © 2000 by Twayne Publishers

All rights reserved. No part of this book may be reproduced or transmitted in any form or by any means, electronic or mechanical, including photocopying, recording, or by any information storage and retrieval system, without permission in writing from the Publisher.

Twayne Publishers
1633 Broadway
New York, NY 10019

Library of Congress Cataloging-in-Publication Data

Marentes, Luis A.
  José Vasconcelos and the writing of the Mexican Revolution / Luis A. Marentes.
      p. cm. — (Twayne's Hispanic Americas series)
  Includes bibliographical references and index.
  ISBN 0-8057-1646-7 (alk. paper)
    1. Vasconcelos, José, 1881–1959. 2. Mexico—History—Revolution, 1910–1920.
3. Mexico—History—1910–1946. 4. Statesmen—Mexico—Biography. 5. Authors,
Mexican—20th century—Biography. I. Title. II. Series.

F1234.V3 M37 2000
972.08′16—dc21   00-042601

This paper meets the requirements of ANSI/NISO Z3948-1992 (Permanence of Paper).

10 9 8 7 6 5 4 3 2 1

Printed in the United States of America

In memory of my brother, Francisco Juan Marentes Dávila (1966–1989)

"La revolución es una desvergüenza"
—Marta Portal

and

Dedicated to all my teachers

Contents

Acknowledgments

I would like to thank those who in one way or another shared with me in the effort to understand the figure of Vasconcelos and his legacy. They are among my friends, teachers, colleagues, students, relatives, and acquaintances who have discussed with me, challenged and questioned me, shared their experience, or read my drafts. Among them, I would like to particularly highlight my dear friend Pedro Bustos Aguilar. This book and I owe much to him. *Un abrazo, Pedro, gracias.* It was he who first encouraged me to look at José Vasconcelos. The others include Hosam Aboul Ela, Rita Cano Alcalá, Luis Avilés, Pedro Barreda, Katherine Bliss, Francisco Borge, Ana Bugallo, Manuel Callahan, Emmanuel Carballo, Guadalupe Cedillos, Sheila Contreras, Nora Cummane, Juliana de Zavalía, Enrique Fierro, Ana María González, Barbara Harlow, Salah Hassan, Haideh Jalali, Rachel Jennings, Doug Kellner, Héctor Lazcano, Angel Loureiro, Jorge Marentes, Glenn Martínez, Raquel Medina, Louis Mendoza, Sidney Monas, Maureen Moynagh, Isolda Ortega Bustamante, Kamala Platt, Emma Rivera, Ignacio Rodeño, Luis Sáenz de Viguera, Farzin Sarabi-Kia, Nina Scott, S. Shankar, Mercedes Soberón, Ilán Stavans, Susana Tablada, Alec Tahmassebi, Arshak Tahmassebi, Alfonso Taracena, Mansour Taradji, Juan Tazón, José Ignacio Vasconcelos, George Yúdice, and Juan Zamora.

I thank my parents and sisters, Luis Jaime, Elena, Rosa Luisa, and Elena Amparo, for the love and support they have given me throughout my life. I also thank my companion, Negar Taradji, for sharing her life with me, for listening and challenging, questioning and suggesting. She and our daughter, Iliana Katayoun, have had great patience as I complete this project.

I would also like to thank the University of Massachusetts Amherst for giving me a Faculty Research Grant that allowed me to spend the summer of 1995 in Austin, Texas, and Mexico City to conclude my research. I am indebted to the personnel of the Benson Latin American Collection in Austin, as well as to the personnel of the Biblioteca Nacional, the Archivo Histórico de la Secretaría de Educación Pública, and the Archivo General de la Nación in Mexico City, for all their help in locating documents. Finally, I would like to thank my editors—Jennifer Farthing and Michelle Kovacs—at Twayne Publishers, copyeditor Sarah Brown, and the staff at Impressions Book and Journal Services for their professionalism, advice, and support throughout the publication process.

Chronology

1882   José Vasconcelos born in Oaxaca, the capital of the southwestern Mexican state of the same name.

1885?   Family moves to the frontier outpost of Sásabe, Sonora, at the border with Arizona.

1888   Family moves to the border town of Piedras Negras, Coahuila. Vasconcelos attends school in neighboring Eagle Pass, Texas.

1895   Family moves to Mexico City and then to Toluca, Estado de México, where Vasconcelos attends school.

1896   Family moves to the southeastern state of Campeche, where Vasconcelos finishes junior high school.

1899   Family returns to Piedras Negras, but Vasconcelos moves to Mexico City to attend high school.

1901   Begins law school in Mexico City.

1905   Graduates from law school with thesis *Teoría dinámica del derecho* (Dynamic theory of law).

1909   Founding member of the *Ateneo de la Juventud.*

1910   Joins Francisco I. Madero's presidential campaign against Porfirio Díaz. Forced into a brief exile in the United States, from where he supports Madero's movement.

1911   Returns to Mexico after Madero's triumph and goes back to his private law practice.

1913   Leaves Mexico after assassination of President Madero and joins the Constitutionalist efforts to overthrow Victoriano Huerta.

1914   Serves as minister of education of the short-lived Government of the Convention, led by Eulalio Gutiérrez.

1915   Again leaves Mexico after the defeat of the Government of the Convention by the forces loyal to Venustiano Carranza.

1920   Returns to Mexico after the overthrow and assassination of Carranza. Appointed president of the National University by provisional President Adolfo de la Huerta.

1921   Gains governmental approval for the creation of a federal ministry of education (*Secretaría de Educación Pública*; SEP) and is appointed minister of education by President Alvaro Obregón.

1924   Resigns as minister of education and leaves Mexico after unsuccessfully running for the governorship of his native state of Oaxaca.

1925   Publishes his racial theory, *La raza cósmica*.

1926   Publishes *Indología*, elaborating the ideas set forth in *La raza cósmica*.

1928   President-elect Obregón is assassinated in Mexico City and Vasconcelos returns to Mexico as candidate for the presidency.

1929   After an electoral defeat tainted by many irregularities, Vasconcelos once again leaves Mexico.

1935   Publishes the first volume of his memoirs, *Ulises criollo*, covering the period spanning from his birth to the assassination of Madero. Also publishes his book about education, *De Robinsón a Odiseo*.

1936   Publishes the second volume of his memoirs, *La tormenta*, covering the period spanning from Madero's assassination to Carranza's assassination.

1937   Publishes his controversial *Breve historia de México*.

1938   Publishes the third volume of his memoirs, *El desastre*, covering his tenure as minister of education and his exile after his resignation. Returns to Mexico.

1939   Publishes the fourth volume of his memoirs, *El proconsulado*, covering his presidential campaign and the following exile.

1948   First Mexican edition of *La raza cósmica*, which includes a new preface.

1959   Dies and is buried with honors in Mexico City.

Chapter One

Introduction: The Many Faces of José Vasconcelos

The life and legacy of José Vasconcelos is one of contrasts and transitions. He is best known as the first minister of education of Mexico's postrevolutionary regime in the early 1920s, a position that in itself represents these elements. Vasconcelos's ministry was meant to bring a cultural transition in a nation full of contrasts. Prior to the outbreak of the revolution in 1910, Mexico had lived through three decades of uninterrupted rule by Porfirio Díaz. Díaz's policies—summarized in the positivist slogan of "order and progress"—had brought about an impressive modernization with relative stability to a country that had lived through more than half a century of violence and destruction as rival factions struggled to obtain and maintain power following the nation's independence from Spain in 1821. Such "order and progress," however, carried a heavy social cost, as the great accumulation of wealth and modern comforts enjoyed by the ruling elite and their foreign associates was not shared by the majority of the population. Quite on the contrary, the expansion of agribusiness, mining, and industry displaced many peasants and artisans, throwing them into utter poverty and landlessness, without recourse to legal redress of their plight.

In 1921, the year Vasconcelos was sworn in as minister of the newly established *Secretaría de Educación Pública,* or SEP (ministry of public education), the nation began a period of relative stability and institutionalization after two decades of bloody and disruptive civil war. It was in November 1910 that many rose in arms behind Francisco I. Madero's *Plan de San Luis* (signed 5 October 1910). The plan's original intentions were not to transform Mexican society in a radical fashion; its main goal was simply to depose Díaz, who had ruled Mexico with an iron fist for more than three decades. The plan saw his "tyranny" as Mexico's greatest problem, condemned what it saw as the country's latest electoral fraud

1

against Madero, and proposed the principle of nonreelectability of the president and vice president as the "Supreme law of the Republic." Madero's call to arms successfully unified thousands of Mexicans, joining together Madero supporters with others who, like the members of the *Partido Liberal Mexicano,* the *Zapatistas,* or the veterans of the strikes of Río Blanco and Cananea, were already mobilized. The *Maderista* uprising was short and effective. By May 1911 Díaz resigned and by 6 November of that year Madero was Mexico's legally constituted president.

The young Vasconcelos had started to make a name for himself in the years immediately prior to this violent transition of power, which marks but the first stage of what would become a long and convulsive civil war, ultimately named the Mexican Revolution. In 1910 he was a young lawyer interested in all sorts of intellectual pursuits. His 1905 law thesis *Teoría dinámica del derecho* (Dynamic theory of law) attempted to find a spiritual component in the law. His inquisitive intellect led him to join the *Ateneo de la Juventud.* Here, with other young intellectuals like Pedro Henríquez Ureña, Alfonso Reyes, Martín Luis Guzmán, and Diego Rivera, Vasconcelos studied the Greco-Latin classics and contemporary philosophy in search of a spiritual alternative for the excessively materialist and scientific positivism, the official ideology of the Díaz regime. Standard histories of Mexico and its revolution look at the *Ateneo* generation as a sort of precursor to the revolution. The young intellectuals' stance against official *científico* positivism marks a transition in their thinking, which had been formed in the official schools. Theirs was a spiritual and aesthetic quest for a value system beyond the pragmatic and crass materialism of the *científico* elite, which justified its privileged position on a social Darwinist belief in the survival of the fittest. This was an emergent generation of intellectuals who would shape official Mexican culture for the next few decades. Their quest for alternative dialogue led them to organize conferences. Particularly notable were those organized to coincide with Mexico's independence centenary in September 1910. In the midst of grand official celebrations with the attendance of many foreign dignitaries and the inauguration of new monuments, the *Ateneo de la Juventud* staged its own alternative intellectual debate.[1]

Vasconcelos's participation in this group reveals a couple of concerns that would remain with him for many years. First and foremost was his interest in a spiritual alternative to positivist materialism. During these years Vasconcelos not only studied the western classics but was also very interested in the teachings of Hinduism, Buddhism, and Theosophy, as he searched for an alternative spiritual explanation to the world and a model for an alternative lifestyle. His interest in these religions crystallized in the publication of his 1920 book *Estudios indostánicos*. Once minister of education, he encouraged a vegetarian diet and breathing exercises taken from his studies of eastern religions. This concern with a spiritual quest would mark, with different shades, his entire career. If at an early age he flirted with spiritualism as an alternative to the positivist materialist official dogma of the Porfirian regime, at a more mature age he would turn to Catholicism for spiritual support and as a marker of a Mexican—and Latin American—identity, which he perceived to be under attack by a North American intrusion in the form of Protestantism and Freemasonry. At another level, his participation in the *Ateneo de la Juventud* reveals Vasconcelos's commitment to a program of national redemption through culture. The lectures sponsored by this organization were not only intended for the *ateneístas* but for a broader public that should be given an alternative to the official school system. The idea of an institution of public service through education was further developed during the short-lived Madero regime, when the *Ateneo* created the *Universidad Popular* (popular university), offering an alternative education to the population of Mexico City. During this period Vasconcelos served as the *Ateneo's* president. It was here that he launched his career as an organizer of public education.

Shortly before the revolution's outbreak, Vasconcelos was a young and successful lawyer for Warner, Johnson and Galston, a firm of New York lawyers whose main tasks in Mexico consisted of "legalization [in Mexico] of purchase and sale agreements of land and mines completed in the United States; organization of corporations {*sociedades anónimas*}; writing of contracts; billings and a little litigation."[2] His work with North American companies was facilitated by his command of English and familiarity with the United States, which he gained attending elementary school in Eagle Pass, Texas. The young lawyer was quick to join Madero's presidential campaign against Díaz. As would be the case in the later stages of the revolution, his work was not that of an armed soldier at the front lines but rather that of an intellectual with multiple functions of diplomat, propagandist, and chronicler. He soon gained a prominent position within the campaign as editor of the Anti-reelectionist Party's weekly paper *El Antireeleccionista*. In his memoirs Vasconcelos claims to have coined Madero's campaign slogan "*Sufragio efectivo, no reelección*" (effective vote and no reelection), a slogan that remains in use to this date in all official documents of the federal government. In the early days, he was able to take advantage of his profession to advance the opposition candidate's campaign, using business trips as an opportunity to spread the *Maderista* cause throughout the republic (*Ulises criollo,* 582–87).

As Díaz realized Madero's popularity, the dictator began cracking down on his opponent's supporters, and Vasconcelos was forced to flee to New York. He was soon able to return to Mexico due to a general amnesty, but after the electoral fraud and Madero's call for a national uprising the young lawyer went into exile again, this time to San Antonio, Washington, D.C., and New Orleans. In the United States Vasconcelos was a *Maderista* spokesman for North American public opinion. During these exiles, one can see the beginning of a trend that would become characteristic of him. In the middle of the political turmoil that faced his country, the future minister of education was able to take advantage of his exile to visit the U.S. libraries and museums that he so admired. In this way, intellectual pursuits and political activism would always be entwined in his career. As a matter of fact, as one reads Vasconcelos's memoirs of the revolutionary period one finds him quite often pursuing his own personal interests—intellectual, romantic, or culinary —instead of engaging full time in the revolutionary struggle. In this regard, Vasconcelos's personal narratives of the Mexican Revolution are often reminiscent of those of his fellow *ateneísta* Martín Luis Guzmán, whose famous *El águila y la serpiente* I will address soon.

While Vasconcelos would become a prominent public official in the early 1920s, this was not the case during Madero's short tenure as president (6 November 1911 to 19 February 1913). During this period the young lawyer remained as an associate of the new president, but he did not hold public office. Instead he returned to his private law practice representing U.S. interests. His newly gained prestige made his job even more lucrative, and it was this possibility of a high income that, according to his memoirs, kept him away from public service (*Ulises criollo,* 652–58). His successful lawyering, however, would not last long, due to circumstances beyond his control and rather related to Madero's demise. The man who was able to organize a broad coalition to depose the Porfirian regime was unable to maintain the coalition once in power. Madero's program, as expressed in his 1910 *Plan de San Luis,* did not envision drastic revolutionary changes. Instead it called for respect for the vote, a prohibition of presidential reelection, and the return to the rule of law. Once in power Madero, perhaps too naively, attempted a national reconciliation without enacting major changes in the law, bureaucracies, or the military. As a result he faced opposition from many fronts. As he refused to overhaul the Porfirian laws and institutions, many *Porfiristas* remained in positions of power and made all efforts to undercut the new regime. His democratic policies permitted an unprecedented freedom of press and speech and the president was constantly besieged by attacks in the newspapers, still controlled by their prerevolutionary owners. Rather than treating the Porfirian armed forces as a defeated army, Madero took them as his own and insisted on the disarmament of those who had fought on his behalf. This greatly upset his supporters. He also lost the support of many allies by imposing, in the opinion of many, the candidacy of José María Pino Suárez for the vice presidency and forming a cabinet with many of his family and friends. Land reform, which had inspired the *Zapatistas* of Morelos to join forces with Madero, had to wait. The peasants who had taken over *hacendado* properties were required to return them to their owners and to pursue any land claims in the courts.

Emiliano Zapata and his peasant armies refused to give up their recently acquired arms and lands and on 28 November 1911 (three weeks after Madero became president) they proclaimed the *Plan de Ayala,* refusing to recognize his presidency. Madero directed troops to quell their rebellion. There were also a series of armed uprisings led by Porfirian forces, the most prominent of which was led by Félix Díaz, nephew of the deposed dictator. Things would come to a head in February 1913, when Félix Díaz and Bernardo Reyes led a coup in Mexico City. After 10 days of violence (known as the *Decena Trágica*), Madero was betrayed by Victoriano Huerta. Madero had appointed Huerta, one of the federal army's best generals, to defend the National Palace from the mutinous soldiers. Instead, Huerta pretended to fight while he secretly negotiated with the rebel camp through the mediation of U.S. Ambassador Henry Lane Wilson. Once he struck an appropriate deal, Huerta had Madero and Pino Suárez arrested and forced to sign their resignations. Through constitutional maneuvers Huerta was appointed president, and despite appeals by their families and friends, the president and vice president were killed under the guise of the *ley fuga,* a law that allowed the execution of prisoners who attempt to escape.

Vasconcelos's life, as that of many other Mexicans, would be drastically changed by the forces unleashed after the *Decena Trágica*. In a practical way, due to his personal association with the murdered president he was forced into exile once again. He departed Mexico City to join the Constitutionalist Army, which, under the leadership of Coahuila Gover-

nor Venustiano Carranza, did not recognize Huerta and challenged the
federal army in the north. After this point the young lawyer would
never return to his private legal practice. He was absorbed into the public arena, where he would remain for the rest of his life. In a more ideological way, Madero would become for this young intellectual an apostle
for democracy and a martyr, victim of the violent forces that, in his
opinion, had ruled Mexico since its independence. Fifteen years later,
when Vasconcelos launched his own candidacy for the presidency, he
would attempt to pick up the mantle of his martyred friend. Furthermore, the future presidential candidate would forever carry a deep
resentment against the United States, as he saw the intervention of U.S.
Ambassador Wilson as a crucial element in the overthrow and assassination of Madero.

Had Madero remained in power, chances are that today we would
not identify his presidential campaign and the insurrection he led as a
revolution. As I have already mentioned, he did not intend to bring
about drastic political, economic, or social changes; rather he proposed a
return to the rule of law. Furthermore, his insurrection was short lived,
with the resignation of Díaz coming shortly after one major battle in
which Díaz's forces were defeated. Madero's short presidency and the
brief armed struggle that led to it represent more of a change in political
leadership than a radical transformation of the nation. This was not the
case in the second stage of the Mexican Revolution. The major battles
and population displacements that are today identified with the Mexican Revolution began in full force in this second stage of the movement.
Vasconcelos's participation, as was the case during the *Maderista* stage,
was not necessarily that of an armed combatant but again that of an
intellectual engaging in propaganda, espionage, and political debate. To
this period of his life the Mexican intellectual dedicates *La tormenta* (The
storm), the second volume of his memoirs, which is in many ways reminiscent of *El águila y la serpiente* (The eagle and the snake), the novelized
memoirs of his contemporary Guzmán dedicated to the same period.

Both Vasconcelos's *La tormenta* and Guzmán's *El águila y la serpiente*
give us a peculiar perspective on the Mexican Revolution. Unlike the
peasant protagonists of Mariano Azuela's *Los de abajo* (The underdogs),
Vasconcelos's and Guzmán's associates are what can be labeled *los de
arriba* (those on top), as they dealt with the upper echelons of the revolutionary armies. The protagonists of Azuela's novel are poor and ignorant peasants who are slowly engulfed by historical circumstances as if
by a tornado. They begin fighting and continue in the armed struggle

out of inertia rather than political ideology or conviction. Vasconcelos, on the other hand, like Guzmán, enters the revolutionary movement with the clear conviction of fighting against injustice and evil. Furthermore, Azuela's characters leave their mark in history with weapons in hand, constantly killing and risking death, living in the fields and mountains, at times foraging for food or taking advantage of the loot of battle. Guzmán and Vasconcelos, while sometimes facing danger and physical need, spend more of their time at receptions, luxurious hotels, and social gatherings with foreign and national dignitaries, journalists, and businessmen. This was for Vasconcelos a time that combined convictions of civic duty with periods of self-indulgence and exploration in Mexico and the United States. Such a contradiction, experienced by many of the intellectuals who joined the revolutionary ranks, is cynically revealed in Gerardo Murillo's (Dr. Atl) short story, *"El hombre que se quedó empeñado"* (The man who remained pawned), which traces the adventures of a pair of Mexican "revolutionaries" in Paris, who in order to raise funds for a revolutionary journal decide to gamble in a casino. After winning much money for their cause they spend it entertaining women and continuing to gamble.

While both Guzmán and Vasconcelos appear to have joined the movement against Huerta's imposition in a sincere and committed fashion, their actual participation in the movement makes them uncomfortable and suspicious. Their original goals are lofty. Enraged by the ignominy of Huerta's coup and his assassination of Madero and Pino Suárez, they head north, where they know that an army is fighting to vindicate the rule of law. As in the case of the *Maderista* uprising, a broad coalition was formed with one unifying principle: the opposition to Huerta. However, as in the previous stage of the revolution, the different factions that joined forces had little more in common, and Huerta's resignation and exile in July 1914 brought factional differences to the fore. Now sides had to be taken within the opposition coalition in order to put forth a project of national reconstruction.

Up until that point Venustiano Carranza had functioned as *Primer Jefe* (first chief) of the Constitutionalist Army. His experience as senator and governor of the northern state of Coahuila gave him the perspective of a pragmatic nation-building statesman. His northern strongholds and the services of experienced brokers allowed him to keep his armies well supplied and to maintain a pragmatic practical dialogue with U.S. business and political leaders despite his sometimes extreme nationalist attitude. On the ground his two best generals were Pancho Villa and Alvaro

Obregón. The legendary Villa's efficient *División del Norte,* which won some of the revolution's crucial battles in Celaya and Zacatecas, was arguably the Constitutionalist Army's strongest contingent. Villa and Carranza, however, distrusted each other. They represented very different backgrounds and expectations for the revolution. Carranza, an elder statesman who had been part of the Porfirian elite, actually sabotaged Villa's march into Mexico City after Huerta's defeat, preferring to allow Obregón to occupy the capital first. Unlike Villa, whose life prior to the revolution was that of a muleteer, cattle rustler, and smuggler, Obregón was a middle-class farmer from the northern state of Sonora with an ideology and education much closer to that of the *Primer Jefe.*

Regarding class and educational background, both chroniclers of the revolution had much more in common with Carranza and Obregón than with Villa or Zapata. Actually, both men originally left Mexico City and headed to San Antonio, Texas, to join the army led by Carranza. However, close contact with the *Primer Jefe* proved disappointing to both. Guzmán depicts Carranza's inner circle as overly concerned with pomp and ceremony and full of adulation to the chief. His close associates appear distant from reality, seeing their struggle as an epic battle of Roman antiquity rather than a particularly Mexican conflict. Vasconcelos, for his part, depicts Carranza as an arrogant, personalist, and corrupt opportunist, attacking him whenever possible in his memoirs. Time and again Vasconcelos paints this man as a shrewd Machiavellian, willing to unleash the most brutal violence against his enemies and amassing in the process an illicit personal fortune. Several times in his memoirs he reminds his readers of the Mexican-coined term *carrancear,* referring to stealing.

Between 10 October and 13 November 1914 the leaders of the various revolutionary factions met in the city of Aguascalientes to reach a consensus now that the common enemy was defeated. Carranza, however, boycotted it. The Convention of Aguascalientes, despite Carranza's absence, created a new national government with General Eulalio Gutiérrez as its president. The lines were now divided, with the forces of the Convention on one side and Carranza's supporters on the other. Vasconcelos remained loyal to the Convention and received the post of minister of education for its government. Such a government, however, existed only on paper, as the nation still remained in chaos. Not only were there still battles raging between the forces of the Convention and the *Carrancistas* but there was great disunity within the group of people loyal to Gutiérrez. Particularly problematic was the tense relationship between the peasant and working-class soldiers and the middle-class urban ideologues and administrators. Villa particularly fascinated Guzmán and Vasconcelos with his military prowess, but they also saw in him a personalist, violent, and capricious leader capable of brutal violence at a whim. His populist policies were based on personal desire rather than the rule of law that these intellectuals purportedly defended. At times of war against a common enemy Villa's military abilities were indispensable for the movement, but his character could not be trusted. Guzmán's description of his troubling first encounter with the general poetically evokes this tension:

> We were escaping Victoriano Huerta, the traitor, the assassin, and were going . . . to fall on Pancho Villa, whose soul, rather than human was that of a jaguar: a jaguar momentarily domesticated for our work, or for what we believed to be our work; a jaguar whose back we carefully caressed, trembling because he could claw us.[3]

The class and cultural abyss that separated intellectuals like Guzmán and Vasconcelos from the peasant and working-class troops of Villa and Zapata is a recurring theme in the memoirs of both writers. Thus, Guzmán poignantly narrates his first encounter with Eufemio Zapata (Emiliano's brother) at the National Palace in December 1914 when the forces of the Convention occupied Mexico City. For the urban intellectual the great southern *caudillo*'s brother appeared as "a porter who shows a rental house." The peasant's incompatibility with the trappings of national power was evident to Guzmán even in his steps:

> There was something in the way his shoe touched the carpet, an incompatibility between carpet and shoe; in the way in which his hand leaned on the banister, an incompatibility between banister and hand. Each time he moved the foot, the foot was surprised by not stumbling on the underbrush; each time he elongated the hand, the hand searched in vain for the tree's bark or the edge in the brute stone. Just by looking at him, one could comprehend that everything that deserved to be around him was lacking, and that, for him, everything which now could be seen around him was too much. (Guzmán, 398–99)

A similarly elitist assessment of Eufemio Zapata is given by Vasconcelos, who in his memoirs remembers his first encounter with Zapata at the National Palace. The forces of the Convention had just taken over Mexico City and they had gathered in the building. Here, the minister of education found a group of *Zapatistas* gathered at a table with Eufemio Zapata at the head. He showed his respects to President Gutiérrez, "but immediately gave in and began asking for cognac."[4] The incompatibility between urban intellectuals and soldiers reached absurd extremes when people like Guzmán retarded and impeded the regular supply of *Zapatista* troops with weapons and trains out of mistrust, although these were supposed to be the soldiers of the Convention. Vasconcelos narrates in *La tormenta* an incident that, although materially less urgent, clearly reflects the differences between the two groups at the ideological level of protocol. He recalls organizing a banquet to receive the diplomatic corps at the National Palace on 1 January 1915. At a time of civil war, for the government of the Convention to hold a public event with the diplomatic corps meant a tacit recognition by the international community. Significantly, Vasconcelos appears extremely uncomfortable about mixing diplomats with Villa, Emiliano Zapata, and their armed escorts. Their arrival at the event appears as completely incongruous and embarrassing, despite the fact that these were the troops that guaranteed the government's existence. Ironically, while Vasconcelos wanted to separate himself from the revolutionary troops, he used the services of an ex-Porfirian consul, Mr. Tinoco, as chief of protocol for the organization of the event (*Tormenta*, 900–905). Such differences between ideologues and soldiers greatly hampered the Convention's government, which was not able to maintain a coalition and fight a war. President Gutiérrez and the forces of the Convention abandoned Mexico City less than a month after the diplomatic reception, leaving the ground open for an ultimate Constitutionalist victory. With Gutiérrez, Vasconcelos left the country for his third exile in the United States.

Vasconcelos's two-year participation in the second stage of the Mexican Revolution left indelible marks on his character and ideology. The years of fratricidal violence gave him a rather pessimistic attitude toward his countrymen, particularly the triumphant politicians. Mexico appears in his later writings as a country condemned to violence. It is what he identifies as the curse of Huitzilopochtli, the Aztec god of war who constantly demanded human sacrifices to quench his thirst for blood. Against this rapacious spirit, Vasconcelos would pose the spirit of Quetzalcóatl, the god of wisdom who left Mexico for a self-imposed exile after he was tempted to sin in a drunken stupor.[5] For Vasconcelos, as he later wrote, a revolution should be like a quick surgery that eliminates damaged tissue. Once the operation is completed, the body politic should return to its normal state and violence should terminate.[6] Such was Madero's program. A regrettable military uprising was necessary exclusively to eliminate the imposition of Díaz, but once the dictator was deposed new elections should be held and the nation should return to its legal status quo. This is not what Vasconcelos saw in this second stage of the revolution. Once Huerta was deposed, rather than resolving their differences in a parliamentary or electoral manner, the intransigent triumphant factions continued addressing their differences in the field of battle. For the rest of his life, the future minister of education would portray Mexican political life as a Manichaean struggle between blood-thirsty militarists, who due to their intellectual mediocrity could only rely on the force of arms, and peace-loving intellectuals, who, like himself, intended to solve the nation's problems through debate and ballots: the eternal conflict between Huitzilopochtli and Quetzalcóatl.

Another aspect of this period of armed struggle that would shape the consciousness of this Mexican intellectual for years to come is the regional origins of the triumphant faction: they were northerners, particularly from the border states of Coahuila and Sonora. Héctor Aguilar Camín, in his study *La frontera nómada,* shows the peculiar border/frontier circumstances that facilitated a victory of the northern faction led by Carranza and Obregón. The border, as Aguilar Camín shows, was a space where Mexican commercial brokers exchanged goods, customs, and ideas with the United States. At the time of a sustained war these brokers were well connected to exchange cattle, grains, or metals for weapons, uniforms, and other commodities desired by the Mexican soldiers. Guzmán eloquently remembers the border town of Nogales, where:

> Those from Nogales [Arizona] equipped us for life and death: they gave us the wine that was consumed in official parties of the Command Post in the same way that they gave us the steel or expansive bullets for our guns, all in exchange for printed little papers that we gave them as currency, and which then served them to take the remains of wealth that the Revolution would cheaply sell for imperative reasons and because it was *"científico* wealth." In this way, [we] revolutionaries returned from Yankee Nogales to Mexican Nogales with everything we needed to continue killing ourselves—and also to solace ourselves a little between combats. But at the same time, the cattle of the Sonoran pastures crossed the dividing line in one herd, a herd that never ended, to go and enrich, for a vile price—it was an uncontainable stream of gold—, the rich *live-stock brokers* of the Far West. The Yankee prohibition to export weapons and ammunition to Mexico—in the *pocho* jargon called *the weapons embargo*—did not diminish this drain of Mexican patrimony, rather it intensified it,

since the risks of contraband, by raising the price of our principal article, was reflected, by sympathy of the market, in the prices of the rest.[7]

Their southern counterparts who, like the *Zapatistas* of Morelos, were away from the borders, had to rely on scavenging weapons from defeated enemies. Beyond the more immediate exchange of weapons for commodities, northern revolutionary agents engaged in a sustained propaganda campaign through publications, speeches, and lobbying in the United States, gaining for their faction a crucial recognition and political support of the more powerful northern neighbor. In this way, the Constitutionalist agents were ultimately able to lift the weapons embargo against their side but maintain one against Villa. Such support, however, came at an important cost: the necessity to please the desires of the United States. For years to come, as an opposition politician Vasconcelos would accuse the triumphant faction of selling out the national interests to the United States.

Despite Vasconcelos's misgivings about the United States, it was there that he again spent most of the next five years in exile, except for a brief hiatus that he spent in Peru teaching English. He did not return to Mexico until 1920. Although a war of factions still continued, the Constitutionalist forces loyal to Carranza controlled most of the nation. In January 1917 a Constitutional Convention promulgated a new constitution and in May of that year Carranza was sworn in as president for the period of 1 December 1916 until 20 November 1920. The president's coalition, however, was fractured. This became evident when the question of Carranza's successor arose. Obregón, his most successful general, expected to play this role, but Carranza selected Ignacio Bonillas, Mexico's ambassador to the United States, for the task. Obregón, nevertheless, launched a presidential campaign, but Bonillas counted on official support. Faced with the impossibility of reaching the presidency through elections, a group of veterans of the revolution from Sonora, including Obregón, proclaimed the *Plan de Agua Prieta* in April and rebelled against the federal government. Carranza was forced to leave Mexico City, and he was assassinated on his way to Veracruz on 21 May 1920. Adolfo de la Huerta, one of the rebellion's leaders, was proclaimed provisional president, and on 5 September Obregón was elected president for the period of 1920 to 1924. It was during this uprising that Vasconcelos, who was living in California, was invited to return to Mexico by de la Huerta himself (*Tormenta*, 1197–98). Although in most of his writings Vasconcelos strongly opposes the use of military force for political purposes, he justifies this uprising by claiming that, like Madero, Obregón had attempted to reach the presidency through a democratic electoral campaign, and that it was not until an electoral fraud became evident that he resorted to the use of force (*Tormenta,* 1190).

With Vasconcelos's return to Mexico began what is considered by most to be the most significant period in his life. Upon his return he was appointed president of the National University by the provisional president. From this forum he successfully lobbied for the creation of a federal ministry of education, which he ultimately led. During his California exile, the future minister of education had participated in long discussions about developments in the newly formed Soviet Union, and he had been particularly impressed by the efforts of Anatolii Lunacharsky and Maxim Gorky to make cultural and educational development at a massive level an integral part of the revolutionary project (*Tormenta,* 1187). Vasconcelos attempted to reproduce this cultural and educational development. For the next three years he led the ministry of education in the building of schools and libraries. He sponsored the publication and distribution of journals and inexpensive editions of classic literary texts; the development of handicrafts, ballets, and orchestras; a volunteer-based literacy campaign; and the development of rural "cultural missions." He also made available many walls of ministry-owned buildings for the work of the Mexican muralists. (Chapter 4 of this study looks at this period of Vasconcelos's life in greater detail.) Political and policy disagreements with Obregón, however, led Vasconcelos to resign his post as minister of education in 1924. He then unsuccessfully ran for governor of his home state, Oaxaca. After his resignation and defeat he once again faced exile in the United States. During this exile he went on an extensive trip through Europe and the Middle East.

Five years later, violent political changes in Mexico concerning a presidential succession again brought Vasconcelos back to his homeland, this time as a candidate for the presidency in 1929. After Obregón's tenure, Obregón's close Sonoran associate, Plutarco Elías Calles, became president for the period of 1924 to 1928. While the 1917 Constitution forbade the reelection of the President—one of the main goals of the movement led by Madero—Calles managed to change the law, thus permitting the reelection of an individual who had stepped down for one presidential period. With the help of this legal change, Obregón was reelected for the 1928 to 1932 period. However, on 17 July 1928 the president-elect was assassinated in Mexico City. Faced with a power vacuum, Calles announced that he would not remain in office. Rather he called on all the revolutionary leaders to join forces for the creation of a new political party and to launch a candidate for the office. In such a way, he claimed, the nation would move away from the politics of strong men into the politics of institutions. The party that was formed, the *Partido Nacional Revolucionario,* or PNR (national revolutionary party), is the same party that has ruled Mexico ever since. (It has undergone two name changes and is now known as *Partido Revolucionario Institucional,* or PRI [revolutionary institutional party].) Vasconcelos returned from his California exile in November 1928 to run against the official party's candidate. (I address this electoral campaign in chapter 5.) Suffice it to say at this point that, despite a very popular and effective campaign, Vasconcelos was defeated by Pascual Ortiz Rubio, the PNR candidate, who counted on blatant government support, political repression, and outright electoral fraud. Once again, Vasconcelos was forced into exile.

The failed presidential campaign was a turning point in the life of Vasconcelos, who emerged from it a deeply bitter and disappointed man. As we will see later in this book, the presidential candidate expected an electoral fraud, but he also expected a massive popular uprising on his behalf once it became clear that such a fraud had been perpetrated. He was correct in his first prediction, but the uprising never took place. The announcement of the electoral results found him in the port city of Guaymas, Sonora, where government troops surrounded him, supposedly for his own personal protection. He soon headed for the United States and published his *Plan de Guaymas,* calling on the Mexican people to rebel. Yet, beyond a few isolated incidents, the Mexican people accepted the official results. Almost two decades of constant armed violence had apparently tired the Mexicans, and they were not ready to embark on this path one more time. The defeated candidate presented himself to the world as the Mexican president-elect, refusing to concede defeat, but, without popular support in his homeland, this was just a rhetorical gesture. Such apparent indifference in Mexico was interpreted by Vasconcelos as both a personal affront and a signal that the Mexican people were not ready for democratic institutions and thus were condemned to live under the despotic regime they deserved. At the same time, he was convinced that the fraud was facilitated by the interference of U.S. Ambassador Dwight W. Morrow, in an echo of Henry Lane Wilson's support of Huerta's coup 16 years earlier.

Beginning with the 1930s the writings and speeches of the man who had once represented the cultural institutions of the radical Mexican revolutionary regime became more and more conservative, even reactionary. If in the 1920s he had enthusiastically prophesied the emergence of a triumphant Mexican and Latin American "cosmic race," product of the *mestizaje* (miscegenation) of all the previously existing races, he now insisted on looking at the salvation of Mexico through its acceptance of its Hispanic heritage. Symptomatic of this perspective is the title he chose for the first volume of his memoirs: *Ulises criollo* (Creole Ulysses), first published in 1935. Particularly prominent in this heritage, for Vasconcelos, was the Catholic tradition. He saw with abhorrence the government's *indigenista*[8] and anticlerical policies that rejected the Mexican Hispanic and Catholic heritage in the name of an exalted Indian past. Such policies, in his opinion, could only serve the interests of the United States by dividing the Mexican nation in what he saw as a process of balkanization. Vasconcelos was particularly outraged by the official closing of Catholic schools as Protestants and Freemasons gained prominence within the ministry of education he had created. Beyond his outright hostility to the ruling regime, his extreme Hispanophile Catholic rhetoric put him at odds even with many intellectuals within the opposition, most of whom were formed within the Mexican Hispanophobic and anticlerical liberal tradition. More and more isolated, the self-proclaimed president-elect became more extreme in his rhetoric, blaming political violence and antidemocratic institutions in Mexico on what he called the country's Aztec heritage of human sacrifices and despotic rule. He concocted international conspiracies linking Jews, Protestants, Freemasons, Bolsheviks, and Wall Street bankers in an effort to rule the world, and expressed his admiration for the fascist regimes of Francisco Franco in Spain and Benito Mussolini in Italy. Such positions only isolated him more, as many of his critics simply dismissed him as a lunatic.

Vasconcelos remained in exile for almost a decade. On 21 September 1938 he returned to Mexico when his U.S. visa expired.[9] By the time of his return the regime of the Mexican Revolution was firmly entrenched and he no longer posed a political threat to it. He spent the last years of his life as an employee of the ministry he had once created, working as librarian in the México Library in Mexico City. From there he continued publishing on a regular basis. He still had a small but faithful group of supporters who continued meeting with him regularly and who published texts in his support. Nevertheless, the zenith of his career was long past, and those who did not have close links to him simply remembered him as that enthusiastic minister of education who created the *Se-*

cretaría de Educación Pública, had literacy campaigns, published inexpensive classics, and gave the ministry's walls to the muralists—now his political enemies. The presidential campaign and the reactionary rhetoric remained better forgotten.

Vasconcelos is a sort of schizophrenic character in the Mexican pantheon of heroes and intellectuals. He represents both extremes of the ideological divide. He is one of the fathers of Mexico's postrevolutionary official *mestizo* nationalism. The slogan he wrote for the National University, *"por mi raza hablará el espíritu"* (through my race the spirit shall speak), is used to this day on every single text coming out of that institution. His emphasis on the *raza* is to this day understood as an insistence on the *mestizo* nature of the national character. *Mestiza* is the aesthetic created by the muralists: Diego Rivera, David Alfaro Siqueiros, José Clemente Orozco, and many others. *Mestiza* is the national food and music. *Mestiza* is the national identity nurtured in every child during the six years of primary education, following the official curriculum and textbooks controlled by the SEP Vasconcelos once led. Yet a brief exposure to this ideal *mestizo,* which defines the Mexican identity in the national imagination through texts, monuments, and public rituals, is definitely skewed in the *indigenista* direction. Just a brief overview of some of the national icons reveals this tendency. Some of these are the Mexican seal, depicting the eagle eating the snake evocative of Tenochtitlan's founding myth, the monument to *la raza* in the shape of a pyramid, even the logo of the Mexican soccer team, which is the Aztec calendar. Such is also the spirit of the use given to *la raza* by the Chicano movement of the 1970s in the United States. In Mexico, in official histories, monuments, and civic holidays, the national narrative is extremely nativist, portraying the Spanish conquest as a national catastrophe, the colonial period as three centuries of obscurantism and exploitation, and the national independence from Spain as the breaking of the chains of oppression. This is also a type of historical narrative often used by Chicanos.[10]

Such a narrative is far removed from the late Vasconcelos's Hispanophile and Catholic one. In his *Breve historia de México* (Brief history of Mexico), he insists that Mexican history as such begins with the conquest. Prior to that, according to Vasconcelos, no Mexican national consciousness as such existed. Such a proposition has alienated him from many Mexican nationalists of the *indigenista* bent. His position, however, is not as far-fetched as it seems, particularly if one considers that despite the fact that one could speak of a populous and complex Mesoamerican civilization, Mexico consisted of a broad array of city-states, empires, regions, linguistic communities, and genders tied in a complex web of cultural, economic, and military relations, often at odds with each other and never a whole nation-state. In fact, it is an anachronism to expect to find human communities identifying themselves as nation-states in fifteenth-century Mexico, when such a notion did not exist. There is in Vasconcelos, however, a rhetoric and positioning in the articulation of this idea that seems to make his statements particularly repulsive to the Mexican liberal tradition. Vasconcelos's statements about Aztec barbarism, ignorance, and brutality make him an outright Indophobe, easily assimilable into the racist tradition of many others like the Argentinean Domingo Faustino Sarmiento. In contrast to him, many Chicanas, such as Adelaida del Castillo and Lucha Corpi, have made similar statements concerning the lack of a cohesive Mexican national identity as such prior to the conquest. For example, in rehabilitating the legacy of *la Malinche,* who as Hernán Cortés's lover and translator is the epitome of treachery in official Mexican history, these Chicanas allude to the fact that this woman had been given away to different rulers and she did not owe any allegiance to those who had given her away as property. She is, thus, often represented as a brave and astute protofeminist, using her multilingual talents in a difficult situation and not as a traitor to a community to which she did not belong.[11] There is not a coherent whole in this world; Malinche must fend for herself. Similarly, the murals by Desiderio Hernández Xochitiotzin at the Government Palace of Tlaxcala narrate a history in which the Tlaxcaltecs are for generations the victims of Aztec imperial aggression and join the Spaniards in their conquest not only of Mexico-Tenochtitlan but also of regions as remote as present-day Honduras, Albuquerque, and the Philippines. In these murals the Tlaxcaltecs appear as a sovereign people, cooperating with the Spaniards and gaining for their cooperation certain royal favors, distinctions, and privileges.[12] Such questioning of a unified Mexican polity and identity, however, fits very well within the *indigenista* and nationalist aesthetic of the Mexican muralist movement. What distinguishes these two examples from Vasconcelos's? What makes the later Vasconcelos so offensive to many?

One of the veins that travels through this study is precisely this problem: there is in Vasconcelos's legacy a long period of what we may call "the ugly Vasconcelos." His intellectual production of this later period turns him into someone who is easily susceptible to racist, reactionary, and Eurocentric epithets. There is the racist Vasconcelos who regularly

puts down the Aztec and broader Indian heritage; the xenophobe who
fears Jewish, North American, and Bolshevik conspiracies; the one who
supported the *cristeros,* considered in the official discourse of his time as
fanatic peasants fighting a supposedly progressive state in the name of
an obscurantist and regressive Catholic faith; and the one who sees the
history of the world in terms of an epic struggle between European civilizations—the Latin and the Anglo-Saxon. I will begin by looking at
this aspect of his legacy, trying to trace relationships between the positions expressed here and those expressed at the peak of Vasconcelos's
revolutionary career. To what degree did these positions change? To
what degree are the changes not fundamental ones, but merely changes
of emphasis and tone? I will also address the way in which the ideology
expressed in his legacy fits within the broader realm of Mexico's official
postrevolutionary ideology, which is the culmination of the liberal project of the nineteenth century.[13] This is the liberal project against which
he disputes, but of which he is a product.

It is my contention that beyond the highly offensive positions the
later Vasconcelos takes, many of the attitudes exacerbated during this
period are present in his early work, at the peak of his liberal revolutionary career. As we will see in chapter 3, a study on the genesis and appro-
priations of Vasconcelos's concept of the "cosmic race," the author's ideology, like that of his liberal predecessors and contemporaries, was
extremely Eurocentric. Liberalism's modernizing zeal provided a European model of national salvation, and its beautifully printed constitu-
tions and laws drew almost exclusively from the European Enlightenment and republican traditions. Native Indians appeared in their
rhetoric as long exploited and/or abandoned victims of a brutal colonial
legacy who had been excluded from the benefits of citizenship and modern developments. The role of a liberal administration was to incorporate them into a modern life in which these benefits would become
available to them. This modern life, however, would attempt to turn
these Indians into westernized citizens, turning to their traditions only
for picturesque folkloric coloring.

Throughout the nineteenth century, solving "the Indian problem"
was one of the liberals' most daunting tasks. In a first instance, Indians
were erased by decree. The repressive caste system, product of colonial
racist exploitation, was by the stroke of a pen dismantled. In the new
republics everyone would be a citizen. The move, supposedly with the
Indians' rights in mind, in theory also erased all the particularities of the
broad mosaic of Mexican ethnicities, languages, and cultural traditions.

The notion of a citizen also brought with it a whole series of assumptions as to what a citizen would be, such as a male adult, often literate, often a property owner. A republic of citizens also assumed in theory certain sorts of legal, social, and economic relations. In the rural world, for example, the ideal organization would consist of small land holdings by individual private farmers, in the European and North American traditions. In this regard, the *Leyes de Reforma* (reform laws), the epitome of Benito Juárez's iconic liberal career, called for the privatization of all communal property. Ostensibly a move against the Catholic Church, such laws completely disregarded Indian communal land tenure traditions and greatly affected entire communities. With liberal economic modernization, the expansion of the railroad, and the growth in agribusiness and mining, many Indians were forced from their lands and thrust into mining or the growing cities. It is very telling that in 1900 nearly half of Mexico City's 500,000 inhabitants were peasants forced to look for employment in the capital.[14] The displaced peasant labor, in a sort of primitive accumulation, had to be turned into a productive modern working force: a national community of citizens working for the good of the country. In practice, however, the theory of national economic redemption was not as utopian. Most migrant peasants found themselves in conditions of squalor in cities to which they were not accustomed. Furthermore, their forced integration into the capitalist system came at the cost of cultural annihilation by the growing cosmopolitan urban centers. Despite the forced dislocations and cultural annihilation, the Indian became a coherent symbol of national identity. But this was an ancient Indian. Monuments and museums, literature and song turned to a glorious Mexican indigenous past, while living Indians remained either exploited or ready for cultural and economic salvation through modernization. Crafts and folklore were encouraged, but always as quaint reminders of a past tradition that defies modernization's onslaught and can therefore be bought and kept as a souvenir of a trip to the exotic "uncontaminated" south. In an ironic turn, living Indians had to be eliminated to become modern citizens with a glorious Indian past. One might cynically say that the slogan for this liberal solution to the Indian problem could well be that statement heard in the Wild West, "A good Indian is a dead Indian."[15]

Such a position is not very different from that of the ugly Vasconcelos. Both saw the Indian as needing some sort of redemption. A major difference, however, remains in the way in which they portray the past. The liberal project, particularly that of the revolution, portrays the Indian past as glorious and the colonial period as a dark hiatus for the national aspirations of the Mexican people. Vasconcelos, for his part, paints a dark Indian past full of human sacrifice and violence, while the colonial period appears to him as one of redemption and glory. The Catholic missionaries and explorers created in America the first hub for international exchange. Their fearless curiosity led them to create an empire where the sun never set. People from all over the world gathered in its realm and communicated in Spanish. The colonial period saw Mexico at the center of commerce between Europe and Asia. Mexican silver coins were the preferred currency in the Far East.[16] While for the liberals Spain had for 300 years impeded the sovereign will of the Mexican people, for Vasconcelos it was the Spanish conquest that created a Mexico, and for that matter a Latin America, as such, leaving a legacy of the Hispanic culture in an entire continent. Such a unity, a result of the Catholic universalizing zeal, is expressed in the common Spanish language. Vasconcelos was not strictly a nationalist, despite the fact that he is considered the patron of post-revolutionary nationalist ideology and culture; rather he was a Latin Americanist. He saw with admiration the success of the former British colonies in the north, which united in a federation rather than seeking their own independent national existence. Latin America, on the other hand, was fractured into a collage of small republics often at odds with each other and with Spain, the mother country. The British colonies had not severed their ties with England. A balkanization of the south meant weakness in the face of the powerful *United* States of America. And a continental unity of the nature proposed by Vasconcelos could not function if splintered along indigenous lines. The unity of southern America came through the Spanish heritage.

As in the modernizing liberal project, the notion of a Latin America proposed by Vasconcelos and by most of his Latin Americanist contemporaries and predecessors was extremely Eurocentric in its nature. The very name "Latin" or "Latino" (preferred by many to the supposedly more Eurocentric "Hispanic" or *"Hispano"*) refers one to the Roman Empire and its Mediterranean civilization. The *arielista* generation to which Vasconcelos belonged had reacted with dismay at the final defeat of the Spanish Empire in Cuba, Puerto Rico, and the Philippines in 1898. Based on Shakespeare's last play, *The Tempest,* José Enrique Rodó's *Ariel* was a call to the Spanish American youth to stand up to the danger of the North American Caliban. Rodó saw in the United States the triumph of practical materialism. North American utilitarianism allowed for the exploding growth of modern production, but at the cost of the spirit. Latin America, represented by Ariel, had much to learn from the United States, a country that Prospero, the essay's narrator, says to admire, but not love.[17] According to him, extreme utilitarianism as seen in the United States facilitates life in the material realm, but it atrophies the spiritual element, making humans incomplete. The Latin tradition, according to Rodó, keeps the spirit alive through religious ritual, aesthetic contemplation, and leisure. He sees a marked cultural divide between two Americas, Latin and Anglo-Saxon. Such a division of the Americas is not exclusive to Rodó. The idea of a Latin America written as an independent noun with its unique identity *(Latinoamérica, América Latina)* emerges from a fully European context as Saintsimonian advisors of Napoleon III view an opportunity to expand their influence in America as part of a pan-Latin project. One of the earliest references to a Latin America in this context (but with the "Latin" as an uncapitalized adjective describing one part of a broader America: *América latina)* is in the writings of Michel Chevalier, who in 1836 published in Paris his impressions of travels in America. In his writings he refers to two Americas, one of Anglo-Saxon Protestant origin and one of Latin Catholic. Despite the broader ethnic, religious, and cultural mosaic, under this perspective the American continent was divided by European parameters, its history and culture an appendix to that in Europe.[18]

A few years before Rodó, the Cuban José Martí talked about *Nuestra América* (our America) in relation to a "European America." While deeply idealist in its utopian aspects, Martí's discussion of *Nuestra América* is very materialist in its romantic emphasis on the land. This emphasis makes him very different from Rodó. Unlike the Uruguayan, the Cuban writer and political activist does not identify Latin culture as the cornerstone of the America he envisions. One must remember, after all, that Martí spent his life, and actually died, struggling for Cuban independence from Spain. In this regard, references to a crucial Spanish heritage in the American identity would be counterproductive. He instead proposes a new perspective in which it is the American space that must be understood and transformed by native intellectuals whom he called "natural men." He saw a danger in the copying of foreign models, particularly European and North American, and thus called for the creation of an American university. Particularly important in his utopian model is the process of miscegenation. Beyond his insistence on an original knowledge corresponding to the American land, Martí's call is also one for racial unity under which the descendants of blacks, Indians, and whites should live in harmony. With this premise, he celebrated an American *mestiza* identity decades before Vasconcelos, and in this spirit his use of *nuestra* (our) to refer to the region of America at hand is much more inclusive than the limiting "Latin" or "Hispanic." Nevertheless, despite this rhetorical distinction, Martí's *Nuestra América* is by implication the region of the world conquered by the Iberian powers and distinct from that conquered by Britain.[19] He saw in the United States a threatening other that he called the "European America." He constantly warned about the dangers of a Pan-American union giving too much power to the already threatening United States. Like Rodó, he was fascinated by North American technical prowess but was scared by the dehumanizing effects of extreme utilitarianism. One can see, for example, his essay *"Nueva York bajo la nieve"* (New York under snow), which expresses his admiration for the metropolis's ability to continue working efficiently just a few hours after a terrible snowstorm. Yet this ability to overcome the obstacles of nature comes at the cost of many victims who must give their existence for the beast to continue its own. However, unlike Rodó's idealist project emphasizing the spiritual leisure of a gifted elite, Martí emphasized social equality across races and the creation of a new intellectual tradition, not an echo of a European model, but one American in its origin.

Vasconcelos's Latin Americanist ideology of the 1920s has much in common with aspects of Martí's and Rodó's. Like these and many other thinkers, ranging from Simón Bolívar to Eugenio María de Hostos and Andrés Bello, he attempts to understand and rehabilitate the part of America newly independent from Spanish colonial rule. Like Martí he puts an emphasis on racial and cultural miscegenation and searches for an original American experience. Like Rodó he emphasizes the Spanish element in his quest for a spiritual superiority. One can see in him a populist aristocrat. If on the one hand his attitudes are extremely elitist, like Rodó's, he spent much of his life following Martí's footsteps, those of an intellectual who delves into the dirty realm of politics. Like both, he was fascinated by the United States but feared their growing hegemony. Like Rodó, he viewed North American culture askance. Considering himself a highly cultured intellectual, he saw the United States as the realm of practical but unrefined "pioneers." Instead of using the Caliban metaphor used by Rodó, he refers to North Americans as "Robinsons," an allusion to Daniel Defoe's Crusoe, a practical man in the wilderness.[20] With the passage of time, however, Vasconcelos's phobia of the United States became almost pathological, as he saw all of Mexico's ills as the result of North American Protestant conspiracies. Although official

Mexican rhetoric is ostensibly anti-American, Vasconcelos's continuous aggressive accusations about the ruling regime's and all its associates' co-optation by the United States greatly ostracized him in later life. His constant pro-Hispanic and pro-Catholic pronouncements turned many liberals against him, although, as I show in chapter 3, such an attitude was present in his earlier texts, which remain popular among the liberal intelligentsia.

One cannot deny that there were major transformations in the thoughts of Vasconcelos. It would be absurd to suggest that his ideas remained unaltered during five decades of public life. I intend to show, however, that despite appearances his core ideology remained surprisingly consistent. What I propose is that what changes drastically is the articulation of his ideas. For my purposes I understand "articulation" in the double sense that Stuart Hall identifies: " 'articulate' means to utter, to speak forth, to be articulate. It carries that sense of language-ing, of expressing, etc. But we also speak of an articulated lorry . . . where the front . . . and the back . . . can, but need not necessarily, be connected to one another."[21] In the "language-ing" sense I refer to the rhetoric, the word choice, the emphasis he gives to his ideas in texts and speeches. In this regard, a series of texts he dedicates to Cuauhtémoc—the last Aztec emperor to challenge the Spanish conquerors and one of the most prominent figures in the nationalist liberal pantheon—is particularly revealing. As I show in chapter 2, despite an apparently extreme difference in the texts, their core understanding of Mexican history and of the place of Indians and Europeans in it remains very consistent. In the more material sense of the "articulated lorry" I refer to the way in which Vasconcelos's legacy is completely intertwined with a series of institutions and organizations, including the *Ateneo de la Juventud,* the *Secretaría de Educación Pública,* the Anti-re-electionist Party, and the Catholic Church, among many others. The range of statements that he made throughout his career was shaped by his relationship with these institutions. Furthermore, our reaction to these statements is also shaped by what we perceive to be his relationship to them. Thus, to give one example that is further explored in chapter 4, today Vasconcelos is remembered by many as the creator of the cultural missions—institutions that were formed to educate the rural, mainly Indian, population. Vasconcelos himself, however, was originally opposed to their particular kind of pedagogy, but was forced into adopting them when the Department of Anthropology, headed by Manuel Gamio, posed a threat to the SEP's control of rural education. Similarly, today Vasconcelos is remembered as the man who first gave walls to the Mexican muralists. It is easy, therefore, to assume that the radical message given by these murals was that intended by the first minister of education, while the fact is that many of them were actually painted decades after Vasconcelos's resignation and that he and the muralists had very important political and aesthetic disagreements. An articulation, therefore, is not limited to the speaker's or writer's will, but to what Hugo Achúgar identifies as the moment of enunciation: the social, political, cultural, economic, and historical context in which a statement is produced and received.[22] Vasconcelos's ideas and slogans, his legacy as a whole, must be understood as it is transformed in different contexts—both in the way in which these contexts affected his legacy as it was being produced and how these contexts affect our reception of this legacy, long after the author's death.

This legacy is particularly enmeshed in the history of the *Secretaría de Educación Pública,* its statements, its schools, its textbooks and buildings. This relationship is studied in chapter 4. Although volume 3 of Vasconcelos's memoirs, *El desastre* (The disaster) would lead us to believe that he almost single-handedly created the ministry, the fact is that he had to work with huge bureaucracies, employees, students, parents, and volunteers. He also had to work within a governmental structure and struggle with other bureaucracies and institutions, often with different agendas, for funding, attention, and prestige. In her study of educational reform during the early Soviet years, Sheila Fitzpatrick has pointed out that the huge bureaucracies inherited by the Bolsheviks from the czarist regime carried with them a heavy load of particular interests. Interbureaucratic struggles that were played out during the czarist regime continued to take place in the early years of Bolshevik power to the extent that "institutions played a far greater role than party factions."[23] While the Mexican bureaucracies were not as large and powerful as their Russian counterparts, they did have an important effect on the way Vasconcelos's ministry ultimately developed. Early in the twentieth century, the sociologist Max Weber had also explored the role of bureaucracies in modern societies. Large state bureaucracies emerge, according to Weber, as a response to rationalizing and leveling tendencies. A bureaucracy implies scientific management, where each bureaucrat performs a specific task with technical mastery. Bureaucracy also implies democratization, he continues, as each individual bureaucrat is in a position not according to a certain inherent privilege, but according to merit. By spreading authority to its limits, no individual member can effect control of the whole organization. Thus, even in times of war or revolution, "A rationally ordered system of officials continues to function smoothly after the enemy has occupied the area: he merely needs to change the top official. This body of officials continues to operate because it is to the vital interest of everyone concerned, including above all the enemy." According to the German sociologist, such organizations make revolution, in the sense of the forceful creation of entirely new formations of authority, technically more and more impossible, "particularly when their rationalizing and leveling forces increase their control of modern means of communication."[24] Such, to a great degree, was the case in Vasconcelos's ministry. Although the central offices in Mexico City insisted upon transformations in local curricula and school administration, it was the local teachers, administrators, parents, and students with entrenched practices who were supposed to implement the changes at the local level, and oftentimes these actors simply ignored the ministry's orders.

Weber's observations about the structural inertia of bureaucracies in the nineteenth and twentieth centuries pose an important challenge to a model that defines revolution as the creation of a new political and economic system. In his classic study *The Old Regime and the French Revolution,* Alexis de Tocqueville argues that despite all its early pageantry announcing a new era, the French Revolution actually strengthened a "State machine [that] had been brought to a high state of perfection" during the Ancient Regime.[25] One can certainly find similarities with this case and that of Mexico during the period that concerns us. In the case of the SEP, when Vasconcelos began to organize a new ministry he had to count on bureaucrats and teachers who, like himself, were formed in the Porfirian regime. On numerous occasions Vasconcelos praises the role and vision of Justo Sierra as minister of education of the Porfirian regime. He also praises the graduates of Sierra's teachers' college *(Normal)* under his supervision. Many of the buildings, books, pedagogical methods, and most other educational materials were also inherited from the Porfirian period. While the ministry was in charge of forming the new cadres to administer the newly created bureaucracies, during its early years it was forced to rely on the existing system. In this regard, as is discussed in chapter 4, we find a significant continuity in the SEP.

The institutional continuity presented by Tocqueville and Weber responds to a great degree to the practical necessities of running a modern society. The state and its bureaucracies, as Weber points out, have become an essential element in society, making it impossible for society to function without municipal utilities, sewage systems, and roads, and without the postal or other communication services, just to mention a few daily activities in which state bureaucracies intervene. In the case of Vasconcelos, schools in Mexico could not function without the infrastructure set in place by the previous regime. This does not exclusively consist of buildings and school supplies but also of a large group of people carrying within itself a heavy baggage of cultural assumptions and practices that do not necessarily change with the arrival of a new regime. As it is the personnel that actually run the institutions, their influence is very significant, often more than that of the minister himself. Recent studies, like Elsie Rockwell's 1994 "Schools of the Revolution: Enacting and Contesting State Forms in Tlaxcala, 1910–1930," indicate that other traditional and newly formed networks, ranging from religious confraternities to parents' associations, also struggled with the institutional bureaucracy to shape the new educational system. In this regard, Rockwell shows us that it is not necessarily at the high official level—in the minister's office—but at the ground level—in the individual schools, households, and communities—that we find many of the crucial struggles that determined the reshaping of Mexico's educational system for years to come. On this point Vasconcelos found himself in what Antonio Gramsci identifies as a war of position, and this is what I discuss in the chapter dedicated to his ministry. We see that the implementation of a new educational system was a struggle at the local level and that one cannot speak of a homogeneous project. Furthermore, we see how some of the ideas that have been identified as Vasconcelos's were actually forced onto him during this struggle.

Chapter 5 takes on the Vasconcelos of the 1929 presidential election. This is the second high point in his career, and indeed a watershed. In this chapter we will see his political and economic project for the nation, which rather than reactionary or even conservative appears as a nationalist sort of social democracy. We also see the relationship his campaign had with the *cristero* uprising, which pitted fervent Catholics of western Mexico, particularly peasants, against the government. The war was the result of the historical confrontation between the Catholic Church and liberal anticlerical intellectuals. Since the mid-nineteenth century, liberal thinkers and administrators had opposed the power of the Catholic Church as a symbol of colonialism and medieval obscurantist opposition to modernity and science. In the mid-1920s radical socialist governors in the states of Yucatán, Guerrero, and Tabasco, with the full support of President Calles, began implementing the 1917 Constitution's anticlerical laws in an extreme fashion, greatly reducing the number of priests who could preach in a given region and even demanding absurdities such as the marriage of Catholic priests in order to practice. The final straw of the confrontation came early in 1925, when a group calling itself *Orden de los Caballeros de Guadalupe* (order of the knights of Guadalupe)—created by the labor union CROM, closely associated with Calles, as an alternative to the Knights of Columbus—took over the Church of the Soledad in Mexico City, proclaiming the creation of the Catholic Apostolic Mexican Church independent of the Vatican. With government support this new church took over six more churches in the states of Puebla, Veracruz, Tabasco, and Oaxaca.[26] The goal of creating a Mexican Catholic Church—independent of the Vatican, as was the case with the Anglican Church in England—had been a dream of liberals for over half a century. Such a proposition proved to be difficult, as not many priests were ready to take on this project and financing a whole national church was beyond the liberal state's means. Promoting Protestant missions appeared to be an easier approach to thwarting the Catholic Church's power. Liberal administrations from Juárez's on had thus confiscated many church buildings, sometimes selling or renting them to Protestant congregations.[27] On this occasion, however, the church hierarchy challenged the government and declared a moratorium on church services. Mexicans, many of them fervent Catholics, could no longer receive the sacraments.

The timing and scope of the confrontation came at a particularly complicated moment in church-state relations in Mexico. Since 1521, despite the appearance of a well-established and transparent relationship between the state and the Catholic Church, which arrived on American shores to legitimize the conquest of the region's peoples, it has always been tainted by tensions and special arrangements. Since colonial times, the Spanish state through the *patronato* had much control over church affairs, nominating officials and managing many of its financial transactions. In the newly independent Mexican state this relationship had to be reconfigured; the church as an institution had sided with the colonial power, going to the extreme of excommunicating many of the nationalist rebels. Nevertheless, one must also remember that some of the most prominent heroes of Mexican nationalism and independence were clerics themselves: for example, Miguel Hidalgo y Costilla and José María Morelos y Pavón, two parish priests who became the undisputed fathers of Mexican Independence (and who were excommunicated); and at a less iconic level, but crucial in the development of a Mexican nationalist ideology, were priests such as Francisco Javier Clavijero and Fray Servando Teresa de Mier. However, despite the radicalism of certain individual priests, or congregations, the Catholic hierarchy in the nineteenth century tended to side with the conservative factions. Particularly damaging to its reputation among liberal nationalists was its support for the imposition of Maximilian, an Austrian archduke, as Mexico's emperor. The liberal administrations, for their part, confiscated church property and sold it, often to foreign investors, to raise revenues. Beginning with the Juárez administration, liberals also attempted to court Protestant groups into Mexico, as an alternative to Catholic power and because a Protestant ethic was seen by many liberals as conducive to modernization. Liberal administrations also took on many of the civic rituals and controls that had traditionally been the church's domain. Thus Juárez opened the national *Registro Civil* (civil registry) for the registration of births, deaths, and marriages. Wresting control of the schools away from the Catholic Church was another big issue on the liberal agenda. In this regard, the general thrust of Calles's anticlerical policies was not new. What was perhaps new was its intensity.

Mexico, despite the most radical liberals' best wishes, is a Catholic nation, where Catholic faith and ritual play an important role in the life of the vast majority—be it the fervent Catholics of the Bajío depicted in Agustín Yáñez's *Al filo del agua,* the millions of devotees of the Virgin of Guadalupe, the urban middle classes who attend mass on a somewhat regular basis, or those who just sometimes participate in a Catholic wedding, funeral, or festivity. Even the ardent anticlerical Ricardo Flores Magón uses the Catholic tale of Judas selling Christ in his short story *"El apóstol."* Hidalgo's flag, like that of the *Zapatistas,* was the Virgin of Guadalupe. One must also bear in mind that during the beginning of the twentieth century the Catholic Church was undergoing its own transformation. Particularly important in Mexico was the 1891 encyclical *Rerum novarum* of Pope Leo XIII calling for an active Catholic participation in the social and political realm, giving birth to new Catholic organizations, ranging from political parties to youth movements and labor unions.[28] Of course, although all these organizations had a Catholic general direction, their goals, tactics, and even conception of Catholicism varied. As the church declared its moratorium on the sacraments, different Catholic organizations reacted in various ways. It was particularly the peasantry that rose up in arms under the slogan of *"Viva Cristo Rey"* (long live Christ the king), thus earning the name *Cristeros.* The church hierarchy did not call for an armed uprising, it just called for a moratorium and waited out the crisis. (As Jean Meyer points out in his fascinating three-volume study of the war, the Catholic Church had been in existence for centuries and viewed the crisis in the long term.) Student and urban Catholic organizations supported the *cristeros* rhetorically and called for civil disobedience and boycotts.

The *cristero* crisis would play a role in the presidential campaign from its beginning. Vasconcelos, always an enemy of political violence, called for a halt in hostilities against Catholics. At the time of Obregón's assassination by José de León Toral, an urban *cristero* supporter, Vasconcelos lived in the United States. From there he had been blaming the massive flow of Mexican emigrants to the north on the violence against Catholics. Once on the campaign trail in Mexico, the candidate even met with *cristero* representatives, and despite his rhetoric of appeasement he secretly counted on their armed support. His strategy was to officially oppose violence, but have it at his disposal in case of electoral fraud. He wanted to follow the pattern set by Madero and Obregón. To his dismay, however, the interim president, Emilio Portes Gil, with the help of U.S. Ambassador Dwight W. Morrow, was able to reach a détente with the Catholic hierarchy and hostilities halted.

Beyond his opposition to outright violence, Vasconcelos now saw Calles's extreme anticlericalism as a threat to the Mexican national identity and sovereignty. A denial of Mexico's Catholicism was for him a denial of its Hispano-Latin identity and a concession to the United States. Particularly alarming to him was the prominence of Protestants and Freemasons in Calles's regime, especially at the ministry he had founded. He also saw with alarm the selective enforcement of anti-foreigner provisions of the 1917 Constitution against Spaniards. He saw the government's anti-Spanish attitude in the name of an *indigenismo* as a tragically divisive mistake. His Hispanophile Catholic pronouncements made him an easy target of the conservative brand—something he certainly would not deny. But in many ways—such as in his call for the nationalization of key industries and natural resources and governmental intervention in the economy and in his concerns for social security—his campaign's program contained many nationalist and populist elements that could easily be linked to the ruling regime's ideology. An easy placing of his Hispanophile Catholic stance as conservative is complicated by this populist and nationalist rhetoric. Vasconcelos did not want to return to a feudal colonial past. Quite on the contrary, he was fascinated by modern technical developments; these were crucial to his model of the cosmic race. He struggled, however, with foreign ownership of Mexico's industry and natural resources and with North American influence on Mexican culture and national identity.

The fourth volume of Vasconcelos's memoirs, *El proconsulado,* speaks of Calles's *Maximato*—the period consisting of his presidency and of his three successors, Emilio Portes Gil, Pascual Ortiz Rubio, and Abelardo Rodríguez, considered by most as his puppets—as a period when Mexico's interests were fully controlled by U.S. ambassadors. In his recollection of this period, Vasconcelos calls these administrations *pochas*—a term used contemptuously by Mexicans to refer to Americanized immigrant Mexicans and Chicanos. In his criticism of these *"pocho"* administrations, Vasconcelos vehemently turns against any sort of Americanization. Ironically, however, it would be among the Mexican expatriate community in the United States that he began his presidential campaign. Of particular interest in chapter 5 is the centrality of what was known then as *el México de Afuera's* (the outside Mexico) in his presidential campaign. His first campaign tour was not in Mexico, but in the southwestern United States among the population of Mexican origin, much of which had recently migrated north due to the political violence and tough economic situation in Mexico. He saw in the Mexicans of the United States evidence that Mexicans could prosper with proper democratic institutions. To him, the huge Mexican migration to the north was shameful proof of the inability of the Mexican regime to fulfill its citizens' basic necessities. Ironically, a man who blamed Mexico's demise on North American interference saw in the United States the blooming of a vibrant Mexican community. He also saw in the United States the emergence of a broader pan-Latin identity, something that he perceived as lacking in his home country.

Vasconcelos's presidential campaign and his ultimate, albeit unfair, defeat turned him into a rabid enemy of the Mexican regime. Exiled for a fifth time, he turned his pen against the triumphant faction. Desperate and bitter, his attacks against the regime became more and more vehement. The main theme of this offensive continued to be two pronged. On the one hand, he condemned what he saw as the state's subservience to U.S. interests to the detriment of a Mexican Hispano-Catholic heritage. He saw in the regime's self-proclaimed radicalism a veneer to enrich its own elites while destroying those traditions that linked Mexico to its glorious colonial past. On the other hand, he denounced the political violence used by the regime to maintain its grip on power. As time passed his rhetoric became more and more provocative, as it found international conspiracies everywhere and attempted to explain Mexican violence through its Aztec past. Such a rhetoric only served to separate him from all but his most ardent supporters. The growth of U.S. power on the international scene only helped to confirm his fears of the triumph of Anglo-Saxon dominance. In this regard, he turned to two dictators, Francisco Franco and Benito Mussolini, as beacons of Latin might. These two figures with strong and charismatic personalities seemed to him to be leading Latin nations back to the glory of the past. Such positions further distanced him from his earlier liberal supporters. Yet the reasons for his support of these dictators are not far removed from the *arielista* positions of his youth. It seems, however, that this connection is not clearly understood by most of his critics. It is for this reason that I turn in chapter 2 to "the ugly Vasconcelos," in an attempt to tackle the most disturbing contradictions early on and then continue looking at their genesis.

The purpose of this book is not necessarily to clarify but rather to disturb the legacy of Vasconcelos and that of the Mexican Revolution. It is too easy to hang on to one of the apparently pure Vasconceloses, be it the radical revolutionary or the reactionary conservative. It does not serve any purpose beyond that of propaganda to dismiss the later Vasconcelos as a crazy and bitter demagogue, completely different from the young man. I intend to explore the ways in which the thought and practice of the later Vasconcelos are intimately related to their earlier incarnations and the way in which this is revealing of the ideological and policy contradictions present in the Mexican liberal nationalist tradition. The contradictions of Vasconcelos remained part of his persona even in his death. Two of his posthumous works reveal these contradictions. Shortly after his death in 1959, *La flama* and *Letanías del atardecer* were published. The first one is the passionate memoir of a public intellectual of civic fervor, criticizing the violent despotism of his country. In it he praised León Toral, the *cristeros,* and those who joined his presidential campaign in search of democracy. It is a bitter polemic against the PRI regime and the United States. At around the same time, *Letanías del atardecer* was published. Here, the man who once had considered himself Prometheus humbled himself before an almighty God, renouncing his filthy body and any human arrogance that led him to desire worldly change. These texts reveal both a man of modern civic democratic zeal and one of medieval, humbling, stoic faith. Vasconcelos was a man of contrasts and transitions, as I pointed out at the beginning of this chapter, product and producer of a time of contrasts and transitions: revolution, globalization, modernization. It is not my desire to praise or condemn Vasconcelos—many others have already done that—but rather to explore through him the transitions and contradictions faced by Mexico's liberal nationalist project in the first half of the twentieth century.

Chapter Two

The Ugly Vasconcelos: José Vasconcelos's Contradictions

In June 1920 José Vasconcelos, the new president of Mexico's National University, gave his inaugural speech. The occasion was a turning point in the young Oaxacan lawyer's political career and in the country's educational history. From his new platform he assessed the state of the institution. On this momentous occasion, as the new Mexican regime officially took over one of the continent's oldest universities, Vasconcelos's assessment began in a rather negative tone. He stated that he arrived "with sadness to [a] pile of ruins," ravaged by "the most stupendous ignorance." He criticized the Carranza regime's disregard for public education and insisted that the university should be a beacon in a "crusade" of "national redemption" through education. Although he believed that the university had some excellent faculty members, the new president envisioned a much more activist type of institution. From his podium Vasconcelos commented on the institution's programs as he observed that it taught French literature and even offered classes on Racine's tragedies. Such classes, he told his audience, would have filled him with pride "were it not for the impression I have in my heart of the spectacle of abandoned children in the neighborhoods of all our cities, of all our hamlets; children that the state should feed and educate, thus recognizing the most elemental duty of a true civilization." Filled with the enthusiasm of a triumphant revolutionary who had followed Lunacharsky's and Gorky's bold leadership of the new Soviet Commissariat for Enlightenment, he insisted that the federal government should create a national ministry of education to attend to the cultural needs of all Mexicans. And although the appreciation and production of what is known as "high culture"—that privileged echelon of world civilization such as Racine's tragedies or Homer's epic poems—was the ultimate goal of an educational program, the lawyer-turned-pedagogue considered more material yet urgent needs, such as nutrition and hygiene, as the most elemental cornerstone in the development of cultured citizens. His was a practical appeal when he said that the university community must "begin with the peasant and the worker. Let us take the peasant under our guardianship and teach him to increase one-hundred-fold his production with the use of better tools and better methods. This is more important than training him in verb conjugations, since culture is a natural fruit of economic development."[1]

The first four university circulars published by him in July 1920 presented practical, literary, and revolutionary goals. The first announced a national literacy campaign. To run it he called on all Mexicans "who have finished third grade or [can] properly certify that they can read and spell in Castilian" to volunteer to teach their illiterate fellow citizens. He also instructed these volunteer teachers to begin their lessons by giving students "elementary advice about hygiene, respiration, diet, clothing, exercise, etc." Only then should they begin to teach in a "simple, clear and direct way, the pronunciation and writing of words and phrases."[2] This was a practical approach to a complex task. The very elemental concern of this campaign is made evident in the title of the university's second circular, "Instrucciones sobre aseo personal e higiene" (Instructions on personal cleanliness and hygiene). In this the president asserted that "often a fist-full of mercury powder against parasites or a bar of soap will be more efficient as base of education than twenty spelling lessons."[3] The third document is a specific appeal for women to participate in the campaign.[4] Only the fourth circular, *"Libros que recomienda la Universidad Nacional"* (Books that the National University recommends), deals with that more privileged realm of world literature. Here the new president recommends "three visionaries whose doctrines must flood the Mexican soul. . . : Benito Pérez Galdós, Romain Rolland and Leo Tolstoy."[5] The lessons in hygiene and basic literacy are stepping-stones to the summit of the fine arts. In the same way, the ad hoc literacy campaign was but the first step in a much more complex project: the creation of a ministry of education at the national level to centrally control Mexico's schools and other cultural institutions. In his inaugural speech Vasconcelos had called "simply stupid" the previous administration's education policy, which turned over federal control of schools to the municipalities. To refederalize education he announced that the university would stop holding classes to dedicate all its efforts to the elaboration of a new education law ("Discurso," 59 – 60). Intellectuals should move out of their ivory towers and put their knowledge at the service of the poorest and least-educated Mexicans. The new university president was a man with a mission, and after an intensive mobilization, he reached his goal when on 3 October 1921 the ministry of education (*Sec-*

retaría de Educación Pública, or SEP) was created, and nine days later, on Columbus Day, Vasconcelos became its first minister.

Vasconcelos's inaugural speech reveals one of the apparent contradictions in his thought. The contradiction is so subtle at this moment that it might pass unperceived. In the speech one sees the liberal dream of modernization in the countryside. The central state has the responsibility to take the benefits of modern science, in the shape of medicine, soap, and nutritional advice, to the backward countryside and urban slums. The ultimate goal is that of creating productive citizens ready to apply modern tools and methods to production. Vasconcelos proposes a holistic approach to education where the state, in the name of knowledge and progress, would regulate through persuasion and education even the most personal aspects of its citizens. Such intervention was not limited to the traditional curricula of schools. It included advice about diet—the university president discouraged Mexicans from eating greasy and spicy food—and even breathing techniques and schedules for people's weekends.[6] Literacy volunteers should recommend that "Saturday afternoons . . . preferably will be dedicated to personal cleanliness, a bath, exercise and some moderate amusement. Sunday morning should be dedicated to studying, and the afternoon to country outings with organized choirs" ("Instrucciones," 107). In such proposals one easily sees the phenomena explored by Foucault in his studies of the prison, the hospital, and insanity in the post-Enlightenment European context. They are interventions of a state that attempts to discipline its subjects' bodies and ideas to an order determined by science.

As other ministers of culture during other revolutions, such as the French, Chinese, Russian, or Iranian, Vasconcelos saw himself as responsible for shaping a whole generation of citizens in a transformed nation-state. Together with the more quotidian and prosaic routines of nutrition and hygiene, the literacy campaign had to fulfill the role announced by its title. The future minister saw in literacy not only the introduction of pupils to the simple mechanics of reading and writing but found also an ideological mission in the process: the introduction of the students to a broader community, that of Spanish speakers—or rather Castilian speakers as the circular says. Nations, after all, as understood in the early twentieth century should share a mother tongue. But Vasconcelos with his characteristic epic and prophetic zeal talked not only about a nation but about the future glories of an entire race. He insisted that the literacy campaign's pupils should be made to understand that:

> Castilian . . . is the language of one of the most illustrious races in the world, [with] between ninety and one hundred million people scattered in the most promising zone on earth . . . [Students should also realize that] this race has a calling for a great destiny. . . . [and that] knowledge of the Castilian language introduces those who have it to the material and moral dominions of this new race, so young and promising. ("Instrucciones," 106)

Beyond the Mexican nation-state, Vasconcelos talks about a race that is united not necessarily by a common genetic background but by a language; and this unifying language is not one of the many native tongues spoken throughout the continent but that of the Castilian conquerors of America. Such references to the Spanish heritage were not limited to the question of language. In his inaugural speech, he had also turned to Mexico's colonial past, pointing to sixteenth-century evangelizing missionaries as a model of commitment for the new literacy volunteers ("Discurso," 61).

In this early speech we see clear examples of Vasconcelos's Hispanophilia, central elements of what would later be labeled as an ultraconservative ideology. However, in the middle of 1920 his practical concern with literacy, nutrition, and health made him look like more of a liberal revolutionary. His emphasis on the Spanish language did not strike a conservative tone. Spanish language education was considered by most liberals as a central element in the forging of a unified nation-state. As E. J. Hobsbawm reminds us in his *Nations and Nationalisms Since 1780,* "for the ideologists of nationalism as it evolved after 1830. . . . language was the soul of a nation, and . . . increasingly the crucial criterion of nationality. . . . All, except the most fortunate governments in multilingual countries, were aware of the explosiveness of the language problem."[7] What for today's observers appears as a blatant Eurocentric approach to a national linguistic policy was in the late nineteenth and early twentieth centuries a pragmatic necessity for national unity. It is revealing to note that in his 1916 *Forjando patria* (Forging a homeland), Manuel Gamio, considered by many as the father of Mexican modern anthropology and *indigenismo,* believed that Spanish language unity was essential to forge a *patria.* For him countries that "enjoy a defined and integrated nationality" share three characteristics: (1) "Ethnic unity in the majority of the population"; (2) "That majority has and uses a common language"; and (3) "The diverse elements, classes or social groups show cultural manifestation of a same essential character." This staunch

defender of Indian rights and culture also saw a threat in Mexico's multilingualism:

> it is well known that the indigenous population appears today as it was
> at the time of the Conquest, divided into more or less numerous group-
> ings. Even if they constitute small *patrias* because of the common link of
> race, language and culture, their mutual rivalries and reciprocal indiffer-
> ence facilitated the sixteenth century conquest and caused their cultural
> stagnation during the colonial period and our times.
>
> The problem is, thus, not to avoid an illusory joint aggression of those
> indigenous groupings, but to direct their now dispersed powerful ener-
> gies, attracting their individual members towards the other [Spanish-
> speaking] social group which they have always considered their enemy,
> incorporating them, merging them with it, tending ultimately to make
> cohesive and homogeneous the national race, unifying the language and
> converging culture.[8]

Any attempt at national unity required almost by definition linguistic
unity, and the common language of Mexico, and for that matter Latin
America, proposed even by defenders of Indian culture like Gamio was
the tongue of Castile proposed by Vasconcelos.

Like Gamio, Vasconcelos sees in linguistic unity something that goes
beyond an administrative nation-state. He sees in it the formation of a
coherent *race*. In this regard, while Gamio's observations point toward a
specific Mexican race and nationality, Vasconcelos sees a much broader
pan-Hispanic race. And here again, Vasconcelos is not alone. Such crucial figures in Latin American intellectual history as Simón Bolívar,
Eugenio María de Hostos, Andrés Bello and even José Martí have proposed the notion of a Latin American unity. At their time they did not
necessarily use the adjective "Latin"; oftentimes they referred simply to
América, or *Nuestra América,* but there is the implication in their rhetoric
that they refer to the former Spanish colonies on the American continent. One must point out that in the nineteenth-century geopolitical
context they advocated for an American culture and identity different
from that of Spain. They were, after all, constructing national imagined
communities different from the colonizing power from which their
nations had just gained independence. Nevertheless, the implied unifying principle for the region known as *América*—with its various modify-
ing adjectives such as *Nuestra, Hispano, Latino, Ibero,* or *Sur,* to mention a
few—was Spanish occupation, Spanish language, and tradition. Thus, in
a very paradoxical way, in his famous 1815 letter from Jamaica, Bolívar

includes among his long list of grievances against the Spanish monarchy its infringement of the "social contract" between Charles V and the Spanish "discoverers, conquerors and inhabitants of America." The descendants of these early European adventurers, the American *Criollos* and *Mestizos* had a birthright in America and they resented imported Spanish administrators running American affairs. Despite this resentment toward Spanish impositions, it is the European background of people like Bolívar that grants them certain rights that, in his rhetoric, do not seem to belong to the American continent itself. "We are," he writes to a Jamaican gentleman, "American by birth, and our rights are those of Europe."[9] American physical reality defines "us—our originality," but the legal and cultural structures that define "us" legally as an entity are still those of the conquerors.

A similar contradiction is evident in Bello's 1847 prologue to his groundbreaking *Gramática de la lengua castellana* (Grammar of the Castilian language). Here he argued that the great transformations in *"Hispano-América"* "call for new signs to express new ideas." His grammar is an effort to document this usage specific to the region, in order to show that "Chile and Venezuela have as much claim as Aragón and Andalucía for the toleration of accidental divergences [in their language], when these are corroborated by the uniform and authentic custom of educated people." Here, as in the case of Bolívar, the American experience produces a specific "originality," but it is ultimately the "Castilian Language" that provides an overall framework that contains it in words. That "originality" must be documented, and Bello's grammar is precisely an attempt at that, basing his observations on the "custom of educated people." In this documentation the author would set limits because an excessive number of neologisms was "the worst of all evils," which "by altering its structure it turns a language into a multitude of irregular, licentious and barbaric dialects." Such multilingualism impaired "enlightenment, law enforcement, state administration and national unity."[10] As did Vasconcelos, despite his efforts to find an originality in America, the Venezuelan-born Chilean minister of education saw the Spanish—or rather Castilian—language as a unifying force in the region he identified as *"Hispano-América."*

The other apparently Hispanophile position in Vasconcelos's speech is his allusion to the evangelizing missionaries as an example for the new teachers in the literacy campaign. These Catholic friars represented a commitment to dedicate one's life to the salvation of others. Their effort was both spiritual, in its dedication to grant salvation to the newly conquered Indians, and practical, in the way that they surmounted natural, cultural, political, and military obstacles in their exploration and proselytizing and pedagogical zeal. They did not limit themselves to isolated contemplation. Rather they went out into the world, built roads, towns, schools, and workshops. They researched the local flora, fauna, languages, and cultural traditions, becoming in a way some of the earliest ethnographers and anthropologists in America, centuries before such disciplines were institutionalized. With religious fervor they built the first universities on the continent, catechized many Indians, and, to echo the title of an article by Antonio Tovar, they "incorporated the New World to western culture."[11] Although Vasconcelos's rhetoric of the time is full of spiritual and religious allusions as he invites Mexicans to participate with "apostolic fervor" and "evangelic ardor" in a project of redemption and salvation, the emphasis of his inaugural speech was more toward a process of cultural and economic incorporation to the modern world. In this regard again, his rhetoric at the time did not strike a conservative tone. Rather, his references to Catholic missionaries were shared by members of the revolutionary Congress. One needs only to look, as an example, to Representative José Gálvez's 1923 legislative project for the creation of Federal Education Missions. Here, the representative also sees Catholic missionaries as examples to emulate in a project of national regeneration through education. The difference is that this time the *maestros misioneros* (missionary teachers) would not spread the word of the medieval Christian God, but that of the new God of science and modernity. Rather than priests, these modern missionaries would be teachers, artisans, scientists, and technicians. They would also take with them the more idealist notion of faith, rearticulating it away from God and toward the nation. It was a turn to a structure of the past to build a modern future.[12]

As the previous examples indicate, Vasconcelos's early ideology as represented in his inaugural speech does include positive references to a Hispanic Catholic past. This Hispanophile attitude can be characterized as Eurocentric and conservative, but in 1920 it did not separate him from the liberal nationalist or Americanist tradition. Rather, such attitudes were shared by many luminaries of that pantheon. Furthermore, Vasconcelos now formed part of a regime that identified itself as revolutionary. "Revolution" implies a historical transition. For a revolution to succeed it cannot stop at the acquisition of power; it must elaborate a new identity that gives it legitimacy. This new identity is imagined in two opposite historical directions. As Raymond Williams points out, the usage of the term "revolution" implies both the "making of a new *human* order" and the "overthrowing of an old order." Since the time of the French Revolution this "new *human* order" has been identified with the notion of "progress." Yet Williams also reminds us that revolutionary thought has also tended to turn to the past in the sense of the "achievement of the ORIGINAL rights of man."[13] The forward "progressive" movement has been represented in utopias and in political, technical, economic, and social programs. The backward-looking glance recasts the past through the reinterpretation and reelaboration of history, traditions, and myths. Vasconcelos's project incorporated these two tendencies. His vision of the future is represented by educational projects, building, and legislating. His vision of the past became a creation myth: the Spanish conquest of America marks the birth of our Hispanic-based *mestiza* identity, nation, continent, and ultimately world civilization.

Vasconcelos's understanding of Mexico's—and Latin America's—historical trajectory was shaped by his early experience in northern Mexico at a time when the region was transforming itself from a frontier into the modern border between Mexico and the United States.[14] The northern frontier was a space at the edge of western civilization. Although he was born in the southwestern state of Oaxaca in 1882, at an early age his family moved to Sásabe, "less than a town, a port in the desert of Sonora, on the limits with Arizona." It was a small bastion of the Mexican nation-state, surrounded by a "vast region of sands and mountain ranges" (*Ulises criollo,* 288). Barry Carr has identified three factors that shaped the Mexican north between 1880 and 1928: (1) its vastness and marginal status within civil and religious administrative structures; (2) the lack of a sedentary Indian population, leading to a lack of the large labor force that was present in the south, and constant armed confrontations between settlers and nomadic tribes; and (3) the growth of a significant economic linkage with U.S. capital.[15] During the *Porfiriato* this region underwent very marked political and economic transformations. The building of railroad lines linked the Mexican capital to the northern regions and the United States, and was accompanied by a significant growth in mining, agribusiness, and cattle raising and the growth of trade with the United States. Such developments reflected a greater interest on the part of federal authorities toward this long-neglected region. It was also a time of consolidation of North American expansion toward the Southwest. As a response, "The Mexican government sent its employees [and] its agencies to face the Yankee . . . *outposts,*" and Vasconcelos's father was one of those sent (*Ulises criollo*, 288, *outposts* in the original).

On both sides of the border, entrepreneurs, capitalists, and government agencies attempted to bring a rational administration to the frontier. Communication networks were established, commerce regulated, bandits and smugglers persecuted, national sovereignties carefully defended. The savage frontier began to be known and dominated, the border between two nation-states more closely defined and regulated. And although settlers like the Vasconceloses were sent to the border to protect the nation from U.S. outposts, both North Americans and Mexicans faced a "common enemy," the Apaches. This nomadic group of the frontier did not respect national borders; it roamed unregulated and posed a threat to national consolidation on both sides of the border. Both groups of settlers—or the "two white dominant castes," as Vasconcelos refers to them—who considered themselves bastions of civilization viewed the Apaches as "savage barbarians" to be tamed or eliminated. It was common knowledge among settlers that Apaches "killed the men, raped the women; they smashed little children on the ground and reserved the older ones for war." This fear so impressed the young Mexican boy that it appears in the first page of his memoirs. However, the text's only actual events that seem an Apache raid turn out to be an armed encounter between Mexican border officials and some smugglers (*Ulises criollo*, 288–89). These smugglers were threats to law and order, but in no way the murdering and pillaging savages of the settlers' imagination, and thus the settlers were relieved. Nevertheless, the real or imagined threat of Apache incursions was an ever-present concern to the settlers on both sides of the border.

Quite different is Vasconcelos's relationship with the United States, which, although also marked by confrontation, is in no way as apocalyptic as the one with the Apaches. The latter is a frontier relationship characterized by a fear, either actual or imagined, felt by a self-proclaimed "civilized" group of settlers facing an unknown nature and untamed human "savagery." These "savages," like the nature to which they belong, must be tamed and dominated, eliminated, or "civilized."[16] The settlers found themselves at the end of the nineteenth century in a situation similar to that of earlier European settlers on the continent, conquerors, missionaries, or pilgrims with a mission of gaining a frontier for western civilization. The United States was a totally different adversary. Here the Mexican settlers, sent north with the specific purpose of representing the nation-state, faced representatives of an opposing nation-state, one that was much more powerful. It was an encounter between two cultures and civilizations; an encounter between equals, albeit the greater military and economic might of the northern neighbor. And although half a century earlier the United States had conquered almost half of Mexico's territory, including the vast frontier where North Americans and Mexicans now faced each other, disputes were more often resolved through legal and diplomatic channels. The threat presented by the United States was no longer military, but rather economic and cultural. Significant in this regard is Vasconcelos's first encounter with the United States, narrated early in his memoirs.

He remembers the arrival of a "North American limits commission," which determined that "our camp, with [the region's only] well, lay under Yankee jurisdiction." The United States, with cartographers and surveyors, scientifically and legally drew a line in the sand. The frontier as a wild unknown was measured and documented. International law had to be respected. A modern border was being drawn. And the Mexicans of Sásabe were instructed to leave by the central government; "we were the weak ones and it was useless to resist" (*Ulises criollo,* 290–91). After a brief stay in Ciudad Juárez, the boy's family was resettled in Piedras Negras, Coahuila, a town that bordered Eagle Pass, Texas. At that time, passports were not needed and people were free to cross the international border. Yet a feeling of mutual suspicion prevented frequent crossings. Instead, Mexicans and North Americans engaged in regular stone-throwing battles across the river, as they yelled insults at each other (*Ulises criollo,* 304–5). Both communities resented each other, but their conflict, as Vasconcelos recalls it, was not as violent and definitive as the one that pitted both nations against the Apaches.

Mexicans resented the occupation of their nation's northern frontier by the United States 50 years earlier, but they also admired their northern neighbors. The United States, the autobiographer remembers, was a country where the rule of law sharply contrasted with Mexico's militarism—its own form of "barbarism," in Vasconcelos's analysis. The United States's democratic institutions and civil liberties created a socioeconomic context where, "Free of the military threat, the neighbors of Eagle Pass built modern and comfortable houses, while we, in Piedras Negras, continued living in a barbaric way." Those Mexicans who were able to save money would rather invest it in the United States out of fear of losing it to an arbitrary Mexican government or possible future revolutionaries. Also, "rebellious [Mexican] characters—the best yeast for progress—escaped whenever they could to the Yankee side which was blessed by a peace nourished by public liberties" (*Ulises criollo,* 304). As a result of peace, liberty and education—another aspect of the United States that Vasconcelos greatly admired—Eagle Pass expanded rapidly. "Four and five-story buildings were erected overnight, avenues were paved." While the people of Eagle Pass "polished and embellished" their town, Piedras Negras was marked by "dumped garbage in the streets and the ruins of an elemental urban construction." Although Piedras Negras had dominated social and economic life for many years, now Eagle Pass leaped ahead. Its ultimate triumph was not marked by violence but rather when Mexican tastes began changing, "it became fashionable to dress in the stores from the other side," and many Mexicans began giving up their traditional wines, preferring instead cocktails, whiskies, and beer, "a liquid that looks like gold but tastes like an unsweetened soup" (*Ulises criollo,* 324–25).[17]

Throughout his memoirs, Vasconcelos narrates with disappointment the way that Mexican cultural practices are transformed by a North American influence. While he looks with admiration at North American technology and democratic institutions, he looks with disdain at many of the northern cultural practices, particularly the culinary. For him these cultural expressions are definitely inferior to the traditional Mexican—that is, Hispanic—ones. Vasconcelos's response to such a perceived inferiority in the United States is an example of the sort of cultural elitism of Rodó's *arielismo.* He admires the U.S.'s modernization, but sees its people as culturally inferior. He recalls that his mother kept some notes from her elementary school that stated that "to the north there lived some rude and red-headed men who put their feet on the table . . . and preached the Protestant heresy" (*Ulises criollo,* 322–23). As in the case of the beer and wine, Vasconcelos's observations are often culinary. He rhetorically insisted that civilization ended where corn oil was used instead of olive, and where barbecuing began in the northern frontier of the Mexican territory. In a turn worthy of Rodó he recalls visiting what had been presented to him as the best restaurant in San Antonio, where they were quickly served a steak with potatoes, ketchup, and coffee from behind a high bar (*Tormenta,* 785–86). Not only is the ketchup-laden meal much inferior to the complex and refined Mexican fare, the emphasis on quick service and consumption is representative of the utilitarianism and lack of leisure in the calibanesque "pioneers" of the north. The emphasis in the north is on efficiency, not pleasure.

Vasconcelos glanced askance at the United States, but ultimately its educational system was an irresistible pull. His parents enrolled him in an Eagle Pass elementary because in Piedras Negras "there was not one acceptable school" (*Ulises criollo*, 304). Here in the microcosm of the classroom and playground, he faced the ambiguities, confrontations, and transitions of the border territory. Here Mexicans and North Americans faced each other. On the playground they fought each other, in the classroom they argued about Texas Independence and the U.S. occupation of Mexico. Vasconcelos remembers that only the teacher's "equanimity" kept a just and disciplined order among the energetic children. The memory of these school days reveals certain aspects of Vasconcelos's personalist cultural elitism. His recollections are of a cultural confrontation with his Anglo-Saxon counterparts. Thus he tells of Anglo students saying things such as "Mexicans are semi-civilized people," and the teacher replying, "But look at Joe, he is a mexican [sic], isn't he civilized?, isn't [sic] he a gentleman?" He also remembers his superior language skills as he was able to spell difficult Mexican words like "Tenochtitlán and Popocatépetl" and those from the United States like "Washington"—a bilingual ability his Anglo-American classmates did not have (*Ulises criollo*, 310–11). He reveals here a characteristic arrogance: it is precisely toward *him*, not his classmates, that the teacher turns as an example of a "civilized" Mexican, it is also *he*, not his classmates, who outdoes North American students in spelling. This is an arrogance that he himself acknowledges, "I knew arrogance before I knew lust. At the age of ten I already felt alone and unique, with a call to lead" (*Ulises criollo*, 320).

A somewhat different type of arrogance is evident in the way Vasconcelos recalls the various types of "Mexicans" in his school. He freely uses the term "Mexican" in an apparently unproblematic manner. Nevertheless, Vasconcelos separates himself from the Texas Mexicans by claiming to be one of the very few "complete Mexicans" in the school. Despite their differences, Vasconcelos sees historical and biological ties linking "complete" and "incomplete" Mexicans. He remembers a Texas history class when such linkages were made evident:

> There were not many Mexicans in the course, but we were determined. Texas Independence and the 1847 War divided the class into rival camps. When I speak of Mexicans I include many who, even living in Texas and having parents with citizenship, joined *my* cause for reasons of blood. And it did not matter whether or not they wanted to, because the Yankees had them classified. (*Ulises criollo*, 311, my emphasis)[18]

It is a Mexican coalition formed around him. It is "them," the Texas Mexicans, who "joined *my* cause," he tells us. It is *his* cause, even if the "incomplete" Texas Mexicans are the ones who bear the burden of occupation after the two North American expansionist wars. It is also the "incomplete" Mexicans who must spend their lives "classified" by the "Yankees," but it is around *him* that he tells us that a coalition was formed.

In this part of his autobiography he uses the term *mexicano* (Mexican) to tautologically refer to people of Mexican descent on both sides of the border and uses the term *norteamericano* (North American) to refer to Anglo-Saxon North Americans—one could assume that Anglo-Saxons born and raised in Mexico with a Mexican cultural upbringing would be considered "Mexicans." Often Vasconcelos uses the term *yanqui* (Yankee) as a synonym for "North American." Both terms—"Mexican" and "North American" or "Yankee"—are freely used by the author almost as binary opposites in a rather arbitrary manner, without accounting for the vast variety of subtle political, cultural, ethnic, economic, gender, and other factors that inform and determine individual and group identities and alliances. He makes some distinctions between the Mexican populations on both sides of the border, but the term remains the same: "Mexican," which is only qualified by an adjective ("complete" or "incomplete"). At other points of his autobiography, and in other texts, Vasconcelos sometimes uses the term *"pocho."* In its general currency, the use of this term is usually associated with linguistic and cultural code switching. Often, as in Vasconcelos's usage, the term carries derogatory connotations. The *pocho* is a grotesque hybrid, the antithesis of a homogeneous national culture.[19] Often in Vasconcelos's writing, *pocho* also signifies all those Mexicans within Mexico who, in his opinion, politically support U.S. influence in Mexican affairs. This accusation usually falls on Calles's supporters.

His Texas Mexican classmates conveniently function as extras in a production in which the *Ulises criollo* is the star. In a characteristically egocentric move of the narrative, it is "a little bilingual Texan" who first approaches Vasconcelos early in the school year, not the other way around. The young boy incites him to fight Jack, an Anglo student. Outside of the classroom the young Texas Mexicans' lives seem to revolve around fighting the Anglo kids, and they are very skillful at it. They are the ones who teach young José to use a knife to intimidate Anglo bullies (*Ulises criollo*, 305–6, 311–13). They are presented as proud and brave Mexican fighters, capable of scaring the strongest Anglos. The young children fight Anglo oppression in the school yard and Vasconcelos learns their skills, but he prefers another forum, that of ideas. The other Mexicans are the troops; he is the ideologue. Vasconcelos appropriates the pain and rage of his "incomplete" Mexican classmates in order to construct himself as redeemer. More than half a century of U.S. occupation of Texas gives him—the heroic, civilized, and complete Mexican—an opportunity to scream the truth. It is he who tells his Anglo classmates "That is not true" when they insult Mexico's dignity. He is the witty and articulate bilingual student who can challenge Yankees to spell "Popocatépetl" as he spells "Washington." Vasconcelos gives a Mexican cosmopolitan voice to the Mexicans under occupation. Like Octavio Paz would do 15 years after the publication of *Ulises criollo,* he finds in Mexicans living in the United States a model for Mexican identity through enraged resistance, but they also seem to be somewhat perverted by their regular contact with North Americans.[20]

Yet despite the tensions between Mexicans and Anglo-Saxons, almost 50 years later Vasconcelos remembers the school with nostalgia, praising the U.S. educational system and his teachers. He considers this system a cornerstone for the fast economic development of the northern nation. What he does criticize is the choice of certain textbooks. Particularly pertinent to our discussion is the narrator's observation about *The Fair God.* With an approach worthy of today's multicultural pedagogues, he identifies the way the North American books like this interpellate minority students, crushing their ethnic pride and identity. Such an observation, however, is disturbingly paradoxical. He critiques this book, not because of its ideological effects on "Mexicans" in the United States but because of its perceived destabilizing effects in Mexico as part of a North American expansionist project. *The Fair God,* he tells us,

> [was] a sort of novel about the Spaniards' arrival to conquer Mexico. . . .
> [I]t was singular that those North Americans, so jealous about the privilege of their white race, when dealing with Mexico always sympathized with the Indians, never with the Spaniards. The thesis of the barbaric Spaniard and the noble Indian . . .

Vasconcelos here seems to exclude Indians from the Mexican equation. Giving him the benefit of the doubt, one could say that his concern rests exclusively on a perceived overprivileging of the Indian. Yet on the previous page Vasconcelos claims that his biggest "irritation" in school was caused by the discussion of Mexicans and Eskimos as "semi-civilized people." Had the comment referred exclusively to the Eskimos, Vasconcelos would certainly agree. His concern here is that Mexicans are paired with Eskimos. Eskimos—a Native American group—are a marker of "semi-civilization." Similarly, on the same page, Vasconcelos refers to the "Aztec massacre" led by Santa Anna at El Alamo. "Aztec" here is a derogatory adjective, synonymous with barbaric (*Ulises criollo,* 311–13). An emphasis on Mexico's Indian past and present is then, by inference, an emphasis on its character as a semicivilized and barbaric nation. Throughout his later career, Vasconcelos would use the adjective "Aztec" to refer to what he perceived to be the bloodthirsty instincts of Mexico's military rulers. Quite different are his thoughts about the Spanish heritage. A foreigner in the schools of a more powerful neighbor, Vasconcelos found solace in what he saw as his country's glorious *past.* Indeed some of his contemporary Mexicans were uncivilized, he thought; for example, those military dictators who put personal interest over that of their country. His parents, concerned about a loss of identity in the United States, provided him with books about Mexico. He particularly mentions the classic *México a través de los siglos* and a historical atlas edited by García Cubas, which

> shows graphically the disaster of our independent history. It depicts Cortés's expeditions until La Paz, in Baja California; those of Albuquerque through New Mexico and the chain of Missions which reached Russian outposts beyond San Francisco. [The atlas] immediately shows the successive losses. A skewed patriotism proclaimed our emancipation from Spain as an unprecedented victory, but it was evident that this was fulfilled through disintegration, not through creation. The maps opened our eyes. . . . Half a nation sacrificed and millions of Mexicans substituted by foreigners in their own territory was the result of the militarist governments of those like Guerrero, Santa Anna and Porfirio Díaz. (*Ulises criollo,* 321)

Such a perspective of Mexico's decay would be prominent throughout the Creole Ulysses's career, nostalgic for a glorious colonial past: a past that saw the first printing press of America in the Viceroyalty of New Spain; a past when sailors left Mexico's ports to explore the world and establish a reliable and efficient transoceanic fleet; a past when the territorial expansion of New Spain and its institutions of higher learning dwarfed their emerging counterparts in New England. Vasconcelos blames the collapse of this glorious past on internal wars, the result of Mexico's militarism during its first independent century. A violence he saw continue in the revolutionary regime that he, by 1935, vehemently opposed.

As he recalls it in 1935, Vasconcelos's family relied on Catholicism, a mark of the Spanish presence in America, as an instrument of resistance both against the Apaches and the Protestant Anglo-Saxons. Yet the role of this religion varies according to the enemy faced. Regarding his fear of the former, the author recalls that his only defense was his mother's religious solace. She advised him that if he ever fell prisoner to the Apaches he should "live with them and serve them, learn their language and speak to them about Our Lord Jesus Christ, who died for us and for them, for all men" (*Ulises criollo,* 290). Vis-à-vis the North Americans, she did not suggest proselytizing. Rather, realizing that her son would constantly interact with them in school, she zealously planted in him the Catholic faith as an inoculation against any "heretic" contamination (*Ulises criollo,* 323). The former is a frontier relationship. Just like the Spanish missionaries of the sixteenth century, she saw a savage and mysterious other, needy of redemption and incorporation into civilization. The latter is a border relationship; also with an other, but one who shares many elements of her civilization. They did not need to be converted or incorporated; rather, the young boy should resist their intrusion.

The Vasconcelos children had a very religious upbringing, praying constantly and reading books about Christianity. And their attitude toward religion went far beyond the dogmas of faith; it represented a whole cultural expression that distinguished Mexicans from North Americans and Apaches. Vasconcelos thus recalls his first trip to Durango during the 1890s. Away from his frontier outpost, in Mexico's colonial interior, Vasconcelos was impressed with the pageantry and mysticism of the Catholic celebration of Holy Week, with candles, bells, processions, choirs, and masses. The magnificent colonial buildings reminded the boy of a more glorious past, when missionaries built new towns and brought Indian populations into the western Christian world. It was in this deeply religious region that the young boy immersed himself in his Hispano-Catholic cultural heritage and understood why his father, deeply rooted in this tradition, would not "suddenly surrender to the Nordic novelties of the railroad and running water." The faith, mysticism, and aesthetic of this ancient Catholic tradition was much more important to him than the simple material comforts provided by modern technology (*Ulises criollo,* 332–37).

The person that the older Vasconcelos evokes is one formed by a border experience, greatly influenced by his mother's lessons on the importance of Catholicism for the maintenance of his Latin Mexican identity, which he must maintain in opposition to his Apache and Anglo-Saxon North American others. The former he sees with fear, but with a spirit of redemption; the latter he fears and resents, but also admires. These emotional attachments and repulsions were prevalent throughout Vasconcelos's public life. During his career's zenith as minister of education, at a time when his Catholic anti-*indigenista* stance was less marked, he endeavored to redeem Mexico's marginalized Indians by bringing western modern and classical culture to them. He was cognizant, however, that this project was not exclusively philanthropic, as the failure to incorporate the Indian majority to the hegemonic culture forebode national disintegration. Concerning the United States, he attempted to incorporate into his educational project North American methods and attitudes that he found useful, but always in an effort to fortify Mexico in the face of U.S. expansionism.

This concern about the situation of Mexico in relation to its Indian population and the United States became less complex, more Manichaean, and very troubling in some of Vasconcelos's polemical writings of the 1930s, texts that have given plenty of material to those who condemn his legacy. These were texts published at the same time as his autobiography, but their purpose was explicitly polemical. Their ultra-conservative political assertions are much more exaggerated and disturbing. With this in mind, I now turn to what can be characterized as Vasconcelos's ugly legacy. I turn here early in the discussion with two purposes: to move beyond the simple dismissal of his later thought under the overused and simplistic epithet of fascist, and to try to find continuities—albeit with varying shades and emphases—in his thought.

"*México en 1950*" (Mexico in 1950) is a curious text, appearing in the 1937 collection *Qué es la revolución* (What is the revolution). It takes us to a parade in Mexico City presided over by "His Excellence Nezahualcóyotl Rosenberg, President of the United Mexican Soviet States." The text represents the fears of a paranoid, grief-stricken Vasconcelos: a Jewish-North-American-Anglo-Saxon-Bolshevik-Banking-Protestant-Masonic conspiracy attempting to take over the world. In Mexico this alliance is represented by a *mestizo* president of Indian and Jewish origin a combination that in the Mexican thinker's celebration of racial mixture should represent a triumph of cosmic miscegenation, but does not in this case. The Judeo-Indian president leads a nation dominated by banks and international trusts. Mexican landowners and industrialists have disappeared as "agrarian property has been socialized" and "all the lands, [and] all the industries belong to the Banks," which are based in "New York and Washington, and a few in London and Paris." The parade marches in front of the monument to the revolution, which now is "surrounded by wretched skyscrapers, disfigured by advertisements of North American trusts."[21]

In texts like this, the cosmopolitan, creative Vasconcelos gives way to a paranoid, racist, and reactionary one. One can understand his fear of North American economic and cultural penetration into Mexico and Latin America: a fear shared by his predecessors and contemporaries like Rodó, Martí, and Mariátegui, among others; a fear justified by U.S. military interventions in Cuba, Puerto Rico, Nicaragua, Panama, and the Dominican Republic during Vasconcelos's life; a fear personally materialized as U.S. ambassador Dwight D. Morrow—of J. P. Morgan—took sides in favor of Pascual Ortiz Rubio, the PNR candidate, in Vasconcelos's questionable electoral defeat. The former presidential candidate, nevertheless, transgresses certain acceptable limits of discourse and analysis and sinks into racism and xenophobia, in an extreme example of a paranoid understanding of a world economy manipulated by a conspiracy of New York Jewish bankers and Russian Jewish Bolsheviks, in collusion with Protestant-Anglo-Saxon interests, in an effort to destroy Hispano-Catholic culture. A clear relationship to justify a plot by such diverse groups is never exposed by the author. It is just assumed, taken for granted, and deployed as a central premise for his preaching. His grotesque caricature of "His Excellence Nezahualcóyotl Rosenberg" clearly denotes a contempt towards Jews and Native Americans. Particularly revealing is his contemptuous use of the name Nezahualcóyotl, that of the king of Texcoco, remembered for his wisdom and poetic talent. If a decade earlier he had defended the refinement of *ancient* Mesoamerican culture, he now mocks even one of its most renowned figures.

Less peculiar, but not less damaging for his reputation, Vasconcelos's attitude toward the Spanish Civil War is an instance in which pronouncements make him vulnerable to accusations of fascism. He sided with Franco's troops in opposition to the Republican government led by the Popular Front. Vasconcelos saw in the Republican government a threat to the Catholic order in Spain, which for him represented a "Saxonizing and reformist project." The anticlericalism of certain factions within the Popular Front government reminded him of the anticlerical tendencies of Calles's regime in Mexico, which culminated in the *Cristero* War. In an effort to take power away from an influential Catholic Church, Mexico's revolutionary regime and the Spanish Republic confiscated Church property and excluded this religious institution from participating in politics and education.

Vasconcelos's fear of a "Saxonizing" anticlericalism was not totally unfounded. As Jean Meyer—who in no way shares Vasconcelos's religious fanaticism and conspiratorial fears—points out in his seminal work on the *Cristero* War, Mexican anticlericals were often Protestants and Masons, full of admiration for the United States, who saw the Catholic Church in Mexico as responsible for a fanaticism that retarded Mexico's development. In this regard they appropriated for themselves "Anglo-Saxon propaganda against Mexico's colonial and Catholic past." While the Mexican Catholic Church was deprived of its traditional educational role, by 1926 the Methodist Church alone ran 200 schools. Meyer reminds us that Episcopal Bishop Moisés Sáenz ran the very ministry that Vasconcelos had created. Concerning the Masonic connection, the same author points out that in this period "Freemasonry and government were tightly related, to the point that it was necessary to be a Freemason to occupy any post of importance." Among Vasconcelos's political enemies, Meyer points out that Pascual Ortiz Rubio—Vasconcelos's PNR opponent for the presidency—was a Freemason, as well as Emilio Portes Gil—provisional president during the campaign . The latter became Grand Master in 1933–1934 (Meyer, 193–97).

Beyond the "Saxonizing" threat, Vasconcelos was extremely concerned about the massive violence unleashed by the most extreme forms of anticlericalism, both in Mexico and in Spain. In Spain churches were looted and burned, priests were summarily shot, and corpses of priests were dug from their graves and mocked in public.[22] Similar acts of violence took place in Mexico, where radical anticlerical forces during the *Cristero* War engaged in extreme and unnecessary provocations, celebrating blasphemous "reverse masses" in Catholic churches, organizing parties in these buildings, dancing with figures of the Virgin, undressing the saints, shooting Christ figures, and having sex, urinating, and defecating in the temples (Meyer, 210). One should, of course, remember that the violence brought about by the religious conflict in both countries responded to much more than simply religious questions. Liberals, more radical anarchists, and communists in both countries considered the Catholic Church a representative of the traditional elite and an obstacle for modernization. In the case of Mexico, the church's opponents also saw in the church an instrument of foreign intervention. The violence unleashed against the church also channeled years of resentment toward the landed elite, longtime allies of the church.

In his 1935 *Ulises criollo,* Vasconcelos is willing to recognize what he considered certain errors in the judgment of the Mexican Catholic hierarchy, such as its decision to support Huerta's overthrow of Madero (*Ulises criollo*, 719). Nevertheless, he saw in the continuous war between liberal governments and the Catholic faithful an unnecessary divisiveness that not only challenged Mexico's identity but also hindered economic development. Even in 1937, the former minister of education does not intend to return to a past order. He is still a supporter of modern economic reform, and thus he admonishes that "With a little religious tolerance, both in Spain and in Mexico, the new economic ideas would have already triumphed," and the countries would not be immersed in fratricidal warfare.[23] Franco's fascist forces represented for Vasconcelos a possibility of order in a Spain that had been plagued by factionalized violence throughout the 1930s.[24] It would be unfair and simplistic, however, to say that Vasconcelos was an outright fascist supporter. In this regard, he writes in the same text that "I detest governments of force and believe that their activities are sterile." Rather, he claims to believe in a civilian-controlled participatory democracy. However, during the 1930s he identifies a greater threat in the chaos he sees in the Spanish Republic than in the fascism espoused by Franco. He thus expresses a qualified understanding of Franco's successful campaign: "the chaos, the insecurity of revolutions, provokes desperate changes of society towards authority; but one should not put one's hopes in the work of dictatorships." He states that upon the overthrow of Azaña's coalition government, he will declare himself against any sort of militarism ("También Francia," 189–90). Rather than specifically sympathizing with Franco's fascist philosophy, Vasconcelos saw in the *Generalísimo* a strong individual who could control the violence and chaos he blamed on the weak Popular Front government.

Here Vasconcelos also expresses his admiration for Italian dictator Benito Mussolini, who, in his opinion, is capable of playing the role of philosopher king. In his defense of the Italian he proposes that *certain* dictators are acceptable. His support is not for a particular philosophy or party, but rather for an individual of genius:

> Today, when in Spain the military triumphs, I can say that I do not expect anything good from a regime that begins imitating Mussolini without having Mussolini's personal genius. The evil of all fascism, as of all communism or every dictatorial regime, rests on the quality of the dictator and his auxiliaries. A genial dictator can do something. A mediocre dictator is the worst plague that a people can suffer.

Referring to the specific case of Mexico, he writes:

If fascism got to signify among us a government of the best, with the object of constructing a country capable of defending its autonomy, its personality, and, with that, its economy, then we could affirm that, at least, we are incorporated into the contemporary face of social development. ("También Francia," 189)

Here his speculative consideration of a Mexican fascism is qualified in two very clear ways. The "at least" seems to indicate reservation in the choosing of the best of two evils. Furthermore, his judgment is based on results—"If fascism got to signify among us . . ." His speculative support, again, is not based on a particular ideology or program, but on a very specific end result.

Texts like this can easily be used to label the Mexican thinker with the epithet of "fascist." With the heavy emotional charge that this term carries, such an accusation can then be used to discredit all of the thought that led to this position. I want to insist, however, that Vasconcelos did not proclaim himself a fascist. In his characteristic personalism, he rather admired particular leaders. He saw in these two dictators, whom he observed from a distance, two *individuals* capable of reinstating order in their countries and of bringing forth economic modernization while maintaining a strong Latin and Catholic national identity. In this regard, one can understand Vasconcelos's sympathy toward Mussolini's regime, with its rhetoric of a return to the glories of the Roman Empire. One notices, for example, that he praises the two Latin fascist dictators, but does not praise the icon of fascism, the German Adolf Hitler.

Throughout his public career, Vasconcelos tended to look at politics on a personal rather than institutional level. It is not parties that matter, but their leaders. His strong criticism of the revolution focuses on individuals rather than whole factions. We see him then praise "the apostle" Madero and attack at a very personal level figures like Carranza, Calles, Wilson, and Morrow. Regarding his own career, he was a dominating individualist who took matters into his own hands. We can remember how it was *he,* the "complete Mexican," who represented his fellow Mexican students in Texas. As minister of education he was a hands-on administrator, pushing his own agenda forward and closely supervising the SEP's activities through regular tours of the republic. He also insisted on personally supervising the ministry's construction projects. The way he ran his presidential campaign is also characteristic of Vasconcelos's personalism. He received the support of various political parties, including Madero's Anti-re-electionist Party, but he never gave in to the party's instructions. His movement was identified as *Vasconcelismo*, not *Antireeleccionismo*. And, at the time of the electoral defeat, he took the lack of an uprising as a personal affront.

The strong personal leader Vasconcelos had in mind for Mexico was none other than himself. The articles in *Qué es la revolución* are full of a bitter arrogance. He is certain that had he assumed the presidency, as he justly deserved, his labor would have been "incomparable" in relation to the destruction caused by the many "inept or evil" characters who held the office.[25] Vasconcelos constructs himself as martyr, leading a life of sacrifice for his people with the printed word as his weapon, of a civilian *caudillo;* an intellectual martyr ready to play the role of philosopher king, but without hopes for a kingdom to rule. As an exiled savior he complains about his destiny, but claims "perhaps more than my own misgivings, weigh the pains of my people for whose tomorrow I fight without rest and hope" ("El amargado," 87). As Martha Robles points out, Vasconcelos tends to construct history as confrontations between good and evil, where he presents himself as a prophet or messiah, announcing the catastrophes awaiting his people and providing the symbol of a new golden age.[26] Vasconcelos's self-assessment as an individual particularly virtuous for prophecy, action, and martyrdom is crucial and prevalent throughout his thought and career, and not particular to his later phase.

Three important poles dominate Vasconcelos's writing of the 1930s that so offended many of his contemporaries and subsequent generations: (1) a self-construction as martyr, prophet, and hero; (2) an orthodox conservative Catholic religious faith; and (3) an obsession with the category of race, which imprisons human beings as an essential marker. All three poles correspond to important categories in his philosophical system, developed long before his "fascist" period. Critics like Max Aub find a radically and unforgivably changed Vasconcelos after 1930.[27] Contrary to this interpretation, I argue that the seed for the thought of the later Vasconcelos, with its rac(ial)ism and xenophobia, was clearly present in his earlier and less controversial period, as he served as minister of education and wrote *La raza cósmica*. His conversion to orthodox Catholicism came after years of intense interest in mysticism and religion. Despite professing a hedonistic heterodoxy in his earlier years, Catholicism was still then central for both his philosophical system and his racial self-construction. His was a Hispanic Catholic heterodoxy.

Central to Vasconcelos's thought is a particular understanding of religion and its intersection with history and politics. The later, paranoid Vasconcelos waves the flag of Catholicism as the only emancipating force able to oppose the Anglo-Saxon-Jewish-Protestant-Banker-Bolshevik conspiracy. The threat he envisions is not limited to economic and material domination, but, even more disturbing to him, it implies the cultural and spiritual demise of the Catholic Latin civilization, and thus, according to his worldview, the foreclosure of the possibility of a truly universal and human race. Vasconcelos, who during the century's first quarter flirted with a playful Catholic heterodoxy, theosophy, eastern religions, and mysticism with a radical edge, by the 1930s aligned himself with conservative orthodox Catholicism. Vasconcelos's alliance with an orthodox and conservative Catholic Church separated him from official nationalists, as well as from liberal and radical opponents of Mexico's regime, largely secular if not outright anticlerical.

Catholicism, for Mexican liberals and radicals, is an anathema; it is the cultural instrument of conservative oppressors, an instrument of the Spanish conquerors, Maximilian, Díaz, the *cristeros,* and, by the 1930s, Franco in Spain. Early in his political career, Vasconcelos's heterodox Catholicism did not interfere with the Sonoran faction's anticlericalism. Despite the important role played by Protestants and Freemasons, as discussed earlier, there was also an important streak of "anticlerical Catholics" who formed part of this faction. One could locate the role of the minister of education within this tradition. After all, as Alan Knight asserts, the Catholic Church, and the Catholic laity in particular, played a central role in the forging of a postrevolutionary political, ideological, and cultural "national synthesis."[28] Knight argues that, while outright support of the Catholic Church is usually considered antithetical to the official nationalist project, ranging from secular to rabidly anticlerical in its liberal and radical traditions, Catholicism is an integral part of Mexican culture and society. Referring to what he identifies as the Mexican "folk" tradition, Knight makes a distinction between Catholic religious and cultural affiliation, on the one hand, and Catholic political activism on the other: "although [the 'folk' tradition] was overwhelmingly Catholic, at least in terms of belief and ritual, [it] was not necessarily *politically* Catholic" (Knight 1990, 233, emphasis in original). Catholicism, as Knight reminds us, is not a monolithic entity; it is open to a multiplicity of interpretations, practices, and levels of commitment, both within and without the official institutions. In a country where Catholicism is the overwhelming religion of the people, liberalism and radicalism often use religious myth and iconography, leading to what Knight identifies as anticlerical Catholicism. Within this tradition, Knight pays particular attention to what he calls "folk liberalism":

> "Folk liberals" were usually Catholic: in ballads and political manifestos (such as Zapata's Plan of Ayala) they invoked God in terms that would have appalled good urban radicals. But they were also staunch liberals, sometimes anticlericals and self-conscious progressives, and usually fierce patriots. They accepted Catholic belief and ritual but rejected clerical authority, which they saw as conservative and antipatriotic.

Knight introduces the concept of anticlerical Catholicism in the following manner:

> Mexico was and remains "Catholic": the census figures are so consistent in this respect that they offer little scope for statistical analyses of de-Christianization. However, the majority of the population were "nominal" Catholic, who, while they subscribed to Catholic belief and ritual, did not necessarily attend Church regularly, did not conform to Catholic doctrinal requirements (e.g., did not marry in the Church), and certainly did not obey the political authority of the Church hierarchy. Catholic by belief or mentality, this majority did not constitute a Catholic political constituency, which conducted its politics according to Catholic criteria. . . . Thus it was entirely possible for many Mexicans, urban and rural, to combine Catholicism and liberalism, even Catholicism and a form of institutional anticlericalism (that is to say, they were, like the anticlericals of Lollardy or the Reformation, against priests—especially rich, socially remote priests—but not against religion per se). (Knight 1990, 233) [29]

The ideology of the early Vasconcelos, while not necessarily "folk," also combined political and religious ideology in a form of anticlerical Catholicism. In a 1958 interview with Emmanuel Carballo, Vasconcelos speaks about moments of *political* rupture with the Catholic Church's hierarchy, particularly after its support of Huerta's 1913 coup against Madero. *Spiritually,* however, he recognizes "moments of doubt," but ultimately affirms his deep faith in Catholic culture and dogma.[30] As will be seen in the next chapters, the minister's early heterodox Catholicism was a central component of his racial philosophy and his educational practice.

As secularism and a more radical anticlericalism gained the upper hand in official circles during the 1920s, affiliation with or rejection of the Catholic Church represented, according to Knight, a "crucial divide"

in Mexican politics, accentuated by the *Cristero* War and the Spanish
Civil War in the 1930s (Knight 1990, 232). Vasconcelos's open alliance
with the Catholic Church after his tenure as minister almost by definition set him in opposition to Calles and his anticlerical supporters. Personal conflicts with Calles further set him apart from established circles.
Finally, the fact that Mexico's population did not rise up in arms to
affirm what he considered the robbery of his legal and democratic election to the presidency in 1929 further alienated Vasconcelos from much
of the Mexican intelligentsia, both official and oppositional. There is no
question that after the 1920s Vasconcelos turned more conservative,
even reactionary. The purpose of this discussion is not to apologize for
Vasconcelos; this has become commonplace in many studies of the
author.[31] It is not my purpose either to provide a psychoanalytic or otherwise ideological or historical explanation for Vasconcelos's marked
conservatism beginning with the 1930s. What concerns my discussion
is the way in which a rac(ial)ist and Catholic ideology and practice,
which in the 1930s would turn into fascist and ultraconservative sympathies, interacted and developed with the secular ideology and practice of
the triumphant liberal and radical factions of the Mexican Revolution.

Hugo Achúgar, in his essay "The Book of Poems as a Social Act,"
insists on the significance of the "historical enunciating situation" surrounding the publication of a book of poems. The usefulness of the category is, however, not limited to poetry books and is applicable to other
cultural products. Attention to the enunciating situation "in addition to
attempting to avoid the reductive emphasis on content that overlooks
the semantic function of the totality of elements constitutive of the book
of poems—considers verbal and social contexts external to the book
itself" (Achúgar, 651–52). As is seen in the following chapters, Vasconcelos's seminal *La raza cósmica* and his tenure at the ministry of education are laden with the rac(ial)ist and Catholic ideology that informs his
later texts and actions. In his later years he became much more vocal in
his conservatism and orthodoxy, and I must insist that his more extreme
statements and allegiances in this period are greatly responsible for his
ostracism. Nevertheless, the continuity of content exists although Vasconcelos's racial and religious pronouncements are received differently
after the 1920s. Not forgetting Vasconcelos's conservative turn, one
must also consider the historical enunciating situations that surround
his pronouncements in both periods. Under which context were they
articulated? How were they both uttered and put into practice? Even
Vasconcelos's Catholicism, antithetical to the official revolutionary ideol-

ogy, under certain circumstances served the institutionalization of the postrevolutionary secular elite's power, and in many ways defines their national(ist) project. Knight warns us against too easy distinctions that immediately relate Catholicism to conservatism and a "false consciousness" imposed by the landed elite on ignorant masses. Catholic ideology, as well as cultural and organizational practices, were used by radicals as well as conservatives during the revolutionary struggle and its later institutionalization.[32]

Central to Vasconcelos's educational project during his ministry, for example, were the cultural missions, which are indicative of such hybrid forms of Catholicism and liberalism. Their inspiration was the Catholic missions used by the Spanish conquerors to convert Native Americans. More than rural schools, the missions should also function as whole cultural centers, teaching both pupils and parents hygiene, nutrition, and other everyday cultural practices in the context of work and leisure beyond the limits of the classroom. As the Spanish conquerors attempted to transform all aspects of indigenous cultural practices in order to incorporate their new subjects into the Christian faith and civilization, now Vasconcelos expected his cultural missions to transform the mainly Indian rural population and incorporate it into the national mainstream. As a more abstract noun, the word "mission" denotes a moral kind of commitment. In terms of the Spanish conquerors, this mission is ideologically construed as the religious duty to God to bring the heathen into the proper religious life; it is a mission of spiritual salvation. This spiritual shade of the term was central for Vasconcelos, as he saw in his educational project a redemptive quality with a scope far broader than literacy and traditional curricula.

For the moment we must point out that Vasconcelos's notion of a redemptive mission corresponds, in more secular terms, to a similar project through education envisioned by liberals, radicals, and even Porfirian positivists. Knight points out that throughout the late nineteenth and early twentieth centuries members of these groups saw in education a way to move Indians out of their "primitive" and "idle" habits and incorporate them into "modern" civilization. The motivations for this incorporation varied. In the view of some, a national system of education would strengthen the nation by raising the national consciousness of Indians, who otherwise remained unaware of their belonging to the Mexican nation-state. For modernizing capitalists, educational projects would prepare a disciplined labor force with a work ethic more conductive to their exploitation. More idealist liberals saw in education a consciousness-raising instrument to help the Mexican masses overcome their wretched conditions, imposed on them due to their ignorance (Knight 1990, 235–36). Under different ideological shades, then, various intellectual circles had shared Vasconcelos's vision of education as a civilizing mission for the regeneration and modernization of the nation. The religious connotations of the term could easily be incorporated into such secular rhetoric and programs. Long after Vasconcelos's retirement from the ministry of education, the cultural missions continued working, often functioning as forums for the anticlerical propaganda of enthusiastic radical young teachers. Ideologically, the conceptualization of education as a civilizing and incorporating mission could be articulated into the postrevolutionary liberal discourse overshadowing its echoes of the Roman Catholic Church and the Spanish conquest.

On a practical level, the institution of the mission fit well into the organizational requirements and conditions of rural Mexico. With limited federal financing, the rural missions provided a public space for a multiplicity of functions. In many towns, school buildings provided a locale for gardens, workshops, meeting halls, offices, markets, and dance halls, in addition to their strictly pedagogical functions.[33] The cultural missions followed a pedagogy that emphasized activism, stressing "the social role of schools and promot[ing] community projects" (Rockwell, 189). Low budgets and insufficient personnel forced the ministry of education to depend on volunteer and local labor and financing. Such an arrangement often empowered local groupings, who used the facilities and political capital of the ministry to advance particular agendas, many times contrary to those of the ministry. Elsie Rockwell's article "Schools of the Revolution: Enacting and Contesting State Forms in Tlaxcala, 1910–1930" describes the intricate networks that negotiated, at a local level, the implementation of the ministry's educational project. Her empirical research shows that, at the provincial level of articulation, the new spaces provided by an activist missionary program of education were heavily contested and produced a variety of results, responding to particular geographic and historical conditions.

Beyond Vasconcelos's—or the regime's—particular religious preferences, during the early 1920s, as during the Porfirian regime, local schools were often administered and financed according to the *cofradía* system, which was originally developed with religious purposes. It is a rotating scheme based on honor, where *mayordomos* are responsible for financing religious festivities through personal contributions or those of their kin. "The arrangement," Rockwell tells us, "was used following the revolution for funding a variety of local projects, such as the restoration of churches or the celebration of patriotic fiestas" (Rockwell, 191). This is just one of many examples of ways in which a traditional organizational system can be articulated for a multiplicity of purposes, at times contradictory to their original purpose. Thus, the *cofradía* system, which had traditionally been used for religious festivities, could also be deployed in often anticlerical patriotic fiestas. Such a secular appropriation of religious ritual and tradition was not limited to the *cofradía* organizational system. "Civic ritual, including altars to Hidalgo and Morelos, had been introduced in the nineteenth century in explicit competition with religious ritual, and the practice continued in the 1920s." Rockwell points out that such a traditional form of politico-religious organization, centered around ritual honor and kinship obligations, "contrasted starkly with the more 'egalitarian' categories of 'citizen' or 'parent,' and with the rules for universal suffrage and taxation proposed by the federal school authorities" (Rockwell, 191–94). However, economic constraints and the lack of a capable professional educational bureaucracy of national scope did not allow for the state to control every single one of its schools, despite Vasconcelos's almost compulsive desire to do precisely that. The complex and multifaceted constellation of forces that struggled to give direction to the new national project is discussed at greater length later. What is important for my argument now is to point out that despite Vasconcelos's intentions, the early stages of educational institutionalization were highly contested. The minister of education helped create a new educational framework, theoretically based on the Catholic Spanish missions. The local articulation of such a framework, however, responded to specific moments of enunciation. The opening of a new school provided a space, the use of which was negotiated at the local level. As Rockwell points out, in some localities schools turned out to be very conservative, in others liberal. This heterogeneity was particularly vital during the early stages of institutionalization, when the old hegemony had collapsed and a new one was forming, in a situation that Knight identifies as one of "multiple sovereignty" (Knight 1994, 30). In and of itself, then, the practical deployment of cultural missions did not by definition offend liberals and radicals, despite the institution's Catholic origins. Similarly, an educational project enacted by a regime with a Jacobin tendency was not necessarily rejected by more traditionally oriented communities. On the contrary, in many instances they were welcomed as vehicles to access power and prestige.[34]

Vasconcelos's racial ideology is the subject of the next chapter, so I will not spend much time on it now. For my present purposes, however, I must make a couple of points. Race, it must be made clear, is a central category of Vasconcelos's thought, even before his utterly offensive racist and anti-Semitic ravings. Spirit and race go hand in hand in his philosophic and political pronouncements. They form part of the National University's motto—*Por mi raza hablará el espíritu* (through my race the spirit shall speak)—which he composed in 1921 and remains in use to this day. As will be discussed at greater length in the next chapter, on the surface Vasconcelos's racial ideology, as articulated in *La raza cósmica,* is a celebration of the racial and cultural miscegenation represented by *mestizaje.* A closer reading of Vasconcelos's texts, however, reveals a very Eurocentric conception of such a cosmic race, where the European races are the sole possessors of science and history. Racial mixture functions almost exclusively as an aesthetic addition to a Latin and Catholic racial and cultural tradition, which overdetermines such a mixture by creating the necessary historical conditions for its appearance.

Nevertheless, Vasconcelos's racial theory is ambiguous enough that it allows for a range of interpretations. The later Vasconcelos, with his close association with Spain and the Catholic Church, is consistent with his early racial theories. Without any problems, he republished *La raza cósmica* in 1948. The book has a new preface, but Vasconcelos takes his earlier words as his, without any apparent contradiction to his new political stance.[35] Articulated in the public sphere, however, and removed from the ideological apparatus that shaped the concept in the author's mind, the concept of *raza cósmica* suffers spectacular transformations unbeknownst to the original author. As a political slogan, the concept of a selected cosmic race fits well into a nationalist discourse. The ambiguity of the terms *raza* and *mestizo* allows for subtle— or not so subtle—changes in emphasis. Just as easily as Vasconcelos foregrounded the Hispanic-Latin part of the cosmic race, *indigenista* proponents foregrounded the Indian. Vasconcelos's suspicion of the United States, which rested on a grand teleological narrative pitting Saxons against Latins in a struggle for human destiny, fit well within official nationalist discourse. Without necessarily considering the grand teleological narrative sustaining Vasconcelos's fears, an assertion of "our" race struggling against a greater menacing "other" is again an efficient political slogan for a populist regime that deploys nationalism as one of its principal legitimating principles. Vasconcelos's privileging of the *raza* was also used in the Chicano movement of the 1960s and 1970s, with the slogan *Por mi raza hablará el espíritu* appearing on the covers of the journal Aztlán and accompanying publications of the Plan de Santa Barbara. Gloria Anzaldúa uses Vasconcelos's notion of the *raza cósmica* in her Chicana feminism. The Chicano movement has been able to articulate fruitfully a privileging of *raza* in certain political contexts, despite the fact that Vasconcelos saw Chicano culture as a threat to the Latin-dominated cosmic race as he conceived it, because of its incorporation of Anglo-Saxon influences and its particular linguistic code switching. Once again, under certain situations of enunciation a concept can take on a new ideological charge and function.

The later Vasconcelos, however, was far less ambiguous in his treatment of the notion of race. Now, he clearly insisted on the preeminence of the category of race. "[F]rom class, in its economic sense, one can exit easily," Vasconcelos writes, assuming an open world of opportunities for socioeconomic mobility within a democratically organized market economy. *"But from class,* [understood] *as race, we cannot exit.* No educational or political effort will turn a black into a white, or an Indian into a Chinese. Race is, in such a way, a relatively fixed mold, within which we must develop ourselves in the best possible way."[36] As was the case with his religious preoccupations, Vasconcelos did not suddenly arrive at racial preoccupations, which formed a prominent part of his early work. What seems to have changed in the decade that separates *La raza cósmica* from this statement is the fixity of the racial category. In the 1920s the Mexican thinker pointed at the cultural aspect of this category, insisting on the role played by missionaries in converting Indians to the Catholic faith and teaching the Spanish language, actions which in themselves seemed to incorporate these new Spanish subjects into a new universal racial category. Now there is not such a prophetic vision of world transformation. His position is rather defensive from purported enemies of Mexico. His is now an unambiguously Hispanic and anti-*indigenista* position. He now declares that his

> thesis of the cosmic race . . . is a way of signaling the phenomenon which we Mexicans constitute. A *mestizaje* that before aspiring to become universal must, first, integrate itself into what it is—a variety of the Hispanic—in which the Indian should not be an opposition as our enemies want, but a bronze vein, which, upon integrating itself in our souls, solidifies the character, iridesces the imagination. ("Conciencia," 104)

Paradoxically, despite his insistence on the determining quality of race, Vasconcelos still argues that Indians can be fused into a "Hispanic" race.

If such a thing is possible, then race is not as fixed as he leads us to believe. Here Vasconcelos finds himself in a paradox faced by many who attempt to define a Hispanic or Latin category both in terms of race and culture.[37] This problem, however, is not exclusive to the later Vasconcelos. As I will show in the next chapter, it is also present in *La raza cósmica,* but with a different emphasis. Furthermore, concern about race and national identity was not limited to this thinker, since, as Knight points out, a "blending of *indigenismo* with nationalism" characterizes the official ideology of the Mexican revolutionary regimes (Knight 1994, 59–60). What distinguishes Vasconcelos's emphasis on race from his counterparts in power is that the former minister privileges a Hispanic-Latin heritage, while official Mexican nationalism privileges— rhetorically and aesthetically, but rarely practically—an Indian heritage.

Particularly bothersome to many of Vasconcelos's critics is his rendering of history. Martha Robles characterizes his 1937 *Breve historia de México* (A brief history of Mexico) as "a broad summary of the nation's anti-history" (Robles, 47). Robles goes on to criticize Vasconcelos's historiographic methodology, which responds more to his whim than to actual research. She, however, is also aware that history and historiography were for Vasconcelos a political and ideological weapon, rather than an exact science. Under this perspective, Vasconcelos's "anti-history" should be seen as an anti-(official-nationalist-liberal-ideological) history, rather than as an anti-(True-Objective) History. Such an ideological emphasis on the critique of his historiography is clearer in Manuel Pedro González's much more personal condemnation of Vasconcelos as a "denigrator of the most noble patriotic figures that the country has produced" (Aub, 45). In his *Breve historia de México,* Vasconcelos denigrates the pantheon of liberal nationalist heroes, like Cuauhtémoc, Hidalgo, and Juárez, praising instead their conservative counterparts Malinche, Cortés, Iturbide, and Alamán, anathema to the liberal pantheon.

Despite the criticism that has befallen Vasconcelos's history of Mexico, Alvaro Matute, in a 1982 reevaluation of the text's legacy, points out that beyond history text books, which have the benefit of captive audiences, Vasconcelos's *Breve historia de México* is "the most read and requested" synthesis of the nation's history.[38] Matute is aware of the book's historiographic shortcomings, particularly viewed with the methodological requirements for historians in the 1980s. Yet he reasons that in 1937 the discipline of history in Mexico was not yet the realm of specialists. At its moment of publication, Vasconcelos's text was but another of a series of interpretations of history, devoid of primary research; part of a rather essayistic tradition that tries to ideologically define the destiny of the country, basing its assertions on the material provided by other history books. With this in mind, he concludes, the text's methodological shortcomings are perfectly understandable. It is, in this regard, a very personal interpretation of Mexico's history, aimed at insisting upon the threat of U.S. intervention in Mexico and foregrounding a glorious Hispanic past. As Matute points out, the text's organization is very telling of Vasconcelos's interpretation of Mexico's history. It begins with Mexico's "discovery" by Spain, then it dedicates its longest section to a narration of the Conquest, passing briefly to a discussion of "Pre-Cortesian"—Vasconcelos's term—Mexico, and a brief discussion of the origins of Mexico's races. After this point, the author begins a discussion of the colonial period and continues chronologically until the present. Such an organization makes it clear that "his departure point is Spain; that indigenous history does not interest him and that he only refers to it to establish the necessity of the Conquest-salvation" (Matute, 147–50). History or anti-history, the controversial point in Vasconcelos's book is not necessarily his research or lack thereof, but its construction of a national history fully dependent upon the Spanish Conquest for its existence. It is at the time of the Conquest that the nation as such is born and expands; it is with independence that the country's borders begin collapsing, victims of the more powerful northern onslaught and militarism and dissension within.

Vasconcelos's nostalgic view of the colonial past makes him build a Manichaean history of the nation, where the Spaniards define civilization and national unity, while the Indians define barbarism and dispersion. Thus, he opens his *Breve historia de México* as follows:

> Mexico's history begins as an episode of the great Odyssey of the discovery and occupation of the New World. Before the Spaniards' arrival Mexico did not exist as a nation; a multitude of tribes, separated by rivers and mountains and the most profound abyss of their three hundred dialects, lived in the regions that today form our homeland's territory. The Aztecs dominated but one zone of the plateau, in constant rivalry with the Tlaxcaltecs, and on the west the Tarascans lived in independent sovereignty, just like the Zapotecs in the south. There was no national idea joining the castes; on the contrary, the most fierce animosity fed a perpetual war, which only the Spanish conquest finished.[39]

Two important themes of Vasconcelos's thought are evident in this opening passage, which sets the tone for his entire book. On the one

hand, the Spanish conquerors represent not only an incorporation of
Mexico into western civilization but they provide a unifying force that
linked a previously separated territory. Concerning the latter, offensive
as his ideas might sound to nationalist Mexicans, the former minister of
education makes an important point. The nation-state as we know it
today, with its modern established borders and the Southwest of the
present United States, did not exist as a coherent social, political, and
cultural whole before the intervention of the Spanish Empire. This cohesiveness was crucial for a man fascinated by synthesis. One can, however, question the level of such cohesiveness. Although today Mexico
stands as an independent nation-state, the plurality of cultures and languages that form it are still far from being synthesized into a homogeneous whole. One need only turn to the modern *Zapatista* movement to
see how the definition of a national culture and identity is still being
contested. Central to Vasconcelos's mission as minister of education was
an effort to encourage such a national homogenization.

At another level, Vasconcelos's insistence on the disunity of Mexico
prior to the Spanish Conquest places great emphasis on military conflict. Throughout his *Breve historia de México,* the former minister refers
to the Aztec civilization as brutal and sanguinary. Yet, as Matute has
pointed out, the purpose of Vasconcelos's book is not to explore the
nature of Native American culture and civilization but rather to celebrate the Hispanic heritage in the country and to explain its contemporary situation. His emphasis on the bloody wars and human sacrifices,
uncritically taken directly from Bernal Díaz del Castillo's eyewitness
account in *Historia verdadera de la conquista de la Nueva España,* functions
as a marker to criticize the revolutionary regime he opposed. Thus,
when discussing the Aztec deities he writes: "The Aztecs' principal god
was a sort of great Moctezuma or a sanguinary [figure], called Huichilobos" (*Historia,* 1428). It does not seem accidental that he uses the
term *jefe máximo* to refer to this sanguinary figure, as it was the term
used by his contemporaries to refer to Calles, his major political enemy.
One of the only redeeming figures in the Aztec religious pantheon was
the figure of Quetzalcóatl, god of knowledge and education, who was
defeated and expelled by his rival Huitzilopochtli (Huichilobos). This
former god is used by Vasconcelos as a symbol of himself and his political allies. Thus, he writes in a clear allusion to his own destiny, "The
struggle between Quetzalcóatl and Huichilobos becomes a summary
and symbol of Mexico's History. Each time that a Quetzalcóatl appears,
he is expelled from the government, or they nullify him through dis-

credit" (*Historia,* 1429). The figure of Huichilobos is linked by Vasconcelos to the Aztec tradition, and he deploys the image time and again as a symbol of the violent methods he ascribed to his political rivals. If at an earlier point in his career the minister of education had seen certain redeemable characteristics in the native traditions, he now uses them as a symbol of the nation's decay, limiting for himself the figure of the noble, but exiled, Quetzalcóatl.

Although at this later stage Vasconcelos appears as an enemy of Indian civilization and a proponent of the Hispanic colonial past, we must insist that Vasconcelos's celebration of the conservative Hispanophile pantheon was present in his early work as minister of education and in his 1925 *La raza cósmica.* The central historical characters in *La raza cósmica*'s teleology are the Spanish conquerors and missionaries. They are the ones who, in his analysis, created the conditions for a unified world. The change after 1930 was in emphasis rather than content. In these years Vasconcelos adds to his Hispanist interpretation of history a much more rabid anti-North Americanism, which makes him deplore anyone who, in his opinion, cooperated in any way with the United States, and any support of Indian autonomy is conceived by him as debilitating to a homogeneous Hispanic nation and thus favoring the United States. Thus, in a polemical reply to a critique of his dethroning of national heroes in his 1937 *Breve historia de México,* Vasconcelos is categorical in his criteria for distinguishing villains and heroes in Mexican history. It is a distinction between

> Those who, whether knowingly or not, have been an instrument of the Poinsett Plan, which intends to replace the Spanish with the Anglo-Saxon in the dominion of Latin America, and those who, whether in full consciousness or by hints, have opposed the Poinsett Plan and have endeavored to act as Mexicans.[40]

At this point in Vasconcelos's life almost every figure in the postrevolutionary government and almost every figure of the liberal pantheon, excluding only Madero, was, according to him, complicit with the "Poinsett Plan." Ironically, by the late 1930s, almost three decades after he participated in the overthrow of Porfirio Díaz in the name of Juárez's liberal Constitution, Vasconcelos now discovered that Juárez was in reality a traitor. Through the Laws of Reform he had taken much property away from the Catholic Church and sold it, oftentimes to foreign investors, many of them from the United States. He also promoted the immigration of Protestant missionaries. Ironically, now he tells us that:

I was the first one surprised to see that [under this standard] Porfirio Díaz came out in a relatively good standing. He continued giving the country's resources to the Poinsett Plan, but in the spiritual realm he refused to consummate de-Hispanization, and he reestablished religious peace. Also, through Limantour's economic policy, he was beginning a timid re-conquest of our economic autonomy. ("Idolos," 154)

With such statements, one cannot underestimate the magnitude of Vasconcelos's ideological shift. We must, however, also recognize that there is a significant shift in the tone and attitude of his writings. While during the 1920s his emphasis was positive and creative, proposing a brighter future, during the 1930s his rhetoric was negative and offensive, criticizing his political enemies and turning to a utopian colonial past.

Particularly revealing of the continuities and transformations in his attitudes both toward race and the liberal nationalist pantheon is a speech he delivered in Rio de Janeiro in 1922. Vasconcelos was Mexico's official representative to the centennial celebrations of Brazilian independence and spoke at the unveiling of a statue of Cuauhtémoc he brought as a gift from the Mexican government to the Brazilian people.[41] The Mexican author dedicates a paragraph to this incident in his 1925 *La raza cósmica*. More attention is given in this narrative to the formalities and celebrations than to the speech or the monument's significance. Vasconcelos writes:

> The speech explained what the hero Cuauhtémoc represents in our history and the intentions which guided us in giving him as a symbol of true independence, not only political, but also moral. I insisted, in this regard, on the necessity to search for the development of our temperament's native traces in order to realize a civilization that would not be only a copy of the European: a spiritual emancipation as a corollary to political emancipation. (*Raza*, 1007–8)

In this narration of the event, he does not debunk Cuauhtémoc. Quite the contrary, as he presents the Aztec emperor as a model of heroism.

The speech about Cuauhtémoc in Brazil is again narrated a decade later in the third volume of Vasconcelos's memoirs, *El desastre* (The disaster), published in 1938. This time the narrative is more cynical and provocative. On this occasion, Vasconcelos complains about the gift's inappropriate nature. In Brazil "there are no Indians," Vasconcelos tells us, so Brazilians would be unable to relate to an Indian figure. A more appropriate gift, he concludes, would be a figure of Latin heritage. In this new rendition of events, Vasconcelos barely relates the speech's content; instead he mocks Cuauhtémoc and other Native American leaders by showing off his ignorance on the subject and relating their exaltation by North American Protestant cultural imperialism:

> I wrote a speech which explained what Cuauhtémoc represented for us. I confess that my ideas on the matter were not very clear. Beyond the school textbook, I did not have any recollection of Cuauhtémoc other than those pilgrimages, in the capital, organized by a North American Protestant pastor, Father Hunt, back during my high school days. This Hunt would collect hundreds of kids and take them to Cuauhtémoc's monument to listen to speeches in the *Aztec language*, which, of course, no one understood. Neither was the object of this ceremony—frankly Poinsettian—guessed by the public, which was content by looking on, passive and lazy as usual. . . . But I put my thought to work and I wrote a speech that had such success precisely, I believe, because it gives a Cuauhtémoc who is a little fantastic, dressed up as a symbol for our wishes for independence, but not from Spain, that has left us in peace after having raised us, but from Monroeism, which is a living and patent threat. A good proof that I did not attain myself to history is that I put in Cuauhtémoc's mouth those words about not wanting to go to heaven if there he would find himself among Spaniards—words which belong to some Antillian *cacique*, if I am not mistaken.[42]

Unlike the 1925 rendition of the speech, Vasconcelos's contempt for Native American history is evident in the tone of this passage. Beyond the racism, the Mexican thinker's disregard for historical fact reveals a central element of Vasconcelos's historiography, which is strategically activist. Political efficacy is privileged over the search for fact. Thus, regarding his mistaken narration of Cuauhtémoc's words, Vasconcelos says "I do not make history; I intend to create a myth" (*Desastre,* 1337).

There is a marked attitudinal change toward the Cuauhtémoc speech in the 13 years that mediate between the publication of *La raza cósmica* and *El desastre.* Giving Vasconcelos the benefit of the doubt, one could argue that the blatant racist contempt of the second narration is just a symptom of his midlife transformation, and foreground instead the earlier, more respectful narrative. While the second narrative mocks liberal nationalist discourse, the first one, with its emphasis on political and moral independence, can very well accommodate itself into this same tradition. The speech itself is closer in spirit to the earlier account; it is very respectful, raising Cuauhtémoc to the level of a moral symbol. It does not contain any of the contemptful mockery of its 1938 narration. Yet, even in the 1922 speech, just beneath the respectful homage to the Aztec emperor, lies a totally Eurocentric ideology. Cuauhtémoc is constructed as brave and moral, but already condemned to historical defeat. He is the silent sentinel of a silenced people:

> A failed hero[43] if he is seen from the point of view of those who only recognize the ideal when it presents itself in Victory's carriage, dominating haughtiness and crushing rebellions; but, for us, a sublime hero because he preferred to succumb before giving in, and because his memory will eternally bother those who are in the habit of pleasing the strong, and are unconditional slaves of success, in any one of its miserable forms. A hero of defeated pain raises in this bronze his erect plume, his flying arrow and his mute mouth, without boastfulness during action and supremely disdainful in defeat.[44]

Against this heroic yet silent and defeated figure appears "the Conqueror, the greatest of all conquerors, the incomparable Hernán Cortés, who defeated with the sword and convinced with the word; after the glorious audacity of burning ships to chain victories, [he] advanced with great armies, illuminated by the aureole of legends" ("Cuauhtémoc," 93).

Cuauhtémoc in this speech appears as a symbol of rebellion; he functions as an inspiration for struggle, but struggle in silent defeat. It is a given in this speech that "Indian power" has "disappeared forever." Europe here appears as a teacher, ready to bring primitive Indians into civilization:

> It is clear that the Mexican nation, in its Cuauhtémoc cult, does not want to become narrow and close its doors to progress; we do not intend to return to the Aztecs' stone age, just as we would not accept to again become any nation's colony. Neither do we renounce Europe, nor are we hostile to it in any way. We thank its teachings, recognize its excellence and will always have open arms for its children: but we want to stop being economic colonies. ("Cuauhtémoc," 95–96)

After singing praises to Europe, Vasconcelos identifies the enemy against which Cuauhtémoc's memory should inspire us to struggle: the United States of America. Cuauhtémoc is a hero, then, only inasmuch as he serves Vasconcelos and allows him to put forth his political project against Anglo-Saxon interference. The speech is indeed a call for Latin American sovereignty. Indeed he rhetorically rejects any colonial condition. Yet, very much like the statue itself is dressed in a Greek toga and taken out of historical context for aesthetic purposes, Vasconcelos dresses Cuauhtémoc as a Hispanophile. One can just wonder what the Aztec emperor would think about such a construction of himself.

Reading the speech and the two later renditions of it indicates that while the author experienced a definite attitudinal change between 1922 and 1938, from a respectful appropriation of Cuauhtémoc's figure to disdainful mockery, even in his most respectful moments Vasconcelos sees the Aztec emperor as a secondary figure in history's passage. The original incident also indicates a very significant dynamic of Vasconcelos's role as minister of education. As representative of the Mexican State, the minister was often forced to function as an official public figure, rather than a private citizen. It is perfectly conceivable that, as Vasconcelos writes in *El desastre,* given the choice he would not have taken a statue of Cuauhtémoc to Brazil. The fact is that giving replicas of this monument had become a sort of tradition for the Mexican government. Similar ones had already been used by the Porfirian regime to represent Mexico at world's fairs in Paris, Chicago, and other places. Ironically for Vasconcelos's anti-Yankee spirit, the replica he took to Brazil was manufactured by Tiffany Company of New York, which gave the Mexican government a discount because of its frequent purchases. On this matter he had no choice. In matters that were under his control, however, he did intervene. Thus, for example, while Alonso Torre Díaz had recommended Aztec motifs for the pavilion that would represent Mexico at the Rio de Janeiro festivities, Vasconcelos insisted on a colonial building in the baroque tradition, representative of a Spanish heritage with Native American influences.[45] Such a decision clearly reveals that, indeed, his preferences for Mexico's representation in Brazil were rather Hispanocentric. Even forgetting the author's later mocking cynicism, the minister's ignorance about Cuauhtémoc's quote in 1922 does indicate that he was not particularly interested in this emperor. He thus dons the emperor with a toga and articulates his image in a Latin versus Anglo narrative that has nothing to do with the last monarch's historical context. The image of Cuauhtémoc is for Vasconcelos a myth, deployed as a tool for the minister's personal political and cultural project.

A similar dynamic took place in relation to Emiliano Zapata, whom Vasconcelos despised. In the racist language characteristic of the later Vasconcelos, he describes *Zapatista* actions in *La tormenta* as "Aztec terror." Zapata and his troops are presented as primitive brutes only capable of violence. Consistent with his conspiracy theories, Vasconcelos sees the peasants of Morelos as being manipulated by foreign interests. Their "*indigenismo,*" he explains, is part of a "Protestant imperialist" project. Obsessed about racializing history and politics, Vasconcelos insists that Zapata was a *mestizo* and Soto y Gama, one of his principal advisers, a *criollo,* thus marking both as vicarious leaders of a supposedly Indian-centered project. Not satisfied with racial slurs, Vasconcelos personally attacks Zapata's character, saying that he, "now the apostle of poor revolutionaries had reserved for his own benefit a good ranch; in another one he installed his brother; in another one a lover, etc., etc." (*Tormenta,* 871–72). Despite his personal hatred for Zapata, Vasconcelos recalls an occasion in 1921 when, as university president, he was politically forced to participate in the commemoration of Zapata's assassination. As he recalls the event in *El desastre*—full of his outright racist attitude, which remained subdued in 1921—he tells of sending just a crown of flowers with only his name on a ribbon, without the university seal. Vasconcelos insists that he distanced himself and the university as much as possible from the event. Nevertheless, he also recognizes his participation in the fallen radical leader's commemoration as a strategic political move. Just as the case with Cuauhtémoc, the university president "gave a gallant tribute to the dead and defeated enemy," and in doing so moved forward his political agenda (*Desastre,* 1239–45).

Beyond his concerns about race and religion, the other aspect that remains constant throughout Vasconcelos's life and work is his extreme personalism. As Sylvia Molloy points out in her study of his autobiography, there is in him "a constant need for recognition; a fervent desire to *do* rivaled only by the desire to *show* himself doing."[46] His "desire to *do*" led him to take matters in his own hands, and his leadership in legislative and administrative tasks was essential in the success of his educational projects in Mexico. It is precisely in the personal passion that Vasconcelos put into his work that many find his merits.[47] Yet his "desire to *show* himself doing" tinged his legacy with a certain arrogance I have already mentioned. I have, for example, talked about his self-construction as martyr and prophet. This self-centeredness is evident in many of his texts. His multivolume autobiography—*Ulises criollo* (1935), *La tormenta* (1936), *El desastre* (1938), *El proconsulado* (1939), and the posthumously published *La flama* (1959)[48]—by definition a self-centered genre, presents a presumptuous individualist.

Such individualism is clearly revealed in his administrative style. Vasconcelos managed the ministry of education in an extremely personal and possessive manner, jealous of any outside intruders in his project. He recalls that "The Ministry I was creating was my exclusive lover" (*Desas-*

tre, 1285). Progenitor and lover, Vasconcelos had a very personal incestuous investment with the institution. Similarly, his recollections of his resignation from the SEP are also marked by intense personal feelings: "At the beginning each change of the plans or the details hurt me, as if they had dishonored my bride" (*Desastre*, 1497). The original in Spanish uses the reflexive construction "*como si me profanasen la novia*," making the burden of the dishonor fall on the speaker. The bride's feelings don't matter; it is the groom's honor that is offended. With such a relationship to his ministry, Vasconcelos was a hands-on administrator who tried to control every single aspect of the new organization, from drafting the legislation instituting it and developing pedagogies and curricula, to personally supervising the design and construction of schools and office buildings. At times in his autobiography Vasconcelos sees himself as single-handedly envisioning and bringing to fruition the new ministry, and indeed his intervention was crucial in the development of the country's contemporary educational system. Nevertheless, as will be seen later, the institutionalization of an educational and cultural infrastructure of the type envisioned by Vasconcelos—an infrastructure that would centrally control schools, libraries, museums, theaters, etc.; an infrastructure responsible for developing a standardized curriculum for the entire nation; an infrastructure that would encompass within its concerns cultural issues ranging from daily nutritional, hygienic, and leisure habits to literacy, technical schooling, and the cultivation of the fine arts—necessarily implied the participation of a broad range of people and groups—the president, Congress, multiple bureaucracies, teachers, construction workers, printers, students, parents, the church, etc.—who struggled with and against Vasconcelos, and with and against each other, to define the nature, role, program, and practices of such an infrastructure. As was the case of the homages to Cuauhtémoc and Zapata, a multiplicity of forces, within and outside the institution, informed the individualist minister's actions. When he lost control of the ministry, he rejected it as a prostituted bride. As we will see, Vasconcelos had a similar personalist attitude toward his presidential campaign.

My early discussion of Vasconcelos focused on the contradictory reception of his texts. In this regard, the contradiction is seen along chronological lines. The early Vasconcelos is welcomed and celebrated; the later one satanized and condemned. Yet, within each one of his texts, one finds a series of contradictory tensions that must now be addressed. One such contradiction has already been touched upon in my discussion of the speech for Cuauhtémoc. Putting aside the mocking attitude toward this speech revealed in *El desastre,* one can find in the original text a certain sincere, if peculiar, admiration for the Aztec hero; an admiration underpinned by a whole series of racist assumptions, but an admiration nonetheless. During this century's first two decades, Vasconcelos struggled to create a culturally and economically sovereign Mexico and Latin America. During this period, his attitude toward Indian customs and culture, like that of many liberals, was sincerely patronizing, seeing in his educational project a redemptive mission.

At another level, in his book *Se llamaba Vasconcelos,* José Joaquín Blanco identifies a series of ideological and methodological "fixed contradictions" prevalent throughout the thinker's work, beginning in his 1907 law thesis *Teoría dinámica del derecho* (A dynamic theory of law) and continuing until his death in 1959. Blanco explains this contradiction using the young law student's thesis as an example. Vasconcelos's "dynamic theory of law" was based on the three "natural" laws: (1) the law of energy development; (2) the law of justice; and (3) the law of equilibrium. "The first law sustained the right of people to the whole development of their energy and postulated the dynamic individual as the ideal human." This law, as Blanco tells us, "was affirmed as a sacred order." The second law, that of justice, dictates that "every organism [should] endure the consequences of its nature and conduct." The third, that of equilibrium, "attributes to every impulse a result equivalent to its degree of energy." As Blanco points out, such a legal—and therefore social—theory, granting cosmically determined privileges as levels of energy, and then determining justice according to these privileges, is symptomatic of an elitism of the worst kind, justifying a social Darwinism of the sort used by the Porfirian *científicos* to theoretically and morally explain their decadently luxurious lifestyles as most of the country's population starved. Such is at least the case in the animal kingdom in an example given in the thesis. As Blanco paraphrases, "if two hungry dogs found themselves in front of a piece of meat, it would be 'justice' for the stronger dog (more energy) to receive the consequences of its nature and conduct and take the piece of meat, since it would only be receiving the result equivalent to its impulse ('equilibrium')" (Blanco, 38). Logically, then, and practically among the fauna, Vasconcelos's legal and social theory justifies the survival of the fittest.

The logical consequences of the young lawyer's "legal Darwinism" match those of the *científicos,* theoretically justifying the power of the ruling class and greatly contradicting his anti-Porfirian political stance. "Reaching this point," Blanco tells us,

> the young Vasconcelos realized that his apology for individualism, spirit and genius, could be understood as a monumentalization of *hacendados* and politicians. Then he forgot the sober and theoretical exposition of his reasoning, and . . . he excommunicated Hispano-American politicians from his theory of dynamic individualism because they were *caudillos* and "we already know that the great warriors are a variety of the criminal type" . . . [and] he also excommunicated [the oligarchy] because . . . the economic aristocracy did not fit in his theory either, since it was not "made," but "inherited" and, also, an unjust and brutal exploitation of others was a variety of barbarism. (Blanco, 37–41)

In Vasconcelos's legal theory, then, we encounter contradictions similar to those in the Cuauhtémoc speech. The theory's ideological underpinnings are extremely elitist, privileging the strong over the weak. Realizing the consequences of his thought, Vasconcelos makes arbitrary and less rigorous exceptions to his theory to match his particular political project of the moment. Vasconcelos's activities in the years preceding the Mexican Revolution are marked by a sincere anti-Porfirian commitment, reflected in his work at the *Ateneo de la Juventud* and by his participation in Madero's Anti-re-electionist Party. Yet his legal and social model remains overall elitist and could have very well been conceived by a staunch supporter of the Porfirian elite.

A similar contradiction is evident in Vasconcelos's construction of race. As is discussed at greater length in the next chapter, Vasconcelos's racial theory as presented in *La raza cósmica* is an impassioned rhetorical celebration of the hybridity of Latin American *mestizaje*. Its theoretical underpinnings, however, are extremely racist in granting historical agency, high culture, technology, and beauty almost exclusively to Europe. At a later stage in his life Vasconcelos would change rhetorical emphasis. The celebration of the *mestizo* gives way to that of the *criollo;* no longer does he celebrate a mixed race but only the descendants of Spanish conquerors in America, and those of Indian, African, Asian, or mixed descent who fell into the fold of a Hispanic culture. Thus, the first volume of his autobiography, published in 1936, is consciously titled *Ulises criollo* and not *Ulises mestizo*. In this construct of a Hispanic race/culture we also find the paradox discussed earlier concerning the relative opposition between the fixity and flexibility of the racial category.

It is one of my contentions that the latter Hispanophile ideological emphasis of Vasconcelos neatly corresponds to the theses set forth in *La raza cósmica*. Consistently throughout his career, however, Vasconcelos constructs himself as an enemy of colonialism. In response to this, he ultimately identifies himself as *criollo*—a person of Spanish origin born in America—and not just any sort of *hispano*. The distinction between Vasconcelos's understanding of both terms is, however, very ambiguous. His construction of a future utopia seems merely to be an attempt to transfer the capital of the ancient Spanish Empire from Madrid to Universópolis—an imaginary city in the Amazonian rim; a transfer of world hegemonic power from European to American Hispanics. In this regard, as I argue in the next chapter, Vasconcelos's project clearly fits within nineteenth-century *criollo* nationalism. At the time of publication, *La raza cósmica* was enthusiastically received by Latin American nationalists and anticolonialists. As Blanco points out—exaggerating in the overcategorical "only," but incisively nevertheless—"Vasconcelos was the only intellectual of his generation who assumed culture as an essentially decolonizing function." In this regard, when Vasconcelos found federal support from Obregón to put his ideas into practice, "he was seen as a decolonizing messiah in all Hispano-America and he achieved the greatest prestige and the most glorious tour that any Mexican had realized in those countries" (Blanco, 41). The question is, decolonizing whom and from whom? Rather than from Europe in general or Spain in particular, Vasconcelos's decolonizing project is against the new kind of cultural, economic, political, and military intervention on the American continent originating in the United States. The people to be decolonized are not the Native Americans who were colonized in the sixteenth century but rather the cultural descendants of the very conquerors. Despite the theory's racist and elitist underpinnings, as a symbol and political slogan, the concept of *raza cósmica* functioned during and after Vasconcelos's life as a liberating anticolonialist mobilizing principle, more often than not representing political agendas different—if not antithetical—from the author's.[49]

Chapter Three

Rac(ial)ist Prophet: Toward a Spanish-American Racial Theory

On 27 April 1921, Vasconcelos, in his capacity as president of the newly formed National University, published a decree establishing the institution's seal. This seal, which to the present day represents UNAM, would consist of "a map of Latin America with the inscription 'Through my race the spirit shall speak'. . . . The seal will be held by an eagle and a condor, all this resting on an allegory of the volcanoes [the Popocatépetl and Iztaccíhuatl] and the Aztec prickly pear {nopal}." The eagle and the prickly pear are distinctively Mexican symbols, appearing on the national flag in remembrance of the Aztec Empire's founding myth. The volcanoes, Popocatépetl and Iztaccíhuatl, are also icons of the Valley of Mexico. The seal's imagery, however, is not limited to exclusively Mexican icons. It includes the whole of Latin America, represented by its map and the condor, typical of South America. In this way then, national boundaries collapse in an expansive gesture that incorporates a whole continent, or rather a section of a continent, since the United States and Canada are not included in the map. Through its motto, the seal also incorporates two categories central to Vasconcelos's thought: race and spirit. The decree explains the motto's significance as "the conviction that our race will elaborate a culture of new tendencies, of a spiritual and absolutely free essence."[1]

In its Spanish original this motto is somewhat ambiguous. It reads: "*Por mi raza hablará el espíritu.*" While I prefer to translate it as "Through my race the spirit shall speak," the preposition "*por*" has a multiplicity of meanings. This word also represents cause or motive, rendering an alternative translation: "Because of my race the spirit shall speak" or "For the sake of my race . . ." The latter is the interpretation given to the phrase by Alberto Trueba Urbina. In my opinion Trueba Urbina's interpretation is, however, limiting, since it completely eliminates the race's agency, rendering it the subject of an omnipotent spirit that intervenes for its redemption. Translating "*por*" as "because," on the other hand, shifts too much agency to the category of race, which now gives voice to the spirit. An understanding of the preposition as "through" solves this problem of agency, providing for two separate categories interacting with each other.

Despite its inaccuracy, the context of Trueba Urbina's interpretation of the university motto is significant in understanding the controversies arising from Vasconcelos's legacy. Trueba Urbina's comments appeared in an article entitled *"Una lección de Gramática para J. Vasconcelos"* (A grammar lesson for J. Vasconcelos), published in Mexican newspapers on 25 November 1952. As the title indicates, the article was a malicious critique of the former minister's grammar, specifically of his use of the preposition *"por."* Grammar, however, was only an excuse to discredit Vasconcelos. At stake was a whole conception of the university's mission. On the 20th of that month, during the inauguration ceremonies for the university's new campus, a group of students unfolded a large placard with the motto *"La Ciencia por la Justicia Social"* (Science for social justice), authored by Trueba Urbina. The motto represented an understanding of the university's mission corresponding to a Jacobin interpretation of the Mexican Revolution, devoid of any spiritualism. Vasconcelos immediately reacted, declaring to the press that, "we, as authentic revolutionaries fought and suffered not only for Stalinist social justice, but also for all the liberties of the spirit." He went on to claim that the proponents of the new motto worked on "the payroll of the most repugnant tyrannies, which have dishonored the Revolution." Taking personal offense at the new proposal, Vasconcelos concluded that, "The day that the University omits my motto, I will feel that it has stopped deserving it" (Taracena, 19–20). The spiritual dimension was, thus, for Vasconcelos an integral part of the university's mission.

Absent from his defense of the university motto is any discussion of the question of race. Trueba Urbina's new proposal also eliminated this category, yet Vasconcelos's reaction exclusively addressed the question of the spirit. In her 1966 study, *José Vasconcelos and His World,* Gabriella de Beer points out that in the late 1930s Vasconcelos's emphasis on race drastically changed. While during the 1910s and 1920s the young thinker emphasized the importance of *mestizaje* in Latin American culture, as years passed his "opinions on racial mixture had changed so radically that in 1944 he publicly admitted that his theory of the emergence of a cosmic race in Latin America was a notorious mistake."[2] The race that the education minister had in mind on April 1921 was a mixed, or cosmic, race, a race that encompassed all the previously existing races to form a superior type of human being. By 1946, in a speech given on 12 October commemorating the "Day of the Race"[3] in San Antonio, Texas, Vasconcelos's emphasis is very different. While the theme of a cosmic race remains on the margins of this speech, his emphasis is on the Hispanic element. Thus, Vasconcelos tells the gathering assembled by the Spanish-language newspaper *La Prensa* that, "For us . . . this is not only Columbus Day, the day of the discovery, but the Day of the Race; that is, the date of homage for the Spanish race, of whose glories we form part because we are part of the Hispanic culture." Of particular significance in this speech is the Catholic tradition, which once again foregrounds the spiritual dimension of the race.[4] The particularities of a specifically Latin American culture are no longer important in this speech; what matters for Vasconcelos is the specifically Spanish heritage.

While in the later stages of his life Vasconcelos turned to a conservative Hispanism, the young thinker devoted much effort to developing a theory of a specifically Latin American race with a liberating edge. In this regard, Germán Posada argues in a 1963 article that he is "the Mexican creator of the idea of America and the precursor of the Mexican and American philosophy about America that is flourishing in our time" (Posada, 380).[5] Leopoldo Zea gives a similar assessment of the early Vasconcelos. Focusing on his participation in the revolution and his tenure with the ministry of education, Zea sees in him the first Mexican thinker to transcend a limited regionalist thought, combining specifically national concerns with broader ones, encompassing the American continent and ultimately becoming universal. According to Zea, prior to Vasconcelos Mexican thought gravitated along two distinct, yet similarly limited, poles: it was either too regional or too imitative of European categories, conceived as universal but with no applicability to the concrete Mexican reality. The 1910 Revolution would change this situation, as Mexican concerns turned inwards, forgetting about "universal" models because of the very specific necessities of the moment. At this time, "Mexico became, without intending it, America's revolutionary leader," and, having "abandoned all models, served as a model to other peoples." This is the context, Zea tells us, in which Vasconcelos's figure fully developed. It is an intersection of very specific and urgent national concerns—concerns that cannot be addressed by foreign models, emerging under very different circumstances—giving Mexico an almost accidental, but very real, leadership position at the continental level.[6]

Due to the revolutionary situation, Vasconcelos is for Zea "a man in which the worlds of action and of thought join. . . . Half politician, half pedagogue. The type of man who distributes his life between the tribune, the battle field or the classroom. Statesman and teacher. Thinker or revolutionary" (Zea, 157). Indeed, his participation in the revolutionary movement was a defining moment in the development of the thinker. His links with the revolutionary leadership gave him an opportunity, as minister of education, to enact his thought at both the national and the continental levels. The next chapter will address Vasconcelos's actions in the ministry. Here, however, we will focus on his American racial thought, which began its development prior to the revolutionary upheaval.

de Beer traces what is "Most likely [Vasconcelos's] first mention of a race theory" to his 1920 play *Prometeo vencedor* (Triumphant Prometheus), where one of the characters, disappointed by the past and the present, looks forward to humanity's future in Latin America, where the best of all cultures will flourish under the Spanish mold (de Beer, 290–91). Posada, however, goes further back, finding "the germ of all of his social thought applicable to the Hispano-American world" in Vasconcelos's 1905 law school thesis, *Teoría dinámica del derecho* (A dynamic theory of law) (Posada, 381). While de Beer focuses on the mixture of cultures, Posada looks at specific spiritual elements that the Mexican thinker identifies as characteristic of the Latin American race:

> We are, according to [Vasconcelos], an idealist race, unable to triumph in a mechanized age like the present; we must resign ourselves to accept this epoch, because it will put wealth at the reach of everyone and will open the road for an ideal future; [however] a spiritual force lives hidden in us, and it will turn us into masters of a future of unlimited knowledge. (Posada, 381)

Both commentators focus on different elements of Vasconcelos's Latin American racial theory to identify its origins, and indeed, both of these elements—miscegenation and spirituality—are crucial in the Mexican's theory. Furthermore, if de Beer and Posada identify two distinct moments when the Mexican thinker actually articulates his racial preoccupations in writing, others, like Fredrick Hart Langhorst, go even further back. Langhorst claims that Vasconcelos's concern about questions of race originates in his childhood on the Mexico-United States border, when he became aware of economic, social, cultural, religious, political, and military differences and tensions along both sides of the river.[7]

While there might be disagreement as to the earliest manifestations of Vasconcelos's racial preoccupations, there is no question as to the date of his first sustained study of the issue. This appears with the 1925 publication in Barcelona of his *La raza cósmica. Misión de la raza iberoamericana* (The cosmic race. The mission of the Ibero-American race).[8] Vasconcelos's argument is that the Latin American continent is the forming ground of a cosmic race. Along very broad lines, the thinker argues that the Spanish Conquest, by facilitating the process of *mestizaje*, first between Native Americans and Spaniards and later incorporating Africans and Asians, opened the possibility for the development of a truly universal race, including features of all the previously existing races. This mixing process, as Posada emphasizes, is "sanguineous and spiritual" (Posada, 387). The new cosmic race would incorporate the best characteristics of all previously existing races, in both genetic features and spiritual tendencies. With this understanding, race is conceived as being formed by an intersection of biological and ideological elements. The actual act of sexual contact between distinct groups brings about physical miscegenation. To this biological act of genetic mixing, however, Vasconcelos adds what he conceives as a universalizing spirit, characteristic of Spanish Catholicism, which materialized in the Spanish missionaries' proselytizing efforts. The fact that the Spaniards did not simply evict Native Americans from their lands but instead endeavored to convert them and thus incorporate them into western culture distinguishes these colonizers, in Vasconcelos's opinion, from the British Puritans who in North America formed their own enclaves, separating themselves as much as possible from the land's previous inhabitants.[9] Furthermore, as the book's subtitle indicates, the concept of a cosmic race is conceived as a historical mission—the concluding phase of a long teleology, the possibility of which is opened by the Spanish colonial project.

Like Vasconcelos's whole career, the racial theory put forth by *La raza cósmica* is full of contradictions. If on the one hand it proposes a liberating theory for Latin America by insisting on the future dominance of its cosmic race, its insistence on the Spanish Conquest's key role in the formation of this race is deeply embedded in a European, racist, colonial paradigm. Hence, while thinkers like Posada and Zea focus on the American emphasis of Vasconcelos's thought, others, like A. Basave Fernández del Valle, focus on its strictly Hispanic dimension. In his 1958 *La filosofía de José Vasconcelos* (José Vasconcelos's philosophy), Basave insists that "Vasconcelos' main message to Spanish America [is that it should] recognize and dignify its Hispanic style."[10] Basave's assessment of the Mexican's message is based not only on *La raza cósmica* but also on his later works. As I have already pointed out, during the 1930s Vasconcelos's thought took a sharp turn, as he rejected his early racial theories and became a radical Hispanophile. Several critics identify this contradiction in Vasconcelos's thought in strictly diachronic terms, identifying changes in his thought as he grew older. Thus, Manuel Pedro González tells us that, "At first he was considered a revolutionary and 'leader' of the center-left, but he ended up becoming a spokesperson of the extreme right and a denigrator of the most noble patriotic figures that the country has produced" (Aub, 45). Nevertheless, while there is no question that the later Vasconcelos became extremely reactionary, his 1925 racial theory is already fraught with colonialist and racist arguments.

Despite its contradictions, in the Latin American context described by Zea, *La raza cósmica* was received with great excitement throughout the region. In 1926, for example, the Peruvian journal *Amauta,* edited by José Carlos Mariátegui, published a very enthusiastic review by Luciano Castillo. In it, Castillo characterized Vasconcelos's text as "the wonderful book of an artist. . . . a book about America."[11] Along similar lines, in his 1928 *Creadores de la nueva América* (Creators of the new America), Benjamín Carrión celebrated Vasconcelos's "Hispano-American theories," claiming that *La raza cósmica* is "a magnificent achievement."[12] Castillo's early review is very characteristic of the book's reception and later interpretations. While the book appears as a sociological, ethnographic, and historic polemic—it is usually anthologized under the author's sociological writings—Castillo finds the work's merit in its artistic and ideological thrust, not in its scientific accuracy:

> The force and faith that Vasconcelos has when he speaks about Iberic America seduces and convinces; and even if his words were only the generous dreams of an artist, which had the virtue of communicating to us Ibero-Americans, particularly the youth, an optimism about the future of the race, and stripping us of all feelings of inferiority, that in itself would make it a great work. (Castillo, 41)

Castillo's review is very positive and, by classifying the text as that of an "artist," he overcomes Vasconcelos's scholarly shortcomings.

In a 1979 study of the Mexican thinker, Margarita Vera argues that Vasconcelos's American theories were very influential on his contemporary Peruvian Marxist José Carlos Mariátegui. She qualifies this influence by emphasizing that there were great differences between the thinkers' racial theories. Of particular importance in these differences is the fact that, while for the Mexican race is the central category, the

Peruvian centered his attention on economics. Furthermore, while the Mexican saw the solution of "the Indian problem" in education, his Peruvian counterpart found it in a change of the land ownership system. What was very valuable for Mariátegui, however, was the role of imagination in Vasconcelos's system. As Vera tells us, Mariátegui insisted on the importance of imagination in Latin America's liberation struggles. The process of American independence would have been impossible, Mariátegui tells us, if leaders like Bolívar had not imagined a free Latin America.[13] In this regard, Mariátegui writes, "No one has imagined America's destiny with a greater ambition or a more vehement hope than José Vasconcelos in the preface to *La raza cósmica.*" Mariátegui's admiration of the Mexican's imagination, however, is tempered by what he identifies as a lack of consciousness of the present:

> The absence that [we] the spirits of the new generation have to confirm with a little sadness and disillusion in Vasconcelos's work is the absence of an acute and awakened sense of the present. The epoch demands a more practical idealism, a more belligerent attitude. Vasconcelos easily and generously keeps us company in condemning the present, but not in understanding it or using it [. . .] Vasconcelos places his utopia too far from us. By probing the future, he loses the habit of looking at the present. (Vera, 225–26)

Like Mariátegui's critique of the Mexican's lack of a "sense of the present," others have criticized his disregard for a rigorous scientific methodology. Many are not as willing as Castillo to accept this shortcoming. In her 1989 study of the author, for example, Martha Robles claims that he "tended to write about matters about which he barely knew." Robles mentions the many instances when the minister moved with apparent comfort from geology to botany and zoology in a single stroke (Robles, 78). Nicandro F. Juárez is similarly critical of Vasconcelos's lack of rigor, claiming that at points "His thought becomes a mixture of insight and error, greatly flawed by the lack of a clear, rational, coherent view of the world."[14] de Beer is also aware of the writer's lack of a coherent and rigorous scientific methodology, but she explains enthusiastic attitudes like Castillo's early review as follows: "[Vasconcelos] ventured into the field of evolution, heredity and eugenics with insufficient scientific preparation and a fair measure of idealism and good will. The result had to be an unscientific fanciful theory, that in its day fell upon very receptive ears and had great appeal for those people of mixed racial stock" (de Beer, 292).

José Joaquín Blanco links Vasconcelos's forays into areas beyond his competence as a particular characteristic of his early formation in Porfirian Mexico. He argues that Vasconcelos is the product of a particular type of an elitist "provincial spirit." According to him, because of the difficulty of criticizing publicly the *Porfiriato*'s official positivism, Vasconcelos and his contemporary critics of the regime found themselves in a cultural vacuum, leading to what Blanco claims is a "self-overvaluation of the author," who does not face the sobering effects of dialogue and polemic. The Vasconcelos Blanco evokes is an arrogant character. Nevertheless, it is precisely in this arrogance that he finds the value of his work: "All of Vasconcelos' philosophical work is worth much more for the passionate and ambitious attitude of its impulse, than for the knowledge that it provides" (Blanco, 34–35). A similar assessment of the thinker's value was made by Octavio Paz in a 1941 review of Vasconcelos's *Páginas escogidas* (Selected works):

> It is, without a doubt, one of the most important books for Ibero-American culture among those published last year. The very name Vasconcelos stirs in any Mexican of our time a series of adhesions and repulsions, of anger and sympathy, that make him Mexico's most living writer. . . . He seems to tell us that literature is not an armchair or a comfortable place; it is a weapon, an instrument of both love and struggle. (Paz, 561)

Like Blanco, Paz emphasizes the writer's committed polemical thrust. Paz sees the value of Vasconcelos's apparent arrogance in the realm of praxis. His literature is a weapon in the making of history. Rather than scholarly works concerned with the accurate and documented representation of history, Vasconcelos's texts are specific interventions in the making of that history. Through their urgent polemical stance, "Vasconcelos' books provoke a dialogue, where others only achieve silent approval" (Paz, 562). In an apparently paradoxical way, the idealist voluntaristic polemics of Vasconcelos are deeply grounded in a material praxis—a praxis that came to full fruition during his tenure as minister of education.

In the specific case of Vasconcelos's racial theories, Abelardo Villegas insists that the polemicist was very aware of their scientific weaknesses. He argues that the minister uses what he calls "the racial fetish" as a polemical weapon to discredit North American racism.[15] This assessment is confirmed by Vasconcelos himself, who in the preface to his 1926 *Indología* writes that his racial theory is "as arbitrary and as fragile as the thesis of the superiority of whites. Science, at least certain science, is still a weapon for combat, and it is our obligation to put it to use" (*Indología*, 1085). Indeed, Vasconcelos uses "scientific" knowledge as a weapon against a particular kind of racism. Nevertheless, his thought is deeply embedded in his own kind of racism. While *La raza cósmica* attacks what Vasconcelos identifies as the Saxon racist project, he has too large an investment in the role of the Spanish—or Latin—peoples for his theory to be a truly cosmic one.

The text of *La raza cósmica* consists of two very different parts. Its first part, which appeared as a preface in the text's early editions and takes the name of *"Mestizaje"* after the 1948 edition, occupies a little less than one-third of the text and consists of a three-part essay elaborating its author's racial theory. The second part is a travel narrative, detailing the author's visit to Brazil and Argentina in 1922 as representative of the Mexican government to the centennial celebrations of Brazil's independence. While the bulk of the text consists of the travel narrative, it is the first part that is by far the most influential and anthologized. It is for this reason that I will focus my discussion on it. However, I must point out a perplexing, but telling, peculiarity of the travel narrative. One is impressed by the fact that in his account of both Brazil and Argentina, Vasconcelos focuses almost exclusively on the Iberian or European cultural aspects of the regions. He, for example, does not seem to notice the African presence in Brazil; rather, he talks at length about its Portuguese architecture and traditions. He also spends many pages narrating his experiences in the Amazon basin and the Iguassu waterfalls, seeing in them examples of the lavish nature of the American tropics. He believes that with the aid of western technology, Latin America's full power will be unleashed and it will become the center of the future world civilization. In these scenes, it is the physical space and its developmental potential, not its *mestizo* inhabitants, that seem to interest him.

La raza cósmica's theoretical exposition on *mestizaje* is an essay, and in that tradition it is situated between the philosophical tract, creative writing, and historical and sociological analysis. In its historical analysis the essay has much more freedom than the strictly academic tract or monograph. The essay—*"ensayo"* in Spanish—is a space to *"ensayar"* (practice) one's ideas without the strict rigors of science or theory. In the spirit of a free putting into practice of ideas, the text is not tied down by the strict parameters of the academic paper. For example, most essays often do not bother to provide footnotes or specific references. Most of the time Vasconcelos's statements are broad generalizations. This, in his view, is an asset of his methodology. He criticizes "scientific" and "empirical" histories' overwhelming focus on specific and trivial details, which do not provide "general conclusions and transcendental hypotheses . . . [thus avoiding] a vast and comprehensive theory." Contrary to this positivist tradition, Vasconcelos's project is "to search for a plan in History." His type of historian, Vasconcelos tells us, looks for "a dynamic, a rhythm and a purpose" in history's events. Grasping this movement is impossible with facts alone, and requires "a leap of the spirit" achievable through "intuition based on history's and science's data" (*Raza,* 908).

As a member of the *Ateneo de la Juventud,* which strongly opposed the Porfirian regime's official ideology of positivism by drawing upon the classical tradition of Greeks and Romans, Vasconcelos tempered what he considered the mundane and specific concerns of science with the subjectivity of intuition, aesthetics, and feelings. In a conference given at the Universidad de San Marcos in Lima, Peru, in 1916, Vasconcelos explained what he saw as his generation's characteristics as follows:

> a generation which deserves to call itself new, not just because of its age, but more legitimately because it is inspired in an aesthetic different from that of its immediate predecessors, an ideal creed which . . . is neither romantic nor modernist, and much less positivist, but a sort of mysticism based on beauty.[16]

Such a mystical aesthetic impulse dominates the argument behind the cosmic race. In this regard, while the text has been called utopian by many, Enrique Krauze proposes an alternative interpretation. "*La raza cósmica* is not a utopia," he tells us. "It does not propose a social architecture, rules of coexistence, methods of earthly happiness and perpetual peace. It is, in the biblical sense of the term, a *vision:* an absolute and irresistible canvas of the future."[17] A similar assessment emphasizing the prophetic and mystical aspects of the text is given by other critics, like Didier T. Jaén and Christopher Domínguez Michael.

Nevertheless, despite their stated opposition to positivism, most *ateneístas* were themselves formed in positivist schools, and held many of their teachers—particularly Justo Sierra, minister of instruction of the Díaz regime—in high regard. Vasconcelos is, therefore, caught between two theoretical frameworks; if, on the one hand, he values the intuitive aspects of his philosophy, he is constantly compelled to support his arguments with scientific evidence, as when he asserts in the very first statement of his essay that "authorized geologists" believe that America is the oldest continent (*Raza,* 906). He similarly imitates the methodology of his positivist nemeses by granting a great determining force to geographic and meteorological conditions on the character and development of the different races. Broad generalizations of this sort dominate Vasconcelos's writing. There is no scientific rigor or discipline in his historical remarks, but he seems to be compelled to frame his discussion in scientific terms. This attempt to move between an intuitive mystical philosophy and contemporary scientific discourse makes the text eclectic and contradictory, leading Jaén to speculate that "Perhaps Vasconcelos' mistake was to have written in a style that emulates science and philosophy, when he pretended to be more than a philosopher or a scientist."[18] However, Vasconcelos was critically addressing scientists or pseudoscientists, specialists in race much in vogue during his period, and he tried to adopt their own language and systems as a weapon, much like Caliban did in Shakespeare's *The Tempest*.

In a prologue added to the 1948 edition of *La raza cósmica,* Vasconcelos defines the purpose of his essay as follows:

> The central thesis of this book is that the different races of the world tend to mix more and more, until they form a new human type, composed from the best of each of the existing peoples. This presage was first published at a time when the Darwinist doctrine of natural selection, which saves the fit and condemns the weak, prevailed in the scientific world; a doctrine which, taken into the social realm by Gobineau, originated the theory of the pure Aryan, defended by the British, and turned into an aberrant imposition by Nazism. (*Raza,* 903)

The incorporation of this prologue over two decades after the text's original publication is significant in a number of ways. First of all, as de Beer points out, it indicates that despite the fact that Vasconcelos had denied in previous years the value of his theses on miscegenation, the political climate after the genocidal atrocities of Nazism made him republish unchanged—beyond the new prologue—his earlier celebration of *mestizaje* (de Beer, 313–14). Secondly, the new prologue adds a more polemical tone to the original essay's prophetic character. It is interesting to note that most editions of *La raza cósmica* do not indicate that the new prologue did not appear in the original. Such is the case with the two most widely circulated versions—the paperback edition by Espasa-Calpe, and the one appearing in the four-volume complete works by Libreros Mexicanos Unidos.

The previously quoted opening lines of the 1948 prologue frame the text in direct confrontation with social Darwinism and the theses of

Count Joseph Arthur de Gobineau, which are specifically linked by the author to the British, and by implication to the United States. Such a frontal attack is not as marked in the original text, where the names of Darwin, Gobineau, or Edmund Spencer—referred to later in the prologue—are not even mentioned. Nevertheless, it is a central thesis of that original *La raza cósmica* that the struggle for world dominion and the future of humanity is a struggle between "[Anglo]-Saxons" and "Latins," and, while the aforementioned proper names are not included in that text, it is evident that Vasconcelos's theses are a response to these men.

Vasconcelos's defense of *mestizaje* is a polemic against two distinct, yet not mutually exclusive, groups. On the one hand, he argues against the Mexican *científico* elite, who, basing its racial ideology on the works of Darwin and Spencer, tautologically justified its position of power over an exploited Indian majority on the basis of the survival of the fittest. Their position of power was for them proof in and of itself of their superiority. On a broader and international level, Vasconcelos's polemic is against doctrines of Anglo-Saxon superiority in favor of Latin virtue. By celebrating miscegenation, Vasconcelos takes on Spencer, one of the most influential thinkers among *científico* circles, who had written against racial mixture, arguing that hybridity "has not been moulded by any social type, and therefore, cannot . . . evolve any social type. Modern Mexico and the South American Republics, with their perpetual revolutions show us the result . . . hybrid societies are imperfectly organisable."[19]

For his part, Gobineau, identified in the new prologue as an originator of social Darwinism, argues that racial mixture implies "degeneracy," responsible for catastrophic periods in history. This process is described by the French thinker as follows:

> a nation is degenerate, when the blood of its founders no longer flows in its veins, but has been gradually deteriorated by successive foreign admixtures; so that the nation, while retaining its original name, is no longer composed of the same elements. The attenuation of the original blood is attended by a modification of the original instincts, or modes of thinking; the new elements assert their influence, and when they have once gained perfect and entire preponderance, the degeneration may be considered as complete. With the last remnant of the original ethnic principle, expires the life of the society and its civilization.[20]

Gobineau's theories are not limited to a condemnation of miscegenation. He also emphasizes that "the various branches of the human family are distinguished by permanent and irradicable differences, both mentally and physically. They are unequal in intellectual capacity, in personal beauty, and in physical strength." Gobineau concludes that of all the races, the black is the inferior, with a "little intellectual and strongly sensual character." The "second in the scale [is] the yellow. . . . [which] seems to form a complete antithesis to the former." Finally, Gobineau identifies the white, among which "we find great physical vigor and capacity of endurance; an intensity of will and desire, but which is balanced and governed by the intellectual faculties" (Gobineau, 439–51). Thus, pure races for Gobineau are the only races capable of civilization, and among the pure races the white is the one capable of the maximum achievement. For him, as for Spencer, races are endowed with essential characteristics that cannot be significantly changed by education or other social institutions. There is, according to their thought, a natural inequality dividing the peoples of the world.[21]

As has already been mentioned, Vasconcelos's defense of miscegenation against positions such as these is shaded by his own celebration of the Latin or Hispanic heritage in America. If during the nineteenth century the United States—having been the first country on the continent to achieve independence from Europe and to form a republican democracy—had been a model emulated by Latin American countries, its rapid expansion throughout the 1800s had turned it into a threat. Not only had the United States invaded and annexed half of the Mexican territory in 1847, in 1898 it gave the final blow to the Spanish transoceanic empire, winning control over Cuba, Puerto Rico, the Philippines, and Guam after the Spanish-American War. By the 1920s it had already intervened militarily in Mexico on several occasions,[22] and in Nicaragua, Panama, and the Dominican Republic, asserting with its Monroe Doctrine the right to dominate the region. The northern country that had once been an ally in keeping at bay the threat of Spanish intervention in its former colonies now loomed as the next possible imperial force in the region, a threat identified by thinkers like José Martí. The publication in 1900 of José Enrique Rodó's *Ariel* came as a wake-up call to the Latin American intelligentsia, indicating that beyond a military threat, the United States represents a cultural threat, as many Latin Americans, sheepishly following North American models, had become victims of "nordomania." Rodó's thought was very popular among the *ateneístas,* it being the subject of one of the early lectures given by Pedro Henríquez Ureña at a forum sponsored by the *Ateneo de la Juventud.*[23] In this regard, Vasconcelos's text follows the tradition of

Rodó's *Ariel*. Like *Ariel*, *La raza cósmica* recognizes with admiration the technological achievements of the Anglo-Saxon or northern civilization, but insists on the spiritual superiority of its Latin or southern counterpart. Unlike *Ariel*, however, Vasconcelos's text incorporates *mestizaje* as a central characteristic of Latin Americans. It also insists upon Latin Americans knowing and dominating their natural environment. In these last two aspects his thought is closer to that of Martí than to that of Rodó.

At a broader, international level, Vasconcelos's defense of the Catholic Latin cultural tradition can be seen as a response to the terms of the racial debates taking place in Europe at this time. In his vast study of the development of the idea of race in the western tradition, Ivan Hannaford shows the way in which the rac(ial)ist theories of thinkers like Gobineau and Spencer emerge from an urge by seventeenth- and eighteenth-century German and British romantics to trace narratives of origin distinct from those inherited from the classical tradition, which had given premium importance to Latin and Catholic lineages. In a search for a distinct lineage, Hannaford tells us, these thinkers deployed new racial theories, basing their arguments on physical anthropology, literary criticism, philology, and history, celebrating the glories of their Germanic ancestors (Hannaford, 187–90). Such a romantic approach to the origins of man reaches its peak, according to Hannaford, with Herder, according to whom peoples are not joined by contractual or political ties, but by spiritual elements, leading to "a people bound together organically by language, religion, education, inherited tradition, folk songs, ritual and speech" (Hannaford, 231). Beginning with the middle of the nineteenth century, Hannaford writes, "the English search for origins . . . [gave rise to] a romantic consciousness of the spiritual forces of race and a scientific hereditarism that both explained and justified the advance of Anglo-Saxon civilization in all corners of the world" (Hannaford, 306). It is, thus, not accidental, beyond the particular political, cultural, and economic reality in Latin America, that Vasconcelos creates a Latin–Anglo-Saxon dichotomy in his racial theory.

Later thinkers, like Ashley Montagu, have deconstructed the very concept of race as being "purely arbitrary and a simple convenience" used by Europeans to classify themselves and other groups.[24] As Montagu tells us in his introduction to the 1964 anthology *The Concept of Race*, "In an age of nationalist and imperialist expansion national pride played no small part in the naming and classification of fossil as well as living forms of men. If the concept of race had not existed it would have had to be invented during this period" (Montagu, xv). National pride—or rather pan-Latin pride—is certainly an element in Vasconcelos's theory of a cosmic race, and, unlike Montagu, his theory does not question the notion of race itself. As a matter of fact, his racial theory, as my discussion will show, is laden with very essentialist notions of race in the Gobineau tradition. The Mexican, for example, gives very definitive characteristics to what he identifies as the four major racial groups: red, yellow, white, and black. Similarly, while Vasconcelos criticizes Darwin's notion of the survival of the fittest, a certain notion of racial selection is central to his thought. The difference is in emphasis. The end result of racial selection, Vasconcelos speculates, will not be the natural survival of the strongest, but the perpetuation of the best elements of each race according to an aesthetic principle.

Despite the essentialist conception of race in Vasconcelos's theory—a perspective that he shares with Gobineau and Spencer—his theory proposes an alternative to theories that privilege pure races. *La raza cósmica* argues that throughout history miscegenation has given an impulse to civilization, rather than the destruction predicted by Gobineau and Spencer. While there is no pure race in his model, Vasconcelos breaks the races of the world into four general categories: (1) red or Indian; (2) yellow or Mongolian; (3) black or African; and (4) white or European. Miscegenation within the same or similar groups has proven very productive, Vasconcelos argues, in civilizations such as the Greek, Roman, and North American.[25] This same mixture among dissimilar races, although much more conflictive in the beginning, has much more potential in the long term. The possibility for this process, he continues, has been opened by European colonization of the world. The Spanish Empire, which included most of the American continent and the Philippines, put all the major races in contact, and, contrary to their British counterparts, Spanish conquerors mixed with native inhabitants. This expansion and racial mixture "set the material and moral bases for the union of all men in a fifth universal race, fruit of previous races and superior to all the past ones" (*Raza*, 909).

One must insist, however, that even at the time of publication Vasconcelos himself doubted the accuracy of his own theories. As mentioned in the previous chapter, in the prologue to his 1926 *Indología*, a published collection of his lectures elaborating the ideas of *La raza cósmica*, Vasconcelos recognizes the arbitrary nature of his thesis and that for him science is an ideological weapon. In his third anthologized lecture in this collection, titled "The Man," the Mexican thinker expresses serious doubts about the future of miscegenation in America. He asserts that miscegenation is the rule throughout the world and that there are no pure races. But, he points out that throughout history racial mixture has taken place among related groups, while *"America's is the first case of an abrupt miscegenation* [among very different groups] *in a large scale"* (*Indología,* 1174, emphasis in original). Such a contrasting mixture, Vasconcelos recognizes, has proven to be conflictive, but he prefers to have hope in the future. His is an act of faith, rather than scientific certainty. Referring to the Catholic Church's recognition of the humanity of Indians in the 1500s and its willingness to grant them the right to receive the sacraments, including marriage, Vasconcelos writes:

> We should not ignore that there are still some who judge as a mistake this legalization of a process which is debatable from an ethnic point of view. Still today many see Latin America's failure precisely in this *mestizaje* which they qualify as inferior, and they see the Saxon success as dependent upon a continuous and severe dominance by the Puritan blood, which has come to constitute a sort of dominating and directing nobility. I do not deny the contrast nor the force of both theses. But just like many have already concentrated on giving arguments in favor of the thesis of a pure race as a dominating factor and, in short, in favor of the thesis which states that *a good Indian is a dead Indian,* I have endeavored to find arguments and, what is more important, proof, that the opposite thesis, the one favoring the *mestizo,* has a foundation and value. . . . This despite the fact that it is so easy to condemn the *mestizo* today that he is threatened by disintegration, while the white power, renewed in North America, expands victoriously throughout the world. (*Indología,* 1175–76)[26]

Further on in his lecture, Vasconcelos returns to the contrast between Latin America and the United States and emphasizes:

> And if we in Latin America suffer the still debatable effects of mixing, the United States maintains alive in their midst the ghastly black problem. The least that can be said about our system, and perhaps also the most that can be said about it, is that it is more humane and more Christian because it brings humans closer to each other. (*Indología,* 1188)

In this way the Mexican thinker clearly expresses the rationale for his racial theories as moral rather than scientific.

Vasconcelos's ambiguous relationship with Latin American *mestizaje* is evident throughout his works dedicated to the subject. While time and again he insists on the importance of racial mixture and the necessity to eliminate any sort of racial hierarchies, as Juárez points out, "La raza cósmica [sic], in the final analysis, did not really reflect a sincere desire to have the racial traits of all peoples blended together. It was rather a hope that those traits Vasconcelos considered inferior would be absorbed and lost in the sea of genes of the superior types" (Juárez, 30). As will be seen shortly, Vasconcelos couched his rhetoric about racial superiority in aesthetic terms, and these are deeply Eurocentric in their nature. His argument gives primacy to European science, technology, history, aesthetics, and philosophy, placing other races, cultures, and civilizations as subsidiary to a larger European process. In one of many examples of slippages characteristic of his thought, Vasconcelos celebrates Mexican churrigueresque architecture as a novel *mestizo* contribution to the world, yet he writes that this style owes its charm to the *"unconscious* contribution of the Indian artist," implying that these Indians were unable to deliberately create a new architectural style (*Indología*, 1214, my emphasis). Similarly, the title of *La raza cósmica*'s sequel, *Indología,* carries within itself the ambiguity characteristic of Vasconcelos's thought. While the title implies an emphasis on the Indian aspect of the American experience, the author is careful in qualifying his word choice within the European tradition:

> All the aspects of thought related to this *{mestizo}* ethnic grouping I comprehend under the name *Indología* because I want to restore our ideal to the prophetic vision of the discoverer of the New World and to his illusion that by stepping on Indian soil he was consummating the circumnavigation of the planet. . . . I do not intend . . . to shelter under this name any intention of predominance favorable to the indigenous tradition of America or to the Indian race of the continent . . . (*Indología,* 1121–23)

It is with this in mind that I now turn to a closer analysis of *La raza cósmica.*

Vasconcelos's racial theory rests on a teleology composed of two parts. On one axis, which I will call the spiritual teleology, the human spirit moves through three stages, leading from the realm of material necessity to that of aesthetic freedom. On the second axis, which I will call the geographic teleology, the dominant human civilization moves from its origins in the warm and fertile tropics to the colder and barren north, only to return once again to the tropics. Of the two narratives, that of spirit forms the model's central core. It corresponds to the essence of Vasconcelos's philosophy.

As Villegas explains in his book, *La filosofía de lo mexicano* (The philosophy of Mexicanness), the first fact of Vasconcelos's philosophical system is the noumenon, or existence itself. The universe is for him one of chaos and constant dissolution. Within this chaos, however, Vasconcelos identifies certain rhythmic structures of energy that constantly repeat themselves. These structures function at three hierarchically arranged levels: (1) that of the atom or physical; (2) that of the cell or biological; and (3) that of the soul or spiritual. Within each of these levels the structures repeat certain rhythms, which vary quantitatively, but never qualitatively. In certain instances, through the process of "revulsion," energy can qualitatively change its rhythm and achieve a higher level. This process cannot be explained rationally; like the first origins, it can only be explained through divine intervention. The higher the level, the broader its possibilities are. Thus, while the atom can merely repeat certain patterns, the cell already has a purpose and a teleology in its efforts to survive. The highest, or spiritual, level can only be achieved by humanity, and it is only at this level that energy can redeem itself through knowledge, which coordinates and constructs the universe (Villegas, 74–83).

Knowledge, for Vasconcelos, goes beyond the rational, which is only one aspect of it. In his system, Villegas tells us, there are three kinds of knowledge, with their respective sciences, corresponding to the three rhythmic stages of energy: (1) "discovery" or physical sciences, yielding knowledge of nature; (2) "invention" sciences, yielding knowledge of humanity; and (3) "spiritual" sciences, yielding aesthetic knowledge. Of the three types of science the spiritual are the superior type. The first two, based on reason, sacrifice real concrete facts for the sake of a universalizing logical or mathematical abstraction. Only aesthetic knowledge can achieve a synthesis between the universal and the concrete. As Villegas puts it, *"The senses put us in contact with the concrete particular; reason, taking its data from the senses, puts us in contact with universal abstract, and art achieves the universal concrete"* (Villegas, 83–85, emphasis in original). Villegas points out that the three stages of human knowledge correspond to the three stages identified by Vasconcelos in human history (Villegas, 93).

In *La raza cósmica* Vasconcelos identifies three social stages in human spiritual history. The first stage Vasconcelos labels the "material" or "warrior" stage. Here brute force and geographic obstacles dominate human life. This is the realm of necessity. The second stage is that of "reason" or "logic." Here science and machinery overcome material necessity, but impose a new obstacle to human freedom by imposing a system of laws, customs, and duties. He identifies such obstacles as follows:

In the name of morality, for example, marriages are imposed which are hard to break by people who do not love each other; in the name of politics private and public liberties are restricted; in the name of religion, which should be sublime inspiration, dogmas and tyrannies are imposed; but each case is justified by reason's dictates, considered the supreme of human activities. (*Raza*, 929)

The overwhelming power of reason, materialized in Mexico by the *científicos'* positivism, was to be overcome in the future by the third stage, named "spiritual" or "aesthetic." Here Vasconcelos finds a complete freedom, where "[n]orms will be given by fantasy, the supreme faculty. . . . [and] people will live without norms." While in the first stage human will is controlled by appetites, and in the second stage by duty, in the third stage it becomes a "passion for beauty" (*Raza*, 928–32). In the teleology's final stage, "reality will be like fantasy" (*Raza*, 925). Fantasy is for him "the superior faculty," which allows humanity to live without norms. It is linked to the human will to express and expand; to break the limits imposed by nature and reason. With this perspective, Vasconcelos pays tribute to Nietzsche's, Wagner's, and Schopenhauer's thrust into the "unintelligible"; their will to break beyond the constraints of reason.[27] In his perspective, fantasy functions as a creative and destructive process; it destroys the norm and enacts its own desires. Like Nietzsche's Zarathustra, Vasconcelos argues for a rupture with the past in the name of superior actions. It is a desire to create new selves; a desire expressed as early as 1905, when in his thesis, *Teoría dinámica del derecho,* he posited the "law of energy's development," according to which individuals should be free to develop their own energy and express it by forming new selves (Blanco, 37–38). This is the ultimate goal of the human spirit, fully achievable in the aesthetic period.

The teleology of spirit is accompanied by another, much more material narrative, which relates the development of the human spirit to its geographic environment. In this geographic narrative Vasconcelos also traces the origins of human civilization through three stages, moving from its emergence in the tropics, through a second period of northern material and ideological dominance, and finally returning to the tropics. While the richer and more fertile lands of the tropics provided the appropriate material conditions for the emergence of early civilizations, the harsher north required the development of fuels for heating purposes. This fuel technology was later applied to machinery, which, with the creation of better means of transportation, set the material base for the linkage of all races. The harsher north also forced the inhabitants of this region to adopt a voluntaristic attitude, helping them to establish a "spiritual" leadership across the entire planet. However, the tropics' rich and beautiful natural resources are an indication to Vasconcelos that civilization must return to this region (*Raza,* 923–26). The two teleological narratives complement each other. The early tropical civilizations correspond to the first material stage. Reason corresponds to the northern stage, where science, through machinery, dominates nature. The return to the subdued tropics corresponds to the aesthetic stage. In a narrative voice reminiscent of modernist utopias, Vasconcelos envisions a future world where "the whites' science" will "utilize condensed snow, or electrochemical currents, or gases of subtle magic, to destroy flies and vermin, to dissipate heat and fever. Then all of humanity will spill itself over the tropics, and in the solemn immensity of its landscapes, souls will conquer plenitude" (*Raza,* 924–25).

In his Americanist spirit, Vasconcelos places his future utopia not in any tropical region of the world but in the Amazon basin, a region he had visited during his tour of Brazil and Argentina and that impressed him with the power concentrated in its rivers and waterfalls. With the faith of a mystical prophet, he does not seem to doubt the appearance of such a place. The only thing that remains in question is who will control the region, and here only two civilizations can vest control—that of the Anglo-Saxons or that of the Latin-based cosmic race. Because of its wealth, Vasconcelos predicts that the future of the world depends on the struggle for control over this region. "It is convenient," he writes, that the Amazons remain "Iberic." In such a way, "With the resources of this zone, the globe's richest in all sorts of treasures," the cosmic race will found Universópolis, and from here "airplanes and armies will go throughout the planet educating people" to create the conditions for a universal "life based on love [which] will express itself in beautiful forms." However, were the region be dominated by the "English . . . either from the [British] islands or the [American] continent," then the new city would be known as Anglotown, a town dominated by white supremacists from where the inhabitants would travel the world to impose on other continents "the predominance of the white blonde man and the extermination of their dark rivals" (*Raza,* 924–25). Thus, despite the theory's "cosmic" pretensions, the future of the world remains in the hands of two European traditions: "Iberic" or "English."

The teleology put forth by Vasconcelos emphasizes the southern tropical regions of the planet as a site for the origins of civilization and for its final triumphant return. These function as a privileged space due to their material wealth and aesthetic bounty. Nevertheless, it is the northern "white" civilization that is responsible for the production of the technologies necessary for a return to the southern paradise. Without the gases and other scientific advancements of the industrialized north, the tropical south is condemned to an existence dominated by vermin and disease. Without the northern (i.e., European) rational system, the southern peoples' possibility for an aesthetic synthesis is foreclosed by filthy animallike conditions. The return to a southern dominance, with the aid of northern technology, opens the possibility for the aesthetic synthesis discussed by Villegas, with the southern natural riches providing the "concrete particular" of the first material stage and the northern technology providing the "universal abstract" of the second rational one.[28]

Just as the southern tropical bounty functions exclusively as a container upon which northern knowledge can achieve an aesthetic synthesis, race—the theory's central category—functions only as the material base upon which a higher quest for beauty is enacted. Divided into four general categories in a system reminiscent of Gobineau, the main races identified by the author are depositories of particular features and attitudes, again reminiscent of Gobineau's essentialist analysis: the red is melancholy and mysterious; the black sensual and lascivious; the yellow observant and creative; the white vigorous and imaginative (*Raza,* 923). While he argues that all races bloomed at some point in the past, he assumes white material and spiritual predominance as an unquestionable fact of his time. Throughout the text, Vasconcelos endeavors to find arguments against the superiority of whites, stating, for example, that "The *mestizo,* the Indian, even the black, are superior to whites in an infinity of specifically spiritual capacities" (*Raza,* 933).[29] These virtues, however, are not specified. Such statements in favor of other races are rare and seem a rhetorical aside. While throughout the text he praises the initiative, bravery, and technological achievements of western civilization, he takes for granted that other groups cannot provide the cultural or scientific leadership for the future cosmic race. He, for example, is unambiguous about the destiny of Indians, who have "but one door to the future, that of modern culture; [they have] only one road, the one already cleared by the Latin civilization." Having set the model of modern civilization for the rest of the world to follow, now whites must "set aside their pride" in order to seek spiritual "progress and redemption" in the soul of the other races (*Raza,* 917). As the southern geography provides the space for the full aesthetic enjoyment of northern technologies, other races provide whites with a possibility of further spiritual development.

Consistent with his aesthetisizing philosophy, Vasconcelos explains the future *mestizaje* in terms of beauty. "In the future," he tells us, "as social conditions improve, blood mixture will become more and more spontaneous, to the point that it will not be subject to necessity, but to taste; in the last instance, to curiosity" (*Raza*, 928). In this realm of freedom Vasconcelos, echoing the eugenicists of his time, envisions the appearance of a new superior race. But the process of selection he envisions departs drastically from that of his contemporary scientists, as it is not intelligence or force that determines the dominant characteristics of the future fifth race. The depuration of the human race, in his view, will respond to aesthetic principles, an aesthetic deeply racist in its premises:

> The species' lower types will be absorbed by the superior type. In this way, for example, the black will be able to slowly redeem himself; through voluntary extinction, the uglier lineages will give way to the prettier. As they become educated, the inferior races will become less prolific, and the better specimens will ascend in a scale of ethnic improvement, the superior type of which is not precisely the white, but a new race, to which even the white will have to aspire as a means to achieve the synthesis. . . . In a few decades of aesthetic eugenics the black could disappear together with other types that the free instinct of beauty will mark as fundamentally recessive or unworthy of perpetuation. (*Raza*, 933)

Statements like these reveal the racist undercurrent in Vasconcelos's thought. Just as he excluded nonwhite races from scientific production, he excludes them from the realm of beauty. While Vasconcelos is emphatic that the new race will not be completely white, his language and assumptions by stating "not precisely white" and "even the white" imply that it will be almost, if not completely, white. These aesthetic assumptions are far removed from the pluralistic premises Vasconcelos's theory implies.

The Mexican believes that by basing his eugenics in beauty and not on the survival of the fittest his arguments are free of the racism he imputes on Darwin's followers. However, time and again his own statements make Vasconcelos's racism evident. In *Indología*, for example, he affirms that the majority of Mexico's *Mestizos* and Indians are ugly. He qualifies his assertion by attributing their unpleasant appearance not to essential hereditary characteristics of their race but to the work regime under which they live. He insists that poor European peasants are also ugly because of their work, and concludes that "Ugliness is a common consequence of misery. Beauty is the fruit of care and luxury" (*Indología*, 1189). According to him, in a more egalitarian system, when whole races and social classes are free of economic exploitation, their potential beauty will bloom. However, such an assertion does not explain why in the previously quoted passage he predicts the voluntary disappearance of the black race. Furthermore, giving him the benefit of the doubt and assuming that he would incorporate physical features of each one of the races, by focusing exclusively on the aesthetic contributions of the various races to the future cosmic race, the text remains silent as to the cultural or intellectual enhancements these races will give to the dominant northern element.

If Vasconcelos's model denies Native Americans—as well as Africans and Asians—a role in the production of modern knowledge and in the possession of physical beauty, a similar kind of privation takes place in the realm of history. Within *La raza cósmica*'s great historical epic a decisive struggle for human destiny will take place in America. The American continent, however, is just a new space for the continuation of a longer, strictly European struggle between Saxons and Latins, dating back to the 1500s, when, armed with the instruments of reason, both groups set forth to conquer the planet.[30] What distinguishes both groups, according to Vasconcelos, is their attitude toward their colonial subjects. While the Spanish conquerors physically and spiritually mixed with the conquered races, the Saxons kept to themselves. It is this distinction that defines the Latin "mission" as nurturer of the cosmic race to be reflected

> in that abundance of love that permitted the Spaniards to create a new race with the Indian and the black, expanding the white lineage through the soldier who engendered an Indian family, and western culture through the missionaries' doctrine and example, putting the Indian in the conditions to enter the new stage; the stage of the One world. (*Raza*, 918)

Vasconcelos disregards the conqueror-conquered dynamic of oppression, celebrating the creation of new families, as if these were consensual relationships and not, as was very often the case, the result of a powerful imposition, war booty, or seigniorial rights. The important fact for him is that this very act engenders a biologically mixed race. And here one must insist on a biologically mixed race because western culture and religious doctrine dominate the ideological aspect of this mixture. The violence of this process is only alluded to when Vasconcelos compares the Spanish-American experience to that of the British. Saxon America, he believes, was able to modernize quickly because of its segregationist policies, which avoided "the contradictory instincts of racial mixtures." The encounter of dissimilar races in Latin America had, at the beginning, violent and chaotic results, undermining in a first instance the possibilities for a rapid growth (*Raza,* 918). The violence of the colonial encounter is, thus, dismissed as just one retarding factor in the longer historical path.

Blaming Latin America's slower economic development vis-à-vis the United States on miscegenation, Vasconcelos praises the economic achievements of the industrialized Saxon north, but qualifies these achievements in a very moralistic tone. In their thrust to dominate the world, he writes, *"they committed the sin of destroying those* [other] *races, while we assimilated them; this gives us new rights and hopes for a mission without precedents in History"* (*Raza,* 918, emphasis in original). By behaving virtuously, Vasconcelos tells us, the Spanish conquerors transformed themselves into the rightful heirs of the future. And, in his grammatical construction of "we assimilated them," he clearly identifies himself as part of the specifically Spanish tradition that assimilated other races.

If in the Spanish Conquest *La raza cósmica* identifies a foundational moment in American and world history, the essay also finds an even more ancient and mystical foundational narrative. According to Vasconcelos, the American continent contains some of the oldest geological formations on the planet and this region was the cradle of the long-disappeared Atlantic civilization, of which Native Americans are the descendants (*Raza,* 906). Such a belief was not Vasconcelos's alone. In 1924 the Carnegie Institute, with his ministry's support, financed Sylvanus Morley's excavations in the Gulf of Mexico to confirm this thesis.[31] While never proved, the Atlantic origins of Native American civilization fit very well in the minister's racial model. It gave legitimacy in antiquity to America, proving his theory that in the distant past—prior even to the classical Greek period—a magnificent civilization had flourished in the region. It is also significant that Atlantis as a foundational myth once again links the history of America to the European tradition, since the notion of Atlantis belongs to European classical antiquity.

The Atlantic theory gives a mythical substratum to *La raza cósmica,* but it is the Spanish Conquest that actually set in motion the ultimate miscegenation project. Central to Vasconcelos's understanding of this historical moment is the role played by the conqueror-explorers and the missionaries. Both of these figures, in their own ways, represent important aspects of his philosophy of history. The conquerors of the American continent are, for Vasconcelos, heroic figures comparable to the mythical figure of el Cid. Brave and inventive, they dared to venture into the unknown, armed by the willpower to challenge the structures accepted by the reason of their time:

> they had the kind of temperament that reforms the very reality by constantly exaggerating and improving it in fantasy and action. Men moved by the mirage of reality; men who do not see what is in front of them because a dream takes them in search of eternal El Dorados that the planet cannot provide, but that the soul creates and destroys at whim. (*Indología*, 1214)

Such an understanding of the conquerors' mentality—inspired by a search for the fantastic—places them as predecessors of the third and final stage in Vasconcelos's teleology of spirit. And the Mexican thinker cannot explain their unprecedented feats in any other terms. He believes that a materialistic search for gold and other riches, in and of itself, cannot explain the conquerors' actions. If this were the case, Vasconcelos reasons, Hernán Cortés could have stayed in the Aztec capital, enjoying his conquest's booty, but instead he continued exploring, reaching as far as the Sea of Cortés, off the Baja California peninsula. Similarly, Pedro de Alvarado could have comfortably stayed as ruler of Guatemala and other regions, but instead he crossed the Central American isthmus and ventured almost to Quito, Ecuador, crossing on horseback territories so harsh that they are rarely visited today. The moving factor behind such apparently absurd actions, Vasconcelos concludes, was "the desire for the contemplation, the charm and the splendor of the most beautiful landscapes in the world" (*Indología*, 1214–15). Rather than warriors or treasure hunters—an attitude too prosaic for the *criollo* Ulysses—the early conquerors were for Vasconcelos explorers in search of an aesthetic gratification of the soul.

Complementing the conquerors' aesthetic mysticism, Vasconcelos identifies the religious zeal of the missionaries who accompanied the explorers in all their adventures. Beyond their essential role as propagators of the Catholic faith, an act which in itself made the conquered peoples equals to their new rulers by incorporating the newly conquered into their civilization, the minister of education emphasizes their pedagogical activities. In this regard, he insists that the education they provided went beyond the teaching of math and language, including lessons in crafts, agriculture, and the care of domestic animals. They were also, according to Vasconcelos, keepers of the Indian knowledge and traditions. He alludes to missionaries like Fray Bernardino de Sahagún, and reminds his readers that these religious men in the early stages of the colonial period systematized many aspects of Indian knowledge in books that to this date provide invaluable information to students of the pre-Columbian past.[32] He insists that most of the destruction of Indian art and traditions was the result of "ignorant militias and narrow fanaticism." The salvaging of knowledge, however, is qualified by Vasconcelos, as he states, "Unfortunately, in our land there were not elements to compete, much less overcome a Christian civilization. The worthless technique and infantile ideology of our Indian myths could not even hold the invaders' curiosity" (*Indología*, 1229–35). Understanding the role of conquerors and missionaries in this way, Vasconcelos concludes that "Religious mysticism and the also mystical desire for natural beauty are for me the principal factors that the Castilian soul contributed to the spirituality and the new consciousness of the continent" (*Indología*, 1215).

The mystical contribution of conquerors and missionaries can then be seen at two levels. On a more obvious level, the role of the missionaries was to preach what Vasconcelos considers to be the true religious faith. One must remember the importance given to the Catholic religion by his mother, who saw in it both a source of spiritual salvation and a defining characteristic of the Hispanic Mexican culture, distinguishing it from both the heathen Apaches and the Protestant North Americans. The mysticism ascribed to the conquerors is somewhat more elusive. It is the spirit of adventure and fantasy characteristic of the third stage of human development; the willingness to break the molds of a given reality and dare to move beyond its limits. This voluntaristic attitude, however, also had very material results, praised also by Vasconcelos. It was these daring men who expanded the map of the Hispanic world empire, circumnavigating the world, leaving the Spanish flag in places as remote as the Magellan Straits and Valdez, Alaska, and establishing a regular trade route between Europe and China, passing through the Philippines, Acapulco, and Veracruz. And as maps and trade expanded, Spain lived its golden age, and printing presses arrived at its American dominion long before they arrived at the northern British colonies. These were the years of glory for the Hispanic civilization; years viewed with nostalgia by a Mexican who sees his country, and that of his fellow Hispanics, torn apart by civil wars and Anglo-Saxon intervention.

A crucial characteristic of these fantastic conqueror-explorers, according to Vasconcelos, was their free spirit. "They all felt as equals before the king," he writes. Only free and creative men like these could achieve the historic feat of the conquest of America. Vasconcelos sees the glories of the Spanish Empire begin to decay as the heroic conquerors were replaced by servile courtiers and bureaucrats:

> Men incapable not only of conquering, but even of defending that which others had conquered with talent and daring; degenerate courtiers, capable of oppressing and humiliating the native, but submissive to royal power; they and their masters did nothing other than ruin the labor of Spanish genius in America. The portentous task begun by the iron-willed conquerors and concluded by the wise and abnegated missionaries was gradually annulled. (*Raza*, 914)

Beyond the courtiers, Vasconcelos identifies another major problem in the land tenure system prevalent in Spanish America, feudal in character and therefore economically inefficient. In his characteristic moralizing spirit, Vasconcelos's critique of this feudal system goes beyond its strictly economic consequences. He criticizes the *encomienda* system as a legalization of slavery and also sees the degenerating effects of subservience to royal will on the spirit of the landowners themselves. Depending on royal favor to control land and people was, in Vasconcelos's view, a humiliation of human dignity. The logical result of a system where a monarch has complete power to grant or take away land and prestige was a society of abject subjects or dissatisfied rebels, both hindrances to a regime's optimum development (*Indología*, 1161–63).

Vasconcelos's critique of the decline of the Spanish Empire in America is, then, not based on its economic exploitation of the region and its people but rather on the moral decay of the Spanish generations that followed the heroic conquerors and missionaries. The Spanish generations that succeeded the original conquerors and missionaries were no longer adventurers willing to risk life and limb in search of new lands and peoples inconceivable by their contemporaries, but servile materialists who gave up the spiritual pride of discovery and conquest in order to maintain their favor and wealth; they lost the fantastic initiative. In this regard, Vasconcelos also criticizes Spanish royal despotism during the colonial period. This, as the authoritarian militarist regimes he saw in his contemporaneous Latin America, he identifies with one of his people's pitfalls, a Caesarist tradition, "the scourge of the Latin race" (*Raza*, 913). In celebrating the mystic zeal of conquerors and missionaries, and in condemning the Caesarist despotism in the region, Vasconcelos once again constructs the history of Latin America in almost exclusively

European terms. His discussion of the colonial period barely touches on the specific contributions of other races to its development, growth, or decay.

As with many of Vasconcelos's texts, *La raza cósmica* and *Indología* cannot be read exclusively as theoretical interpretations of a distant past. They are also conscious interventions in the sociopolitical reality surrounding their publication. In this regard, Vasconcelos's texts are a call to Latin American unity and a reaction to attacks against the Hispanic heritage of the region. Their celebration of a glorious Spanish American empire linking under one authority most of the continent greatly contrasts with the Latin America of Vasconcelos's time, deeply divided by petty nationalisms. Like his predecessor, José Martí, he believed that regionalisms and desire for local power divided and weakened Latin America. Furthermore, if disintegration within America had atrophied the region, the antagonistic rhetoric of the independent American nations toward Spain was a crucial mistake. Breaking with Spain implied breaking with Latin America's history, culture, and tradition, and opened the region to easy manipulation, first by Great Britain and later by the United States. Denying the Spanish heritage also separated Latin Americans from their creative thrust as they turned into imitators of the Anglo-Saxon powers, the "nordomania" against which Rodó had warned.

In *La raza cósmica,* Vasconcelos recognizes that the independentist leaders of the early 1800s had a legitimate gripe against monarchical tyranny. Yet the American colonies were not the only victims of such despotism; peninsular Spaniards were also affected. In this regard, the struggle against the monarchy should have been constructed as a political act, linking democrats on both sides of the Atlantic. The struggle should never have been constructed as one between America and Spain. Vasconcelos would have preferred to follow the path of the British American colonies, which, despite breaking politically from the metropolis, never denied their British cultural and ethnic lineage. Such a relationship allowed Anglo-Saxon power to expand across the planet, creating a world situation in which, as Vasconcelos presents it, "what is not conquered by the English from the islands is taken and kept by the English of the new continent" (*Raza,* 915). Under this perspective, however, Vasconcelos does not seem to be aware of another one of the contradictions in his thought. Indeed, the United States has not nurtured an anti-British tradition in the way the Latin American republics have nurtured an anti-Spanish tradition. However, as Vasconcelos himself recognizes, the colonists who created the United States of America at the turn of the eighteenth century did not consider miscegenation with the Native American and black population of their colonies as part of their identity either. They were white, no questions asked. In the Latin case, Vasconcelos would have preferred to see a transatlantic Hispanic federation emerging from the failed republican attempt of the *Cortes de Cádiz*. And, since that did not happen, he now urgently calls for pan-Hispanic reconciliation in the present, moving beyond the limiting concerns of nationalisms. At one point he recognizes the Conquest's "trace of spilled blood; the cursed blood that centuries do not erase." But he insists on reconciliation, arguing that a "common danger must eliminate these [traces]. There is no other way" (*Raza*, 915–18; *Indología*, 1219–20). And, particularly important for the unity of Latin America in Vasconcelos's thought is the propagation of the Spanish language. Vasconcelos recognizes the linguistic plurality of the continent, but characterizes Indian languages as "dialects without any connection between them, and which lack written expression and power of diffusion." He believes that these languages have enriched the Spanish language, but in a modern era that tends to simplification they are condemned to disappear. Furthermore, Vasconcelos identifies polyglotism as one of the principal causes of nationalist conflict in Europe and believes that linguistic unity will function as a "synthesizing vehicle" for the American continent, which would otherwise remain divided (*Indología*, 1190–98).[33]

As has been seen in my discussion of *La raza cósmica* and *Indología*, Vasconcelos's racial theories in the mid-1920s were rhetorical celebrations of *mestizaje*, but their premises were deeply Eurocentric. Nonetheless, many of those who are quick to condemn the later conservative Vasconcelos still celebrate his notion of a cosmic race as a pluralistic and all-inclusive understanding of Latin American race and culture. As Nancy Leys Stepan has pointed out in her study of eugenics in Latin America, the idea of the cosmic race has become one of Mexico's revolutionary myths. Vasconcelos's celebration of *mestizaje* has been taken at face value without a critical examination, despite the fact that the theory "was fundamentally structured by the racism of the period."[34] This was a racism that often cloaked itself in a discourse celebratory of Mexico's Indians, but which, nevertheless, oftentimes relegated them to strategic ideological tokens in an otherwise exclusively European worldview. In this regard, Vasconcelos's contradictory rhetorical celebration of *mestizaje* can be better understood in the context of *criollo* nationalism and nine-

teenth-century liberal pro-*mestizo* ideology, two distinct but closely
related movements deployed by Mexico's intellectual elite in an effort to
construct a uniquely Mexican national identity. Vasconcelos's racial theory emerges from, and dialogues with, these traditions.

As David Brading points out in his seminal study of the origins of
Mexican nationalism, three important elements constituted the early
attempts of Mexican *criollos* to distinguish themselves from peninsular
Spaniards, whom they saw as foreigners in a land that they now considered legitimately theirs: a denigration of Spaniards and the conquest, an
exaltation of the Indian past, and a unity around the Catholic faith.[35]
Although, as we have seen, Vasconcelos would be very critical of any
denigration of Mexico's Spanish heritage, his glorification of the Indian
past—in terms of the mythical Atlantis—and his insistence on a
Catholic identity fall neatly into this tradition. Two examples of *criollo*
nationalism should be illustrative of the ideological underpinnings this
tradition shares with Vasconcelos's racial theory.

In 1780, for example, the Jesuit Francisco Javier Clavijero, who like
other Jesuits had been expelled from New Spain by the Bourbon monarchy, published his *Historia antigua de México* (Ancient history of Mexico)
as a polemic against those European intellectuals who posited a natural
inferiority of Americans. His text is a comprehensive study of Mesoamerican civilization. He endeavors to describe a uniquely American
experience. In the early chapters he describes at great length a distinctively American nature, but he cannot resist westernizing the culture
and civilization of the region's inhabitants. Thus, as Brading points out,
Clavijero constantly compares Native American civilization to the classical European past, turning Texcoco into the Athens of Anáhuac, Cholula
into the Rome of Anáhuac, and Quetzalcóatl into the Mexican Saturn
(Brading, 37–38).

Along similar lines, Fray Servando Teresa de Mier, one of the fathers
of Mexican nationalism, also praised the artistic and technical achievements of a pre-Columbian past.[36] However, Fray Servando did not limit
himself to a discussion of the advancements of the ancient Mexican civilization. He went one step further by claiming that scientific research
gave reasons to believe that the holy image of the Virgin of Guadalupe
did not appear on the peasant Juan Diego's cape, as Catholic authorities
claimed, but on the cape of the Indian god Quetzalcóatl. His version,
which was not new and had already been considered by Carlos de
Sigüenza y Góngora in the seventeenth century, argued that shortly
after Jesus's death the Apostle Thomas took the name of Quetzalcóatl

and proselytized in America. In 1794, Fray Servando dared to make these assertions specifically on 12 December—the anniversary of the supposed appearance of the Virgin of Guadalupe—and was soon detained for blasphemy and sent to Spain by the Inquisition. Using official Church ideology, Fray Servando had placed the origins of American Christianity in the Apostle Thomas/Quetzalcóatl and not the Spanish conquerors. As exposing Native Americans to Christianity was the main legitimating principle for the Conquest, the existence of a pre-Spanish American Christianity legitimated the possibility for an American independence. This, however, is ironically achieved by westernizing the Indian past; assuming that it was western before the western—or actually eastern in Indian terms—invaders arrived. A similar attempt to westernize Mexico's Indian heritage is evident in the monument to Cuauhtémoc on the Paseo de la Reforma, in Mexico City (see chapter 2, note 41).

In all of these cases, what *criollo* nationalists emphasize is a glorious native *past,* and they remain silent about an Indian *present.* Furthermore, even as they praise the past achievements of Mesoamerican civilizations, they feel compelled to westernize them, be it through the comparison with classical antiquity or through the Christianization of their traditions. Such is also the gesture that Vasconcelos makes as he writes America's origins in the muted memory of the mythical—and Hellenic—Atlantis. Unlike Fray Servando, however, Vasconcelos would not blame the destruction of Indian civilization on the Spanish Conquest. Quite on the contrary; according to the ex-minister, the glories of the Atlantic civilization in America had already decayed by the time of the conquerors' arrival. In this regard, one must consider the very different contexts of each one of these thinkers. Fray Servando was a publicist for Mexican independence and as such needed to demonize his political and military enemies. By the time of Vasconcelos's writings, Mexico had been independent for over a century, and now the greater threat was North American expansionism.

If Fray Servando, Clavijero, and other *criollo* nationalists deployed the image of a glorious but toga-clad Indian *past* to legitimate their project of Mexican independence, it would be the task of the liberal thinkers of the nineteenth century to deal with the very pressing reality of the Indian *present.* In their efforts to integrate the marginalized Indian population into national life, they would also attempt to dress it in western garb; not necessarily in the toga of Greek and Roman classicism but in the overalls of the modern worker or farmer. In a very paradoxical turn,

the liberals who advocated for Indian rights actually advocated their disappearance as a distinct group in order for them to become absorbed in
a modern and homogeneous nation-state. After all, with the gaining of
independence, liberal thinkers argued that all Mexicans were supposed
to become equal citizens. The highly elaborate caste system developed
by the Spaniards was conceived by the newly emerged republican leaders as a marker of Spanish oppression. The notion of an "Indian" was a
misnomer coined when Columbus thought he had reached the Indies.
The role of a progressive government was to strive for a situation where
all citizens were equal, without any of the caste classifications of the
Spanish oppressors. Furthermore, they attributed what they saw as the
backward living conditions of the majority of Indians to 300 years of
Spanish rule. The introduction of western agricultural, hygienic, and
medical techniques through education would, in their mind, modernize
the Indians and save them from the effects of colonial oppression.[37]

At another level, the leaders of the new Mexican independent state
saw themselves in a problematic situation particular to many postcolonial nations: the forging of a new national identity. A nation-state
encompassing the broad territory and cultures contained between California, Nevada, and Utah in the north and the Central American isthmus in the south had never existed as such. These borders did not
respond to a cultural historical continuity but to the administrative
desires of the Spanish Empire. As Agustín Basave Benítez points out,
after independence, Latin American states—as governing structures—
emerged first and then the "nations" had to be created, "imagined," like
Benedict Anderson would say.[38] Latin America did not have the com-
monality of language, religion, culture, or ethnic background around
which nineteenth-century European nationalist movements rallied.
What linked this space was the common Spanish colonial heritage,
which at least among certain sectors of the population, and particularly
in the urban centers, had spread the Spanish language, the Catholic religion, and cultural practices that, although hybridized by the trans-
culturation that took place over three centuries of colonial rule, were
Hispano-Latin in their core. Most of the broader Mesoamerican cultural
networks in place prior to the Conquest had been destroyed, marginaliz-
ing Indian cultural practices and institutions to a very localized level
(Bonfil Batalla, 50).

The nineteenth-century liberal ideology of *mestizaje* functions as a
two-pronged effort to homogenize the national population and create
Mexican citizens. While the term, particularly in its current usage,

implies racial and cultural mixture, it actually implies, as Bonfil Batalla argues, a project of "de-Indianizing the Indian." On the one hand, throughout the nineteenth century, many liberal thinkers like Lorenzo de Zavala, Justo Sierra O'Reilly, José María Luis Mora, Sebastián Lerdo de Tejada, and even Mexico's "Indian president" Benito Juárez actively promoted European and North American immigration into Mexico in order to colonize "empty territories," bring in European and North American modern knowledge, and hopefully whiten the Indian population of Mexico through intermarriage—an idea put forth in the early years of the colony by Bartolomé de las Casas, a staunch defender of Indian rights. The other prong of this approach is cultural; an attempt to rid the Indian of his or her culture through a westernizing education. It is to this effort that I turn to in the next chapter, which addresses Vasconcelos's tenure as minister of education, an experience he claims informed his racial theory.

Chapter Four
Cultural Missionary: Vasconcelos's Ministry of Education

The third volume of Vasconcelos's autobiography, *El desastre*, begins with the narrator on a mission as a "traveling salesman of culture." These opening images of the future minister touring the country by train in 1920 to gather support for the formation of a national ministry of education aptly represent the tone of Vasconcelos's understanding of his role during that period. Riding in the "oldest and most modest private car of the National Railroads," Vasconcelos and his entourage of intellectuals crisscross the country with the message of culture. From his very first discussion of the project, the narrator distinguishes himself from the "victorious generals" for whom the most luxurious train cars are reserved. Despite this difference, Vasconcelos, who had just returned to the country after Carranza's assassination, counted on the support of Generals Adolfo de la Huerta and Alvaro Obregón—interim president and president-elect—for his project (*Desastre,* 1218–20). "The most modest private car" was a railroad car nevertheless, put at the disposal of the future minister by the new authorities of the nation.

Three decades before Vasconcelos's railroad tour of the republic, Justo Sierra presided over the First National Congress of Instruction (*Primer Congreso Nacional de Instrucción,* 29 November 1889–31 March 1890). Liberals for the most part, the participants proposed for the nation an "integral" education that would foster the harmonic development of students' physical, intellectual, and moral attributes. It also recommended the creation of a unified national system of "popular education," which should be free, mandatory, and secular.[1] This congress would, according to historian Josefina Vázquez, "inaugurate a new epoch in the history of the country's educational policy," as prior to the congress's initiative, education in Mexico was administered at the local level. Furthermore, the congress saw in popular education an instrument of the state, with the responsibility of developing marginalized social groups—particularly peasants and Indians—into citizens, capable of participating in the economic and civil life of a modern nation-state

(Gallo, 93–94). Sierra's "social pedagogy" greatly differed from a traditional book-based pedagogy with its emphasis on classroom education. Instead, his method encouraged the active participation of both students and teachers, the former by exploring and interacting with their physical surrounding, the latter by actively shaping the pupils' relationship to the world. A positivist thinker, Sierra also saw as a duty of education the promotion of scientific thought over "superstitions," something that he saw as particularly prevalent in the peasantry. Finally, a popular education should create "moral" people who "acquire, by intimate conviction, and not by the memorization of manuals' phrases, the habit of feeling responsible for their actions, discerning the good from the bad." A "social pedagogy," capable of producing literate and moral citizens, was seen by Sierra as necessary "to make our democracy move from the ideal realm into political reality" (Gallo, 54–55).

Behind Sierra's beautiful words of democracy and moral citizenship lies the very pragmatic reality, emphasized by Alan Knight, of gaining the ideological allegiance of populations that were often even unaware of the existence of the nation-state or its official language. An effective educational system should also prepare a disciplined labor force out of peasants whose perceived "carefree" habits were incompatible with the regimented requirements of modern production (Knight 1990, 237–38). One cannot but think of Foucault when reading Sierra's emphasis on the subject's internalization of a social morality and turning it into an "intimate conviction" or even a reflexive "habit" as citizens now "impose upon themselves" their social duties.

A little over 30 years after the congress, armed with official support and the enthusiasm and expectations raised by the revolution, Vasconcelos crisscrossed the country by train, endeavoring to bring his precursors' educational project to fruition. Like his predecessors, Vasconcelos saw in a centrally coordinated national education infrastructure an indispensable instrument for the consolidation of the nation. The future minister of education was, however, even more ambitious than the participants of the first congress; the enthusiastic young intellectual saw his project as a crucial step in the affirmation of the cosmic race's cultural and material ascendance.

Like in many other moments of his life, Vasconcelos was often forced to improvise as minister of education. A lawyer by formation, Vasconcelos did not have much practical or theoretical experience in pedagogy or school administration. His 1935 book on pedagogy, *De Robinsón a Odiseo*

(From Robinson to Odysseus), is based on his experience as minister of
education. The text provides an interesting combination of theory and
practice. The first part sets forth Vasconcelos's theory, based on his particular philosophical understanding of the three levels of energy and his
conception of the sociopolitical and historical role of education, particularly in relation to his construction of the Latin-based cosmic race. The
second part discusses the organizational framework of Vasconcelos's
ministry and the pedagogical methods put into practice in the schools
and other cultural institutions of the ministry. This book is very helpful
in understanding the institutionalization of cultural networks during
Vasconcelos's tenure, but one must bear in mind the date of its publication. Published over a decade after his service, the text is often charged
with its author's later, more conservative and religious ideology. Nevertheless, the book is a useful stepping-stone into our discussion of Vasconcelos's ministry.

De Robinsón a Odiseo was published as a polemic against John Dewey's
progressive educational philosophy. Dewey's pedagogy was very influential in what came to be known as the "School of Action" during Vasconcelos's tenure, and his complete dismissal of this influence is symptomatic of the author's later rabid criticism of the United States.
Nevertheless, Dewey's methods were adapted to the minister's broader
project. The book's title refers to Robinson Crusoe and Odysseus, who
represent alternative pedagogical paradigms. The former, who must
learn by himself to survive on a desert island, represents Dewey's pedagogy, which emphasized the independent and practical role of the student, who must discover the lessons on his or her own with minimal
interference from the teacher. The latter, while also an adventurer, relied
not only on his practical skills but also on a traditional and ancient wisdom, unavailable on a secluded island. Robinson Crusoe comes to represent a practical man, able to solve immediate material problems without
necessarily being concerned about spiritual or aesthetic questions. He
represents in Vasconcelos's mind a practical North American attitude,
characteristic of the machine age and devoid of a spiritual dimension:

> The fundamental mistake of activism is found, it seems to me, in not per-
> ceiving that the contemporary child lives in a super-civilized technical
> milieu, and not in the desert of the *pioneer* robinsons [sic] who eighty
> years ago improvised and "learned in the making" . . . The intense
> exchange of commodities and ideas is a characteristic of our era, and such
> a life system surpasses the simplistic understanding of the island's tool-
> building Robinson and of the "Taylorized" robinsons [sic] of the Ford

factories. The modern age's conditions demand a more international Odysseus, more international and universal. A traveler who explores and acts, discovers and creates, not only with the hands, and never only with the hands, because neither can he nor does he want to dispose of the baggage that widens his soul, the ingenuity and the treasures of a millenarian culture. We need an Odysseus who does not begin his journey, as Robinson did, from Bacon, but from much farther back; from Aristotle and Yajnavalkia, the legendary Hindu; from Moses, the founder of our civilization. Our century's Odysseus will easily surpass the Homeric Odysseus because of the extension of his knowledge. . . . It is towards a new Odysseus that the epoch's virile ambition should tend. Not towards robinsons [sic].[2]

The Robinson-Odysseus dichotomy represents the divide Vasconcelos sees between a Saxon and a Latin project. The former represents mechanized efficiency in understanding and dominating the material environment, while the latter represents much more universal spiritual and aesthetic concerns. It is, of course, the model of Odysseus that the self-proclaimed *Ulises criollo* chooses as his own.

The text's early sections serve Vasconcelos to present his opposition to what he identifies as "naturalist" approaches to pedagogy, which he traces back to Rousseau and that he finds in Dewey. Under such an approach, Vasconcelos tells us,

Beginning with Rousseau, educators preoccupy themselves with taking from schooling its character of a rule imposed on the consciousness from without. They please themselves imagining that the child in liberty, just like the hypothetical natural man, will develop the most hidden treasures of his particular idiosyncrasy. On the way, they accuse schooling of not making any other thing than suffocating the impetus from the marvelous seed. (*Robinsón,* 1498)

Against such an approach to education, which assumes that every human is potentially good, Vasconcelos poses what he identifies as the "Christian thesis of original sin." "According to this profound cosmic vision, each man is born with the stigma of his fall, and, therefore, each one needs correction and redemption" (*Robinsón,* 1498). A belief in natural individual virtue is substituted in Vasconcelos's model by a belief in the ambiguity of human nature and in its tendency toward corruption. Against this corruption stand the teachers, who must mold the soul and conscience of their students. Anchoring his pedagogy on a religious concept allows Vasconcelos to present his model as cosmic, overflowing the earthly limitations of a nature-based approach. The *Ulises criollo,* however, does not want to limit his argument to theological concerns; his positivist formation forces him to search for a "scientific" premise for his argument and he finds this in Jung, a psychoanalyst—therefore scientist—obsessed by the mythic component of human consciousness:

> for a while science has been officially evolutionist, and evolutionism, in the penultimate of its versions, tells us through Jung's mouth that the child is nothing else than the development of the embryo, and this consists on an organized portion of the species' general plasma. In the nucleus of this plasma portion there is a subconscious, where all the experiences of the remote predecessors remain latent: the monkey's astuteness and also the tiger's fierceness, the instinct's radiance and the brute's corruptions; in sum, all the zoology as a sediment of our impure and confused humanity. This is what science says in clamorous opposition to the vagueness and sentimentality of a pedagogy derived from Rousseau. Experimental science contradicts the thesis of original perfection, implicit in modern pedagogy, which began with Rousseau who improvised it and continued until Dewey who did not deepen it but did dogmatize it. (*Robinsón,* 1498–99)

As these passages indicate, Vasconcelos's pedagogical vision responds to the universalizing tendency of his worldview. He grounds his vision on both the ethereal realm of religion, by invoking original sin, and on the material realm of science, by invoking Jung and the physical carriage of instincts in the embryonic plasma. The universality of his model is both synchronic and diachronic. At any particular moment the embryonic plasma carries all of the present possibilities; at the mystic level it carries within itself the ever-present moral struggle of good against evil. As a reflection of historical development, this same embryonic plasma carries within itself the historical experience of humanity, dating back not only to human experience as we know it but to the much longer experience of animal life and instinct. The teacher functions in his model as arbitrator, censor, and carrier of tradition. Human intervention depurates the limitations, dangers, and obstacles imposed by nature. The teacher functions as a depository of human wisdom who must tame and direct the students' natural development. Such a wisdom is encompassed in what Vasconcelos identifies as "culture." Vasconcelos uses a gardening metaphor to explain this concept: "From the garden which abandoned to itself is overcome by weeds, to man's conscience which when it lacks the light of another's knowledge falls into bestiality, there is not one case in which culture does not represent an effort to reorient the natural and to intervene in its development." Remaining within this metaphor, the Mexican pedagogue identifies two specific tasks of the gardener/teacher: (1) the gardener removes undesirable weeds and plagues from the garden; (2) the gardener also interferes in the natural process to improve the plants. Thus, the author tells us, characteristically focusing on the aesthetic rose rather than on nutritional corn or wheat, "A garden rose is a deformed wild rose, but, from the human point of view, improved" (*Robinsón,* 1499–500).

Despite Vasconcelos's use of a natural metaphor to explain his conception of education, the Mexican thinker draws a clear distinction between the natural and human realms. In a move reminiscent of Giambatista Vico, Vasconcelos argues for the impossibility of understanding of nature separated from human intervention: "The natural can be conceived as subsistent without us, but only as a hypothesis; in reality, everything that we know is the unbreakable tie of our action upon the world." Furthermore, he argues that "the natural becomes human when it is touched by man's impetus" (*Robinsón,* 1500). The teacher, with his or her accumulated human knowledge, must break the child away from her natural impulses and endow her with humanity. Like the gardener, the teacher must also carefully exclude all kinds of "weeds" and "plagues" from the pupils' consciousness, as these undesirable instincts attempt against human civilization, pulling humanity back into its natural and bestial condition.

The process of education shapes its pupils like the gardener shapes the rose. Vasconcelos is unambiguous; the educational process is highly ideological, because it is moral:

> In certain sense, each pedagogy is coercion . . . In any case, school has a morality that it aspires to impose, and this is enough to make the educator's impartiality fictitious and the supposed respect of infantile consciousness false. With more or less frankness, those who administer schools try to gain the power reserves contained in the young generations for their party. (*Robinsón,* 1503)

Gone is the Rousseauian notion of natural goodness. Vasconcelos sees in education a political instrument able to channel youthful energy toward specific pragmatic objectives. Furthermore, Vasconcelos insists that "all pedagogy . . . is the putting into action of a metaphysics" (*Robinsón,* 1505). Political program and metaphysics are clearly linked in Vasconcelos's pedagogy, the former appearing as an earthly expression and instrument of the latter.

Like his historical teleology and his discussion of the states of energy, Vasconcelos's metaphysics in relation to education consists of a three-stage process, moving from the clean, to the dirty, and then to the radiant. Such a movement is motored by the category of "disgust."[3] As with his theory of revulsion, discussed in chapter 3, Vasconcelos traces a movement from the mineral to the animal and ultimately the spiritual and aesthetic realms. Minerals are considered clean by Vasconcelos, but devoid of life. Life is engendered in plants and animals—plants functioning in his model as a transition between minerals and animals. Contrary to minerals, the latter contain juices and secretions, the necessary by-products of organisms that require outside nourishment for survival. Vasconcelos is eloquent in expressing his disgust for these reminders of our material existence:

> Juices and saps circulate inside the plant; the viscous element, which tends to give aromatic essences, is engendered. But the animal is born— worse if it is of our species—and the glands appear with their entourage of repugnant secretions. Our disposal matter is poisonous and we live surrounded by a mephitic aura. There exists then, according to the penetrating perception of disgust, a sort of damnation more remote than that of Adam which accompanies the zoological cell from the moment when it separates itself from the polyp realm; ever since, separated from the solid coral, it searches for food in the waters.

Against a disgusting bodily reality, Vasconcelos posits the "soul," which rejects the dirty realm and moves into the radiant:

> In man, the secretionary dejection mechanism is shameful; here lies our original sin and the impossibility of loving ourselves just the way we are. The soul, closed into these impure vessels, spends its existence loving what we should be and feeling repugnance for our state. In its zeal to escape, the soul creates the image: improved substitute for reality; we think because of it, and in the image we anoint our reality with adoration, we redeem it by loving it. In such a way, through imaginary construction which is one form of divine construction, we exit our zoology and recreate ourselves in a spirituality foreign to disgust. (*Robinsón,* 1504–5)

Vasconcelos's idealism jumps at one's eyes as one reads these passages. His metaphysics reject the human condition of living beings, requiring nutrition, digestion, and secretion, as disgusting. It is in imagination—the conscious rejection of a material human condition—that Vasconcelos places the highest aspirations of humanity. The highest state even gives up consciousness, which would "immediately extinguish [itself] . . ., abandoned to itself, but slowly discovering the art of opening the windows through which the stream of infinite energy enters. Spiritual power; with it we construct the scaffolding of culture; the world of illusion which we need, just like the fish needs the water and the bird needs the wind." At this point there appears to be a contradiction in Vasconcelos's argument. On the one hand, in his polemic against Dewey and the "naturalist" school, Vasconcelos speaks about the important role of the teacher, who must shape the pupils. On the other hand, Vasconcelos's metaphysics privilege imagination at a very individual level, separated from teachers or any other outside interference. In the radiant stage, "the being is self-sufficient; it no longer reflects exterior light like the diamond; instead it illuminates" (*Robinsón,* 1505). The role of the teacher, however, is to prepare the pupils for the radiant stage by introducing them to the cultural tradition of previous generations, which, in their aesthetic pursuits, have endeavored to reach this stage.

The minister's idealist metaphysics, however, seem to directly clash with the practical tasks required from the ministry of education in the early 1920s; they also seem to clash with the "rational" emphasis given to education by the new political elite. In 1910, before the outbreak of the revolution, 84 percent of the country's population was illiterate (Vázquez, 107). Vasconcelos's quest for the radiant stage required pupils well acquainted with a traditional humanist canon, written in texts most Mexicans could not decipher. Beyond the very pressing concerns with illiteracy, a decade of civil war had destroyed much of the nation's infrastructure, which needed to be rebuilt. The postrevolutionary regime faced a great lack of financial, human, and infrastructural resources— one of the main obstacles for the development of a national educational system. Vasconcelos's idealist search for spiritual and aesthetic oblivion requires a leisure, valued by the thinker but unavailable after 10 years of revolutionary bloodshed and destruction, particularly in a country that prior to the revolutionary upheaval had most of its population in abject poverty. How could a pedagogy with such idealist premises function to institutionalize the postrevolutionary educational system with so many urgent practical demands? The answer to this question lies in two directions: (1) in Vasconcelos's ability to mobilize the population; and (2) in the fact that despite its idealism, Vasconcelos's metaphysics—and therefore pedagogy—contains within itself a very practical dimension.

In her assessment of Vasconcelos's role as minister of education, Vázquez insists that the minister "achieved something truly incredible: to rouse and mobilize the Mexican people. . . . [and] to convert almost every person who knew how to read into a teacher" (Vázquez, 156–57). Such an assessment is shared by Guadalupe Monroy Huitron, who, writing about the minister's efforts to mobilize the nation's population, tells that during his tenure "there really was an evangelical zeal to teach one's fellows how to read and write; back then one really felt it in the chest."[4] Vasconcelos's criticism of purely material concerns led him to give great importance to "representation." He criticizes the utilitarian nature of Dewey's pedagogy, saying that while "[s]ometimes we have objects in front of us, other times we reflect over representations of objects." The ultimate goal of Vasconcelos's pedagogy is for the student to manipulate not objects themselves but their representation (*Robinsón*, 1521). Within the mystic and religious discourse of the 1935 *De Robinsón a Odiseo,* the author's emphasis on representations seems to be very far removed from the concrete necessities of a postrevolutionary regime. Yet a politically astute manipulation of representations proved to be a very useful instrument in the mobilization of national and international support for the new regime. In the previous chapters I have discussed the minister's manipulation of the images of Cuauhtémoc and Zapata and the category of race for very practical political goals. In these cases, Vasconcelos's emphasis on imagination and representations allows him to put forth an "imagined community" around which to mobilize the emergent nation. As Mariátegui had pointed out, Vasconcelos was able to imagine a better future, and his eloquence and zeal inspired many to partake in his project.

Vasconcelos's privileging of imagination goes hand in hand with his emphasis on emotions and other impulses: "passions . . . which awaken the soul." He tells us "school is fortified when it shares the enthusiasm of gregarious impulses like faith in progress and patriotism" (*Robinsón,* 1522). Fostering this type of excitement was very useful in the consolidation of the new regime. Youthful enthusiasm, with its desire to break molds and its impulse toward novelty, was particularly valuable for Vasconcelos, not only during his ministry but also during his presidential campaign, which received widespread support from youth. Moved from the realm of metaphysics to the realm of history, the enthusiastic impulse functions in his model like "revulsion" and "disgust." As I have discussed earlier, these categories function as motors for qualitative transformations: the theory of revulsion explains the transformation of energy from the mineral to the animal and the spiritual realm; the theory of disgust explains the soul's rejection of material constraints in search of a superior imaginary reality. In the realm of history, the impulse functions as a denial of the present in the name of a better future. Such an impulse, then, is the motor of historical transformation. In regard to the school's historical mission, the Mexican thinker tells us, "every pedagogy implies a thesis about destiny, and not only a science of things" (*Robinsón*, 1530). It was toward his own understanding of historical destiny that the minister of education would try to guide the enthusiasm of pupils and volunteers throughout Mexico.

Vasconcelos's idealism turns him into an iconoclast, questioning reality in favor of a distinct and better future. Yet in a characteristic contradiction of his thought, Vasconcelos is better qualified by the apparent oxymoron of a conservative iconoclast. Within his pedagogy, the enthusiastic impulse must be kept in check: "The educator's magic consists of joining, in live synthesis, tradition and impulse" (*Robinsón*, 1522). While Vasconcelos privileges iconoclastic and transformational impulses, this transformation cannot take place in a vacuum. Vasconcelos's historical model is teleological, with a beginning, a middle, and an end; later generations must necessarily build upon the inheritance of their predecessors. Vasconcelos critiques Dewey's emphasis on children's independent experimentation and discovery. There is a certain cultural accumulation that the teacher must pass on to the student. The teacher should be a guide, acting as Virgil in Dante's *Divine Comedy* (*Robinsón*, 1511). Mocking Dewey, and relating him to the Anglo-Saxon tradition, Vasconcelos speaks of his pedagogy as appropriate for the "pioneers"—a word he consistently writes in English—for whom the discovery of a log, a pond, or a rabbit is of utmost importance. Such an approach, Vasconcelos tells us, is laudable and necessary in a cultural desert, "but this cannot be the case in an already established society" (*Robinsón*, 1521).

Outside of the "pioneers' settlement," in the context of a historical cultural tradition, "school should be the summary of humanity's general experience" (*Robinsón*, 1514). Such an experience encompasses a broad spectrum of knowledge, divisible into three general groupings, corresponding to Vasconcelos's other triads: physical, ethical, and aesthetic. Knowledge acquisition within the physical realm—the area that according to Vasconcelos was emphasized in Dewey's pedagogy—is "active," within the ethical realm it is "normative," and in the aesthetic "contagious" (*Robinsón*, 1538). To a degree, children can discover the physical world through independent activity. In the ethical realm, however, children require the teacher's experience, which establishes the moral rules and regulations of social coexistence, according to the dominant ideology. Aesthetic knowledge cannot be regulated, but a teacher is also necessary; a teacher whose aesthetic enthusiasm is transmitted to the students by contagion. While Vasconcelos privileges bookish over practical learning, a complete curriculum must address all three areas of knowledge. Thus Vasconcelos proposes the following courses for an elementary education:

Objective knowledge or science of facts:
    Mathematics.
    Geography.
    Natural History.
    Physics and Chemistry.
    Logic.
Ethical knowledge or science of conduct:
    Biology.
    Physiology.
    Psychology.
    Moral-History.
    Sociology.
Aesthetic knowledge or science of the spirit:
    Plastic Arts.
    Music.
    Poetics.
    Philosophy.
    Religion. (*Robinsón*, 1539)[5]

Rhetorically, Vasconcelos—particularly the later one—is a radical opponent of Dewey's pragmatic pedagogy and its utilitarian emphasis. Yet Vasconcelos does not have a gripe with utilitarianism itself. He is fearful of a strictly technical and utilitarian education, seeing this as the result of machinist and technical tendencies in the United States, culminating with paradigms like Taylorism and Fordism. Nonetheless, one must insist that Vasconcelos also had very practical aims for his educational system. Although his long-term project envisioned the mystical goal of the radiant stage, we must remember that in his metaphysics each stage must necessarily follow the previous one. As in *La raza cósmica,* Vasconcelos saw the necessity of the knowledge acquired by the northern intellectual state in order to reach the final aesthetic synthesis; students must be exposed to all the forms of knowledge in order to reach the ultimate radiant synthesis. Symbolic of this concern is his second memo as university president, dealing with one of the most material of concerns, hygiene. In this memo he reminded all teachers that "many times a fistful of mercury powder, to fight parasites, or a bar of soap will be a more efficient educational starting point than twenty spelling lessons" ("Instrucciones," 104–5). Similarly, when referring to the students' enthusiasm, he praises "progress" and "patriotism," qualities of the second stage that are necessary to build the bases for the future in a third stage. Vasconcelos saw in front of him what he considered a primitive and barbarous Mexico. Atrophied by internal strife, Mexico—and most of Latin America—needed a historical leap that required the appropriation of a knowledge, developed by historical necessity in foreign lands, but nevertheless necessary as part of a common human arsenal of knowledge. Vasconcelos's ministry, then, functions as a transitional institution, responsible for bringing a backward population into modern civilization, to then overcome modernity in an aesthetic synthesis. Before embarking on the task of reaching his high spiritual goals, Vasconcelos first had to complete the project envisioned by Sierra and his liberal and positivist colleagues. A modern nation had to be built before the establishment of a future utopia. Despite Vasconcelos's apparent disdain for technology and labor, Universópolis—the utopian city of *La raza cósmica*—depends on the most modern machinery for its existence. In response to such a necessity, despite what *De Robinsón a Odiseo*'s theoretical framework might lead us to think, technical education received much attention during his tenure.[6]

In opposition to the utilitarian pedagogy of Dewey, associated by him with an Anglo-Saxon tradition, Vasconcelos proposes a model based on the Hispanic cultural heritage. From the Spanish heritage the roles that Vasconcelos values most are those of conqueror and missionary. Around their figures he creates a myth of initiative and zeal that will shape his labor as minister of education. From the mythic conqueror he takes the military discipline, the imagination, the strength, and the free will; from the missionary the commitment to culture and to others. Vasconcelos is more often related to the latter, oftentimes being referred to as missionary, prophet, and martyr. Nevertheless, Martha Robles, José Joaquín Blanco, and Claude Fell, among others, have identified in the minister of education his will to power and spirit of adventure, which links him to his admired conquerors.

As an adventurer, as Blanco proposes, Vasconcelos was very active in the formation of a new structure. Like Columbus, Vasconcelos obtained the state's mentorship to launch a new adventure. Unlike him, however,

Vasconcelos was not in search of natural resources but of the Mexican mind. Vasconcelos as a minister embodied the individualism he admired in his mythic conqueror. He disliked assemblies and other consultative bodies that "function at best to give a suggestion; but in essence, ratify and legalize the work of a brain, which, in its creative moments, must feel alone and feel responsible at the individual level" (*Desastre*, 1225). Like his mythic conquerors, who drew cities and scriptures, Vasconcelos drew and built schools and libraries, theaters and museums, laws and memoranda. Like those same conquerors, he traveled the country on horse, foot, or any available conveyance as he led his missionaries in a redemptive campaign of the nation's poor and ignorant.

The military image of the conquerors was appropriately fitting to a country emerging from a decade of armed struggle. Vasconcelos's ministry thus used military metaphors and structures in its early organization. An example of this is the "Children's Army," consisting of fourth, fifth, and sixth graders, whose purpose was to participate in the literacy campaign. In 1922 the ministry of education claimed that its 5,000 member strong Children's Army had trained almost 9,000 others. The Army's incentive system was very similar to that of its military counterparts, consisting of appeals to patriotism and honor, bestowed with diplomas instead of medals.[7] The early literacy campaign is couched in military terms. "On the eve of war," Vasconcelos tells his compatriots as he encourages them to volunteer their services, "countries call all their inhabitants to public service. The campaign we are ready to begin is more important than many wars; we hope that our compatriots will know how to respond to the country's urgent calling" ("Campaña," 103). He appropriated the military parade's fanfare, proposing the "Alphabet *Fiesta,*" in which all those who had been taught by volunteers outside of the school system would parade in a show of the campaign's victories (*Desastre*, 1326–28; Fell, 28).[8] Vasconcelos in this way borrows an old tradition, not necessarily related to education, and rearticulates it in a different direction. The institution of the popular parade has both military and religious origins. Parades have provided a space for armies to represent their disciplined might and for religious communities to express their cohesiveness and faith. Vasconcelos is very successful in building upon and manipulating these preexistent institutions. As he insisted, his pedagogy was not new; it was efficient (*Robinsón*, 1501).

The military metaphors, one must point out, did not remain in the ministry's vocabulary for a long time, as such a language went against Vasconcelos's vehement opposition to militarism, but he did use them at the beginning of his campaign; a reflection, perhaps, of his times. However, Vasconcelos shared with the military tradition an almost compulsive obsession with discipline, enacted in a multitude of choreographed activities. Throughout the republic, the ministry's schools organized spectacles involving large groups of well-coordinated students. Such events reached their maximum expression the day the National Stadium, one of the minister's pet projects, was inaugurated. On that occasion male and female athletes paraded and performed a series of choreographed exercises, a choir of 12,000 children sang, and 1,000 couples danced to traditional Mexican and Spanish songs (*Desastre*, 1455–56). Such activities instilled discipline and a group spirit among the participants. Many of the performances, as that at the National Stadium, emphasized dances and music from the Mexican and Hispanic tradition in an effort to foster a cultural pride among the participants (*Indología*, 1261–63).

Vasconcelos's ministry's zeal in disciplining the human body went far beyond these choreographed performances, intervening even in the quotidian practices of the students. It was in this spirit that Vasconcelos's second memo as president of the university insisted upon a comprehensive training of the students in the literacy campaign. Basing his proposal on his studies of the cultures of India, he proposed a program that would incorporate proper breathing exercises and a new diet, free of alcohol and excessive greases and spices and consisting mainly of vegetables. The regimentation Vasconcelos wanted enacted even considered a programmed schedule for the weekends. Saturday afternoons should be dedicated to personal hygiene, exercise, and moderate entertainment. Sunday mornings would be dedicated to study and the afternoon to strolls in the countryside, where choirs would be organized ("Instrucciones," 104–7).

Vasconcelos's admiration of the conquerors and missionaries was based in great part on what he saw as their capacity to build. "Upon a victory," he writes about the conquerors, "they traced new cities and wrote their founding scriptures" (*Raza*, 914). Similarly, the missionaries built temples and monasteries, schools and hospitals. This attitude showed a pragmatism the minister attempted to imitate, one that reveals a man much more practical than his theoretical idealism might suggest. One of his first concerns as minister was to obtain an appropriate building for the ministry. From this point on he would be constantly preoccupied with obtaining buildings and funding from the state (*Desastre*, 1228–33). This very material concern was markedly present in his daily labors. He tells us that every day after an early breakfast, "at eight [he] was already visiting the construction sites, climbing scaffolding, urging expediency, noting what was missing to hasten its arrival. At nine [he] arrived to [his] office splattered with lime" (*Desastre,* 1278).

The sophisticated and refined philosopher, whose goal was to reach the radiant stage of contemplation, acknowledges that the technical education branch was "the Ministry's most important contribution to national culture" (*Desastre,* 1268), reflecting an understanding of culture that recognizes material and technical developments as crucial. As the missionaries had taught new crafts to the colonized peoples of America, so did the Schools of Work—or of Action—of the SEP. In rural villages elementary schools had orchards and domestic animals where students and teachers worked in unison. In urban centers these schools had workshops where students acquired technical skills ranging from sewing and cooking, to food packaging, soap making, and technical drawing. At the secondary level schools prepared technicians in the construction, chemical, and electric industries, among other fields (*Indología,* 1248–50).

During his tenure, Vasconcelos often addressed specifically material issues. One of his most pressing concerns was the fostering of hygienic habits among the student population and their parents. He also sponsored the establishment of free school breakfast programs for indigent children, as he recognized that malnourished pupils could not take advantage of the school's educational resources. These breakfasts consisted of a cup of milk with coffee, two small loafs of wheat bread, and a portion of beans, and were originally financed through voluntary payroll deductions from teachers and staff.[9] Vasconcelos's concern with diet is multifaceted. At one level, as in the school breakfasts' case, his concern is with fulfilling the students' basic nutritional needs. In other cases, as I have discussed in earlier chapters, diet functions as a cultural marker. Thus he announces with pride his "zeal to reform our people's eating habits," insisting on the preparation of stews and grain dishes, cooked with olive oil, which he identified with the Hispanic tradition, instead of with lard, which he saw as a Yankee influence (*Desastre,* 1448). Eating in general was a subject of numerous articles in *El maestro* (The teacher), one of the journals edited by the SEP. The articles' focus ranged from the benefits of a vegetarian diet to the proper way to set a table with a white linen tablecloth, a bouquet of flowers, and clean china. "If the tablecloth is dirty and the table is set carelessly, the room messy and everything in disorder," the journal warns, "there is little tendency towards culture and good manners. If on the contrary, everything is orderly, everything in the house can play an educational role."[10] In this regard, Fell also finds a moral component in Vasconcelos's dietary concerns (Fell, 30–31).

As a missionary the minister enacted broad collective projects, involving local communities in the schools' daily activities. The school of the Bolsa neighborhood is a pertinent example, described by Vasconcelos in the following way:

> In the Bolsa neighborhood, one of the most abandoned and miserable of the time, we ran a school which was an exercise in the redemption of the very underworld; the poorest and most dishonest part of a great city. By renting a ravaged house and a large contiguous lot, we started to gain the collaboration of neighbors, who organized themselves in brigades to sweep the streets and clean the sewage. We did not even consult the city hall, eternally dedicated to the politics and estates of people, who, after a year in office, sported cars and properties, but never even visited the plebeian ghettos. Without the resources to implement sanitation measures, we succeeded in getting parents and students to dedicate Saturday afternoons to cleaning the filth and burning the trash. We placed a bath and barber shop in the school. And the first campaign was not for the alphabet, but the extirpation of lice, the curing of scabies, and the washing of the little ones' clothes. Immediately after, as hunger was the cause of their mental slowness and physical ills, we took advantage of a small grant and gave free breakfasts to all students. Initially, this measure was highly opposed, as it was considered unprecedented and uneconomical: giving helpless creatures a little milk and bread. Nevertheless, similar things were being done at a greater scale in Argentina, and they continue. It was impressive to contemplate the results within a few months of the school's establishment. (*Desastre*, 1260)[11]

I would like to stop to look at two of this narrative's central elements at the point of contact between individual and collective praxis. As mentioned earlier, Vasconcelos's thought is centered on individual responsibility. One is then surprised to find the emphasis on collectivity in these lines. Not only are most of the school's ancillary institutions—cleaning and sanitary brigades, school kitchens, etc.—developed collectively, the author's narrative voice is the collective "we," referring to the ministry as a whole, working in cooperation with students, parents, and neighbors. This collective impulse is, however, tempered by the minister's missionary zeal. Like his ideal Spanish missionaries, the minister of education mixed with the native community in the actual construction of a cultural infrastructure. Yet his discourse, like that of the missionaries, is monological. As missionaries brought the Christian faith, the ministry of education brought culture, nutrition, and hygiene. In this regard, the school is privileged over the community, functioning as "the collective's head, the avant-garde of customs reform" (*Robinsón,* 1550). As the will to power is the conqueror's motor, selfless compassion is that of the missionary. In this operational mode, Vasconcelos turns to the church's rhetoric, as the ministry's mission was the "redemption of the very underworld." Early in his tenure Vasconcelos moved away from military terminology, preferring to couch his rhetoric in a Christian discourse. Words like sacrifice, crusade, humility, self-denial, mission, missionary, redemption, and faith fill his pages, in the place of their more belligerent counterparts (Fell, 20, 33). Although one should, of course, remember the belligerent connotations of the term "crusade" and of the militant positions of some of the overenthusiastic missionaries.

This redemptive discourse is, however, also charged by a very arrogant and paternalistic streak of condescension. While in the early twenties sanitation was indeed a pressing problem,[12] Vasconcelos's language reveals a certain elitist aesthetics of poverty. He is most impressed by the Bolsa's crime and vice and by the external markers of poverty present in filth, trash, scabies, and lice. It takes the more refined consciousness of the missionary to organize the ignorant masses for their redemption. It is up to the missionaries to protect these "helpless creatures." Vasconcelos's focus on the filth of poverty refers us to the metaphysical bases of his pedagogy, tracing a movement from "the dirty," through "the clean," to "the radiant." The emphasis placed on filth in the discussion of the Bolsa school clearly places these people in the realm of animal necessity. It is the role of the enlightened missionary to point the way first to cleanliness before he can even begin to address the movement into contemplation. One must also notice that these missionaries emerge from the ministry of education itself. Vasconcelos's apparently humble narration of the ministry's involvement in the Bolsa school clearly degrades municipal and legislative participation in the process, labeling them as corrupt and inefficient. He insisted on as much independence as possible for his institution and greatly enjoyed whenever the ministry outdid the other bureaucracies.

In certain ways the ministry's agencies worked as charitable institutions where a cultural and economic elite could channel their services for the redemption of the country. In this spirit, Vasconcelos proudly states that he recruited his staff from professionals like himself, with successful private practices, who did not depend on the ministry for their financial well-being (*Desastre,* 1275). He and his ministry are an aristocracy of culture with enough knowledge and leisure to turn to the missionary's path. The overall mission is couched by Vasconcelos in terms of charity. Yet, within the bureaucracy itself he is ruthless in his elitism.

Charity or school, the Bolsa school was an astounding success, and as a response the ministry created similar schools in Mexico City, Orizaba, and Puebla. These schools combined a classical education in art and literature with a practical training in crafts and trades useful to the community. Fell tells us that they had two objectives: "establishing an embryonic social network in highly populated zones, almost totally lacking an educational and cultural infrastructure; in second place, to a degree, they played the role of experimental centers for the investigation of pedagogical methods." In 1923 the Francisco I. Madero school had a production and sale cooperative, including also sanitary and social services. The Belisario Domínguez experimental school included a special educational program on nutrition (Fell, 42–43).

Individual agencies such as these could be mobilized at a national level to achieve very practical aims in the struggle for national sovereignty. With this aim, Vasconcelos emphasized import substitution, using the ministry's shops to produce, whenever possible, the necessary supplies, ranging from books to furniture (*Desastre,* 1285–86). Projects such as these fulfilled two purposes: pedagogical, as the students learned the crafts necessary to produce the objects in question; and economical, as the ministry saved the money necessary to buy those objects, and, in the case of import substitution, set the basis for a national industry. Students learned by both making and using the products. This production also gave the ministry a certain independence from the state and private industry.

Governmental support of the publishing industry dates to the Carranza regime, which in a 1919 decree encouraged the publication of textbooks in Mexico to substitute for North American ones that, through the New York based company, Appleton, controlled most of the Mexican market. In 1919, the call for a Mexican textbook was based in great part on the argument that the books by Appleton lacked a sufficient Mexican specificity, as they were designed to be used throughout all of Latin America (Vázquez, 152–59). Vasconcelos's publishing endeavors, however, went beyond the production of school textbooks. The ministry printed and distributed a collection of "classics" at cheap prices. The volumes were produced in editions of 20,000 to 25,000 issues, and were sold for 50 cents each. Among the texts published were *The Iliad, The Odyssey, The Divine Comedy, Faust, The Lives* by Romain Rolland, the

Gospels, anthologies of Esquilius, Euripides, Plotinus, and Tagore, and three volumes of Plato and two of Plutarch. At the time of his departure an edition of the *Romancero,* an anthology of Latin American literature and one of Lope de Vega were in the process of production. They also had already planned publication of books by Calderón de la Barca, Shakespeare, Ibsen, Bernard Shaw, and Reclus. Beyond the classics the ministry published 1,000,000 elementary reading books, 500,000 educational pamphlets, over 2,000,000 alphabet cards, editions of Justo Sierra's Mexican and world history books, a collection of readings for women edited by Gabriela Mistral, and a collection of classics for children (*Indología,* 1252–54). The minister was mocked for his publication of the classics in a country where the majority of the population was illiterate, but this did not stop him. He strongly believed that once the country was literate publications like these would greatly increase its culture. His inspiration for this project was based on similar activities taking place in the newly formed Soviet Union under the guidance of Lunacharsky and Gorky (*Desastre,* 1252–53; *Tormenta,* 1187). Judging from the selections of texts for the collection, we can once again see his Eurocentric understanding of culture. Beyond the texts by Tagore, all other books belonged to the western tradition.

The publications project was complemented by a great emphasis on the construction of libraries in the country. Libraries were revered buildings for Vasconcelos, buildings that he compared with sanctuaries.[13] From his youth in Piedras Negras he remembered the Carnegie libraries in Eagle Pass, and they were an example that he tried to imitate (*Indología,* 1250–51). The SEP had one department specifically dedicated to their development, having as its goal the establishment of one library in each location with more than 3,000 inhabitants. Among the members of the Libraries Department were some of the most prominent intellectuals of the time, including Jaime Torres Bodet, Julio Torri, Carlos Pellicer, Rafael Heliodoro Valle, Pedro Henríquez Ureña, Gabriela Mistral, Francisco Monterde, Alfonso Taracena, Xavier Villaurrutia, Salvador Novo, and Bernardo Ortiz de Montellano. The libraries were divided into six different kinds: (1) mobile libraries, which would take books, often on horseback or donkey, to the most remote areas of the country; (2) rural libraries; (3) school libraries, with books specially targeted to children; (4) urban libraries, for localities with populations of more than 5,000 and often placed in working-class neighborhoods; (5) specialized libraries, for institutions of secondary and higher education; and (6) public libraries, with eclectic collections. Beyond these categories was the national library to function as an archive for the nation as a whole. By December 1923 a total of 1,976 new libraries had been established throughout the country, holding a total of 182,514 volumes (*Indología*, 100–110). The distribution of books was not limited to Mexico. Vasconcelos's project, as we have pointed out, was ultimately continental. In this regard the SEP's archives are full of requests for books and other printed material from schools throughout Latin America. Similar requests were made by Mexican organizations in the United States, such as the *Sociedad Mutualista Mexicana* (Mexican mutual aid society) in Pittsburg (sic), California, the *Club Cuauhtémoc* from Los Angeles, and the *Escuela libre para mexicanos* (free school for Mexicans) in San Diego.[14]

Central to Vasconcelos's educational project are the "cultural missions" *(misiones culturales)*. These centers for rural education were, according to Vasconcelos, the theoretical seed for the ideas put forth in *La raza cósmica* (*Desastre*, 1329). They are qualified by Vázquez as "one of the most successful Mexican institutions" (Vázquez, 157). The cultural mission program was the most ambitious effort for the implementation of a national rural educational system since independence. In *El desastre*, Vasconcelos is unambiguous about the origins of this project; he unquestionably gives all credit to the Spanish missionaries, in comparison to whom his modern missionaries could only be second (*Desastre*, 1328–31). Remembering the events 15 years after the fact, Vasconcelos sees in the Spanish missionaries two qualities that his personnel lacked: celibacy and spirituality. The former, he reasons, by taking away the burden of a family allowed the religious to dedicate full attention to their redemptive mission and bond with their assigned communities.[15] The latter gave the missionaries a transcendental sense of mission that greatly increased their zeal.

Closer to Vasconcelos's tenure, the government of Francisco León de la Barra—interim president between Porfirio Díaz and Francisco I. Madero—attempted to deploy by decree a system of "rudimentary schools" *(escuelas rudimentarias)* as an effort to incorporate the rural, largely Indian, population into the national mainstream.[16] An idea of Sierra, as their name indicates, these schools' main purpose was to teach very basic Spanish literacy, arithmetic, and citizenship. Low budgets, more pressing political and economic concerns, and their very limited scope undermined any possibility of success for the venture. They never achieved the comprehensiveness and scope of their Spanish predecessors or of the later SEP program (Fell, 203–4; Gallo, 53–55; Vázquez, 107–8).

Like the colonial Catholic missions and the rudimentary schools, these twentieth-century missions targeted the largely Indian rural population. More than just rural schools, these missions were whole cultural centers, designed to fulfill a variety of purposes. Through the training provided by them, the poor inhabitants of rural Mexico were supposed to acquire the technical skills necessary for their incorporation into the modern capitalist economy. Through their insistence on teaching Spanish—or "national language" as it was often called—and citizenship, the missions were supposed to incorporate their pupils into the broader national community and to foster patriotism. In their best instances, the missions included a group of teachers and social workers competent in a variety of fields, including hygiene, physical education, first aid, literature, music, agriculture, pedagogy, and crafts. Traveling teachers moved from one mission to another, temporally sharing their particular knowledge. To provide competent teachers, a network of "regional teachers' colleges" *(normales regionales)* was established throughout the country. Reflecting the broad scope of the cultural missions, schools were rebaptized as "Houses of the People" *(Casas del Pueblo)*, becoming cultural and social centers for the whole community. These missions also became important economic spaces, fostering the development of local natural resources and combining academic education with technical and agricultural training.[17] The law, which incorporated the missions program, foresaw that the model mission would include, in addition to the teachers, the following personnel:

1 Director, who will be responsible and in charge of the organization and direction of the mission;

1 Medical doctor in charge of the population's health and the anthropological study of the [region's] race. He will also be the director of physical education and sports;

1 Agronomist, who will have under his charge everything related to field work and the propagation of useful plants and animals, will study the region's flora, fauna and geology, will direct the construction of buildings and roads to communicate the mission with the railroad or with other towns;

1 Teacher of aesthetic culture;

1 Teacher of small industries, and particularly in charge of improving the regional industries (basket weaving, work with palm trees, fibers, etc.);

1 Carpenter;

1 Blacksmith;

1 Potter;

1 Construction expert;

1 Tanner;

1 Soap maker;

1 Gardener;

1 [Female] Teacher in charge particularly of teaching feminine labors (use of loom and sewing machine) and to give the girls some notions of child rearing and home economics;

1 Cook who will teach cooking and baking.

Each member of the mission, in addition to instructing the natives of the region in their particular area of expertise, had the responsibility of teaching the Spanish language (Gálvez, 21).

The law project encouraged these teachers to "find inspiration in the spirit of the Franciscan missionaries who Christianized the Indians." As the Spanish missionaries of the sixteenth century, the modern missionaries had a double mission. Not only were they supposed to educate their pupils, they themselves were assigned the task of gathering information about the region and the population to which they were assigned. They were expected to provide the SEP with detailed information about the region's geographic and meteorological conditions, the social structure—paying attention to the prominent inhabitants who could aid through their influence—and the conditions of the school, if one existed. They were also expected to compile vocabulary lists of the languages they encountered in their region. Playing the role of ethnographers, they were assigned to gather as much information as possible about the "Indigenous races" they encountered, including:

> Percentage of indigenous population. Races. Historical and archeological data. Description of the races. Nutrition. Dress. Shelter. Languages and dialects. Religion. Superstitions. Customs. Hygienic conditions in which they live. Furniture and utensils. Their occupations. Their vices. Their virtues. Data about noteworthy events in their individual and collective life. Diseases that kill them. Influences that damage them and influences that benefit them. Their artistic inclinations. The census. The school-age population. General economic conditions and suggestions of means that can be used to improve them.

Beyond the distribution and gathering of information, the cultural missions had a social role in promoting local, regional, and national cohesion. For this purpose the teachers of the missions were expected to visit with parents and organize a wide variety of public events, including conferences, films, dances, picnics, patriotic festivals, choirs, exhibits, and "the great corn *fiesta*" at the end of the harvest season. To sponsor regional understanding, the teachers were supposed to organize excursions, competitions, and exchanges of school projects with neighboring communities. It was also recommended that newspaper-reading gatherings be organized to inform the local residents of world events. As social activists, the teachers would also help organize work and saving cooperatives in their areas (Gálvez, 22–25).

Despite Vasconcelos's later criticism of Dewey's practical approach to education, the memoranda distributed by the SEP concerning rural education placed a great emphasis on what it identified as the "school of action," a pedagogical method in which all of the students' subjects would be organized around practical experiences. The curriculum of the rural schools was designed around two principal areas: "Study of Nature" and "Handicrafts in relation to the environment in which the school is located." "The study of Nature," one memorandum stated, "shall not be theoretical. Instead it will be based on observed facts and on the experiences provoked by this." If students studied geography or arithmetic, this should be linked to the more practical concerns of agriculture or other crafts. Similarly, the language lessons would be related to the animals, plants, and other things in the surrounding environment. *"The type of teacher that only explains,"* concluded this memo, *"the theorizing teacher, is not the type needed in these schools, instead we need the teacher who can promote the students' activities, who produces, who teaches working."*[18]

The cultural missions, with their emphasis on multidisciplinary communal activism, are very similar to the Bolsa school in Mexico City. However, their constituency—mainly Indian—makes them very different. In the racial double bind I discussed earlier, the cultural missions are special schools for Native Americans within a system that claims to be racially blind. *"Los misioneros modernos"* (The modern missionaries), the chapter of *El desastre* specifically dedicated to this institution, opens with the narrator declaring that "[t]he inspiration for the education of the Indians came to us, as was natural, from the Spanish tradition." Expressing his constant concern for national unity under the Hispanic tradition, Vasconcelos praises the Spanish missionaries, who, according to him, "rather than school segregation, established the fusion of races in school and worship. The homogeneity of our national race, the races' relative cohesion, has resulted from that fusion" (*Desastre,* 1328–29). Within this statement the racial double bind of Indian integration into a united national culture becomes evident. Vasconcelos first celebrates the creation of cultural missions as an instrument to specifically address Indian needs, only to immediately state that this doctrine's merit is its emphasis on incorporation into the national mainstream. In his autobiography, Vasconcelos insists that the Department of Indian Education *(Enseñanza Indígena)* was an exclusively auxiliary and temporal branch of his ministry, which, like the Literacy Department *(Departamento de Desanalfabetización)*, would disappear once its task had been achieved. Like many mainstreaming projects in the United States today, the department "had no other purpose than preparing the Indian for admission into common schools, having given him notions of the Spanish language." The minister did not believe in the elaboration of a permanent system of education specifically targeted at the Indian population. Such a system seemed to Vasconcelos to represent a segregationist approach to education, which he associated with North American anthropologists, the U.S. Bureau of Indian Affairs, and what he called the North American "reservation" mentality. Furthermore, he reasons, "Fortunately, here [in Mexico] we stop being Indians the day we are baptized. Baptism gave our predecessors the status of reasonable people *{gente de razón}*" *(Desastre,* 1226–27). Yet despite Vasconcelos's categorical statements, the *Casas del Pueblo* were specifically designed to fulfill the needs of the Indians. Their rules required that at least 60 percent of their students fell under this category.[19]

Claude Fell points out that the initiative for the Department of Indian Education did not come from Vasconcelos's ministry but from the *Partido Liberal Constitucionalista.* The minister, Fell tells us, "accepts this measure without much enthusiasm, since he thinks that it breaks his system's harmony and could retard the Indian's integration" (Fell, 217). Within the bill that Vasconcelos had originally presented to Congress in October 1920, the subject of an Indian education is briefly mentioned in a call for "special Indian schools in all the regions with indigenous populations which will teach Castilian with rudiments of hygiene and economics, lessons of harvesting and the application of machines in agriculture" (Fell, 204). As Fell points out, at this early stage, Vasconcelos's conception of a rural Indian education was not far removed from the earlier projects for "rudimentary schools." Once political pressures forced Vasconcelos to put more emphasis on rural Indian education, the image of the Catholic Spanish mission nicely fit his Hispanophile-Anglophobe political paradigm. Whenever Vasconcelos mentions the cultural mission he insists that it represents the Hispanic ideal of multiethnic inclusion through the evangelical process. The mission is for him a transitional institution, preparing Indians for their incorporation into society at large. As a dangerous polar opposite to this system, Vasconcelos finds the "North American" system to which he often refers as a "reservation" system, which, according to him, is "based on positivist ethnography, which exaggerates the differences among races and makes a separate being out of the savage, a sort of link between the monkey and man" (*Desastre,* 1328). His project is one of inclusion, or rather absorption, since without the cultural missions Vasconcelos conceives of Indians as fellow humans, but as savage humans, needy of the redemptive help the missionaries will provide.

Vasconcelos's critique of the "reservation" system rested on two distinct premises. On the one hand, within the United States the system represented to the Mexican a sort of protoapartheid, a system that consciously separated human beings along racial lines. Within this system the minister of education saw the economic and power differential between the white elite and the excluded blacks and Native Americans who had no access to the resources of society at large. It was an example of the racism that he claimed distinguished the Anglo-Saxon tradition from the Hispanic. In Mexico, however, the problem of the "reservation" system took a different shade. Not only did it represent Anglo-Saxon racism, it was also a threat to national cohesiveness. He uses the term "reservation" against Mexican thinkers like Pedro Lamicq, who in his 1913 *Piedad para el indio* (Pity for the Indian) identified Spanish colonialism as the culprit for Mexico's Indians' wretched condition and called for greater sovereignty for them. Such a policy, Vasconcelos reasoned, would fan historical hatreds and foster divisions at the national level, opening up Mexico to North American intervention. We must remember that for him the two world powers were the Latin and the Anglo-Saxon civilizations, with other groups functioning almost exclusively as pawns. As Fell aptly points out, "[f]or Vasconcelos, there does not exist a midway between the 'reservation' and the pure and simple 'incorporation'; the latter option is, for him, the first requirement for the formation of a 'national soul' " (Fell, 206). Like Saxons and Latins culturally represent two binary opposites, "reservations" and "missions" are pedagogical and social binary opposites.

Left to his own devices, Vasconcelos's policy for the cultural missions would have been exclusively a transitory stage in an effort to westernize the Indians and forge a Eurocentric national identity. Nevertheless, Vasconcelos did not work in a vacuum and he reacted to the politics and policies of his period. A particularly fruitful, yet contradictory, relationship took place between Vasconcelos's ministry and the Department of Anthropology *(Dirección de Antropología)*—a branch of the ministry of agriculture and development—headed by Manuel Gamio since 1917. These two entities had distinct agendas, but oftentimes dealt with similar issues. The Department of Anthropology studied Indian cultures; it placed great emphasis on improving the economic and educational situation of its subjects, stepping onto the turf of Vasconcelos's ministry. Oftentimes Gamio had to be a vocal advocate for his department in order to gain funds and to avoid its absorption by the National University or the SEP. The relationship between the bureaucratic entities, just like that between their respective leaders, was confrontational; but, ironically, as Fell indicates, both "instead of coordinating their activities, apply parallel policies inspired, without confessing it, on each other" (Fell, 211–16).

Manuel Gamio was an example of the intellectual most despised by Vasconcelos: an empirical anthropologist, educated in the United States. In 1920 he obtained a Ph.D. in anthropology from Columbia University, where he studied under the mentorship of Franz Boas.[20] Like Vasconcelos, Gamio had a strong interest in the national unity of Mexico, but unlike the minister of education the anthropologist paid much more attention to the Indian element in Mexico's culture. In 1916 he published his classic, *Forjando patria* (Forging a homeland), in which he insisted upon the necessity of understanding the Indian population of Mexico in order to build a coherent nation. Early in this text Gamio recognizes that 75 percent of Latin America's population is Indian, but it is represented by the 25 percent that is culturally and linguistically European. Of great concern for Gamio is the fact that this ruling elite is completely ignorant of the language, culture, and ideas of the majority of the continent's population, the existence of which passes unnoticed (Gamio, 7). Anthropology, for him, would provide "the basic knowledge for good government, because through it one knows the population which is the raw material with which one governs and for whom one governs" (Gamio, 15). In this regard, Gamio's project assumes that the Indian population is to be governed, leading commentators like David Brading to identify in him an ultimate impulse to absorb the Indian population into western culture in a redemptive gesture parallel to those of the nineteenth-century liberals.[21]

Like nineteenth-century liberal and nationalist thinkers, Gamio understood the concept of nation as consisting of a unity of ethnicity, language, and cultural practices. Mexico—and Latin America—represented for him a society consisting of a plurality of homelands. His project of forging a homeland foresaw the forging of a unified national culture. Otherwise, division and violence would plague the nation. The problem of the nation, Gamio wrote in 1916, consists of:

> channeling the powerful energies [of Indian groups] which today are dispersed, attracting their individuals to the other social group that they have always considered as enemy, incorporating them, fusing them with it, tending, finally, to make the national race coherent and homogeneous, unifying the language and converging the culture. (Gamio, 10)

Gamio's project is, then, not very different from Vasconcelos's in its ultimate goals. But, for Gamio, the incorporation of the Indians into national life implied a far greater understanding of their cultures, history, and traditions—albeit to better govern them—than that proposed by Vasconcelos. "Contemporary European civilization," Gamio wrote,

> has not been able to infiltrate our indigenous population because of two important reasons: first, because of the natural resistance which that population opposes to a cultural change; second, because we do not know the motives of such a resistance, we do not know how the Indian thinks, we ignore his true aspirations, we prejudge him with our criteria, when we should understand his to comprehend him and make him comprehend us. We must forge for ourselves—even if just temporarily—an Indian soul. Then we will be able to labor for the advancement of the Indian class. This task does not belong neither to the governor nor the pedagogue, nor the sociologist; it is destined exclusively for the anthropologist and particularly to the ethnographer. (Gamio, 25)

To Vasconcelos's horror, such anthropologists would not base their methodology on the Spanish missions, but on the U.S. Bureau of Indian Affairs (Fell, 210–11).

Under Gamio's leadership, the Department of Anthropology coordinated a series of research projects, beginning with the region of Teotihuacan (1920–1922), documenting and cataloging the specific living conditions of indigenous populations, as well as their languages, customs, rituals, traditions, and other aspects of life of interest to the anthropological field. Despite Vasconcelos's open opposition to such projects, the work of the Department of Anthropology greatly influenced his own project. To a great degree, as Fell has pointed out, the competition between teachers and anthropologists to dominate the destiny of the incorporated Indians made them imitate each other. The thorough research of Indian communities conducted by the cultural missions is one example of the replication of work by both institutions. And, despite Vasconcelos's professed distaste for ethnographers and anthropologists, one must remember that his admired Spanish missionaries were some of the earliest anthropological researchers to stand on the American continent (Ricard, 39–60). Any serious attempt to incorporate Native Americans into the broader national community requires a certain level of knowledge of their specific languages, beliefs, and traditions, as well as of their specific material resources and necessities, even if the incorporation implies the absorption envisioned by Vasconcelos. At the most elemental linguistic level, even if Vasconcelos wanted everyone to speak Spanish, some teachers had to know Indian languages to begin teaching monolingual students. For this reason, despite what the minister would later write, teachers who spoke Indian languages were preferred for the position of traveling missionary.[22]

Gamio's anthropologists were but one group among the many who interacted in the actual articulation of cultural missions in rural Mexico. In a rather official assessment of the cultural missions, published in a 1962 four-volume anthology commemorating the fiftieth anniversary of the revolution, Víctor Gallo insists that in these missions the work "developed in the classrooms is a mere complement, since unity of work is integrated with the social labor that tends towards economic improvement . . ." Gallo continues with half a page of clauses describing the vast array of social and economic functions played by the missions, ranging from technical training, to public hygiene and physical fitness programs, the construction of roads, public illumination and irrigation projects, home improvements, and the fostering of civic and family values (Gallo, 65). Almost four decades after the minister's tenure and three years after his death, the cultural missions that Vasconcelos had envisioned as transitory institutions were now a central element of the regime's project for technical development, the classroom, Vasconcelos's final goal, only playing the role of a "mere complement."

Gallo's assessment, however, reflects an understanding of the cultural missions as they developed after Vasconcelos's tenure. Yet one may ask, what was the situation of the cultural missions during their early stages? Reading only Vasconcelos one would believe that they were extremely coherent organizations, functioning in unison, with enthusiastic volunteers working with a single will to complete the minister's utopia. Yet, as our discussion of the Department of Anthropology indicates, different

governmental institutions jockeyed for positions in the deployment of
the institutions. Far from the central government, in the actual rural
locations where the missions were established, a whole new series of
actors also engaged in what Antonio Gramsci terms a "War of Position."[23] In a recent study of educational transformation in the revolutionary period, "Schools of the Revolution: Enacting and Contesting
State Forms in Tlaxcala, 1910–1930," Elsie Rockwell argues against
interpretations of a very coherent and well-organized educational policy
during the first decades of postrevolutionary regimes. Rockwell insists
that during this period "the pre-Revolutionary state was effectively dis-
solved. . . . [giving] way to diverse regional conflicts and realignments,"
which would take decades to stabilize again (Rockwell, 171). Her article
warns against an excessive reliance on "documented history" in an
assessment of the period's educational reforms:

> Historical analyses of schooling that draw exclusively on the documenta-
> tion of official public discourse (laws, reports, programs, and textbooks)
> sometimes assume that school systems actually accomplish what govern-
> ments claim—such as constituting free citizens or disseminating a ratio-
> nal world view—and that they change uniformly when central policies
> are modified. In reality, school practices are extraordinarily diverse and
> often at odds with official policy. Furthermore, the state's educational
> proposals at any given moment are not necessarily coherent, and they are
> redefined as they filter down through the respective governing agencies.
> . . . In my view, ethnography should attempt to uncover the "undocu-
> mented history". . . . A school's "undocumented history" consists of
> those socio-cultural contexts and resources—both constraining and
> enabling—that structure social action. At any given moment in school
> history, persistent local practices and beliefs interact with government
> initiatives to mold school life. (Rockwell, 173–74)

Such an understanding of schooling's place within local social history
leads Rockwell to one of her "key arguments . . . that the development
of rural schools in the post-Revolutionary years owed as much to popular claims and resources as to any 'rational' designs of the newly forming
state" (Rockwell, 191).

Despite Vasconcelos's efforts to centrally control schools through the
federal government, in practice school administration was divided into a
multiplicity of networks. Vasconcelos, in *El desastre,* tells of a multitiered
administrative structure under which the states managed urban schools,
municipalities managed—with federal support—preexistent schools under

their jurisdiction, and the federal government took charge of rural schools and those in the Federal District (Mexico City); the ministry also certified private schools that followed certain requirements of its programs (*Desastre*, 1227–28). Thus different schools fell under different jurisdictions. According to Rockwell's analysis—which is limited to Tlaxcala, the first state to federalize education—there were two immediate effects resulting from Vasconcelos's educational reforms: communal activism and a reconfiguration of forces, empowering localities in relation to the state.[24] An interesting intersection takes place between local, state, and federal authorities. The influx of funds and young teachers, some from other states, greatly improved local schools in relation to their urban counterparts administered by the state. While some of the young teachers were rejected by local communities, their activist approach was welcomed by many. Responsible to the federal government, they functioned as new channels to articulate local demands. Federal support of local projects helped municipalities overstep state authorities, giving them a sense of empowerment and leading communities to demand their own schools, with their concomitant funding and teachers. While influential, the teachers themselves did not unilaterally determine the localities' demands and agendas but became one more force within often conflicting patronage networks, developed, among many other factors, along political, kin, economic, gender, age, or religious lines (Rockwell, 186–90).

Prior to the revolution, municipal schools were financed and administered at the local level, with villagers paying fees or contributing in kind or labor. More sophisticated traditional financing mechanisms, like the *cofradía* system, based on kinship and *barrio* networks, were also available to villagers. Under this system, local principals *(mayordomos)* are selected on a rotating basis. These give significant contributions on their own and gather other pledges from kin and friends. While this form of organization was traditionally used to finance religious festivities, it was used after the revolution for a variety of more secular purposes. Rockwell documents several cases in which *cofradías* alternately financed both school and church projects. In other cases, schools were financed by the local *hacendado* landowner.[25] Young new teachers, often emerging from families with liberal traditions, interacted with these more traditional politico-religious organizations in the forging of a new educational system. At times teachers worked with local groupings, or factions thereof, at others in opposition to them. Even considering the cases when teachers were opposed by local communities, Rockwell warns that "it would be inaccurate to polarize an account of schooling by assuming, as it were, that a uniform traditional 'society' always opposed the [federal] 'state' schools, represented by the teachers" (Rockwell, 191–97). Rockwell insists on the difficulty of generalizing this process, as it responds to the particular conditions of each locality. Thus, she points out that in case of central Tlaxcala, despite the general acceptance of "popular Catholicism," most villages lacked resident priests, leaving a space open for teachers to take on a role of social and moral leadership, foreclosed to them in regions, like Jalisco, with a strong tradition of resident priests intervening in the daily lives of the parishioners (Rockwell, 200).[26]

The "hidden record," Rockwell argues, shows a whole series of points of contention that need to be negotiated in each locality for the establishment of an alternative educational system. At stake are not only curricula and pedagogies. Particularly in the early stages, when the fledgling ministry was overburdened by lack of material and human resources and lacked the professional institutional mechanisms to administer schooling, different local factions struggled to define the use of time and space in the new schools. Despite Vasconcelos's compulsive concern with architecture, often villagers chose the style of the buildings they would help construct. Rural school buildings provided alternative spaces, which could be used after hours for a multiplicity of purposes, such as workshops, dance halls, and markets. Such alternative uses were often contested, control of the school keys being a jealously guarded privilege. Often schools attempted to regiment time through clocks and bells, to encourage punctuality as a virtue of modern society. Nevertheless, local authorities permitted flexibility to teachers and students to run errands or go home for lunch " 'in accordance with the local custom.' " Local authorities also unilaterally canceled classes for religious or local holidays, unaccounted for in the federal calendar. Despite Vasconcelos's insistence on the Spanish language, teachers in Tlaxcala who knew Nahuatl played particularly important brokerage roles. The shared used of classroom space by both girls and boys, despite many parents' complaints, altered in significant ways relations between the genders. Classroom teaching also created new networks among children who, although ultimately subject to school and parental authorities, also played a role in the negotiating process (Rockwell, 195–204).

Throughout the republic the nature of the curriculum and the conflicts that arose varied. In the southeastern sate of Yucatán, for example, where the *Partido Socialista del Sureste* (socialist party of the southeast) controlled the government, the educational programs, based on the rationalist pedagogy of the Spanish anarchist José de la Luz Mena, were much more radical than those recommended by the SEP. The educational authorities of that state, for example, foresaw the establishment of "Red Mondays" *(Lunes rojos)* for the education of workers along socialist and atheistic lines. The subjects to be included in the weekly conferences were divided along ten broad categories: (1) religion and atheism; (2) socialism; (3) feminism; (4) the different kinds of love; (5) production and consumption; (6) modern art and events; (7) criminality, its causes, and its solutions; (8) educational systems; (9) Mayan history, culture, and language; (10) defanatization *(desfanatización)* to eliminate religious superstition.[27] The ideal school for the proponents of the rationalist project would be closer to Dewey's model criticized by Vasconcelos, in that students would learn not necessarily through lessons but through the example set by adults performing their daily activities. Students should be encouraged to explore their interests, and grades would not be given, as this would feed the vanity of the smarter students. Under this pedagogy students would not take exams but would instead complete projects in which the necessary knowledge of their field would be applied. With its marked concern about the freedom of the students—a signal of its anarchist origins—programs of study would not have a set timetable, as students were supposed to be at liberty to move at their own pace.[28] Atheistic, scientific, and free was the proposed educational model of the rationalists; very different from the mystic, spiritual, and disciplined method proposed by Vasconcelos. Furthermore, reflecting the interests of the Mayan constituents of the *Partido Socialista del Sureste,* great attention was given by Yucatán's rationalists to the study of the particular language, culture, and tradition of this group.

Although the rationalist project was quite different to the one proposed by Vasconcelos, its radical premises were often used by opponents of the federalization of a lay educational system to discredit it. Thus, for example, in November 1922 an article in the Colima local newspaper, *El restaurador,* warned teachers about the perilous effects of the SEP's educational proposals, basing its attack on the proceedings of a rationalist convention. Calling rationalist education "impious and perverse and abominable to the extreme" and labeling it "Bolshevik," J. Jesus Ursua claimed that the rural schools sponsored by the ministry of education would dissolve the social structure of Colima.[29] In this regard, V. V. Ibarra, the SEP's delegate to Colima, complained to the head of the school department in Mexico City that such campaigns, labeling the new program as Bolshevik, had been successful in swaying public opinion against his efforts. Furthermore, he reports that a Catholic association had founded its own school with the specific purpose of undermining the ministry's "Carrillo" school. To make matters worse, Ibarra claimed that many people distrusted his efforts, because educational programs similar to the ones the SEP intended to implement had been promised to them in 1910, but they never actually had been set in place.[30]

If V. V. Ibarra faced the opposition of the conservative press of his state, in Angamacútiro, Michoacán, the missionary teacher Ciro Esquivel had to struggle against the local power elite. In September 1923 Domingo Sámano filed a complaint against the appointment by Mr. Esquivel of Carlos Martínez as rural teacher for the school located on his ranch. According to Sámano, Martínez had a bad reputation in the region and 30 of the ranch's inhabitants had complained to him about this teacher. The ministry of education requested Esquivel to solve the problem. Upon investigating the situation, the missionary teacher reached the conclusion that the opposition to Martínez was based on political disagreements. According to him, the local priest had threatened to excommunicate Sámano if he allowed Martínez to teach at the school. The local priest, according to Esquivel, insisted on continuing the traditional Catholic education and saw the federal lay school as a "Protestant" influence. Sámano, fearful of the priest, threatened to expel from his land those parents who allowed their children to attend the school. Furthermore, Esquivel claimed that Martínez had had conflicts with Sámano over certain land claims. In this way, the missionary teacher presents Sámano's opposition to Martínez as the opposition of the landed Catholic elite to the progressive measures proposed by the ministry of education. Despite Esquivel's defense of his teacher, the ministry of education recommended that he transfer Martínez in order to avoid confrontation. The final resolution of this conflict is unclear in the information available at the SEP's archives.[31] Furthermore, one cannot really know whose claims were more true. However, for the purposes of my discussion, it is significant to notice the types of confrontations that the missionary teachers encountered in the fulfillment of their duties.

In other cases, the confrontations pitted workers of the ministry of education against each other. Such is the case of a conflict between missionary teacher Margarita Avila and José Lundes Martínez, director of the rural school in Janitzio, Michoacán. Throughout her correspondence with the ministry of education, Avila complained about Lundes Martínez's bad work habits and teaching methods. She claimed that he had interests in the local fishing industry and he dedicated much more attention to this than to the rural school. She also accuses him of permitting the school children to continue studying the Catholic catechism and to use the San Miguel spelling handbook. Lundes Martínez, for his part, claimed that Avila had complained about him because they had different pedagogical approaches and that his, the result of greater experience with the local community, was more appropriate to the region. He believed that Ms. Avila's insistence on implementing a standardized national pedagogy in Janitzio was unfeasible. He would rather move slowly in order to address the region's specific necessities. According to him, the local students would not even understand the books suggested by Avila. In addition, he writes that were he to eliminate catechism and the San Miguel handbook from the curriculum, students would stop attending school.[32]

As in the previous case, the little correspondence that is available in the archives does not allow one to clearly understand who was right in this discussion. But, once again, this confrontation allows us to understand the multiplicity of contradictions present in the implementation of a national educational system. Some conflicts might simply reflect personality clashes. Others had to do with pedagogical approaches, or with new imported missionary teachers intervening in a territory already controlled by well-established teachers. Furthermore, Avila's accusation of Lundes Martínez's personal stake in a local business, whether true or false, raises another important problem, recognized in José Gálvez's legislative project for the official implementation of the cultural mission program. In his effort to better regulate the program, Gálvez points at the inexperience of many of the teachers, and to the fact that many of the teachers had developed political careers and dedicated themselves to "business and vice" (Gálvez, 13–14). Furthermore, one must point out, financing of teachers' salaries was a constant concern. This might have caused many teachers to seek other forms of compensation. V. V. Ibarra's reports from Colima to the ministry's office in Mexico City are full of pleas for money. He claims that teachers have not received compensation for over 50 days on average and that he does not have money to buy necessary furniture. He warns the ministry that teachers have been resigning and moving to other states where they are better compensated.[33]

Under monetary pressure, the implementers of the new educational system had to find alternatives. Ibarra reports implementing creative fund-raising schemes such as lotteries, festivals, and the sale of "bonds" by school children that would give their bearers discounts at movies, theaters, bullfights, and other activities. He also reports about teachers improvising furniture and teaching under the shade of trees.[34] The missionary teacher José A. Bazán reports from Michoacán that a local *hacienda* is financing a school on its premises and the ministry has only to give the supplies. He also reports about several cases in which local communities donated a house and land for the establishment of a school or a *Casa del Pueblo*.[35] Similar reports appear in the file of Esquivel. He reports that a local community has donated land, labor, and animals for a *Casa del Pueblo*.[36] From the northern state of Chihuahua, Martín Jiménez reports about local businesses—particularly mining—that finance schools. He also reports about a cooperative society of workers that intends to open 27 schools and is simply requesting school supplies. Another voluntary association, the *"Centro cultural Amado Nervo,"* was formed in Ciudad Camargo with the purpose of teaching literacy, fine arts, and music. It survived with a little library of donated books, a small gymnasium, baths, a functions hall, and a printing press to publish its newspaper *"La Idea."* It was requesting from the ministry a supply of books for its library.[37] Other organizations, like the *Ligas Patriótico-Moralizadoras de la República* (patriotic and moralizing leagues of the republic), offered their help in organizing conferences and donating popular libraries, patriotic altars, free tutoring to school children, and other types of help to materially improve schools.[38] In this way, the ministry's centralizing project found itself interacting with a great variety of groups who brought their own initiative to the fore.

Yet, despite the blossoming of the personal initiative, there still remained confrontations among different governmental or private institutions over control. In Mexico City, for example, where buildings for schools were in short supply, often important conflicts erupted over the control of such buildings. Thus, in October 1921 the principal and teachers of Municipal School #52, who had refused to give control of the school to federal authorities, were forcefully expelled from the school building by armed police.[39] Carranza's education law of 1917—the one harshly criticized by Vasconcelos—had given control of schools that once belonged to the federation to the municipalities. With Vasconcelos's educational reform these schools would once again turn back to the federation, but some administrators and teachers, like those of Municipal School #52, did not want to give up what they considered theirs. At times conflict over school control took much more overtly political shades. Such was the case of the *Colegio Mexicano* in Mexico City. President Alvaro Obregón claimed that as a private institution this school "rather than a Cultural Center, has been a Speculation Center for a business enterprise," which has exploited the parents through tuition. Vasconcelos defended the school, claiming that at a time of urgent necessities for schools it was illogical to get rid of one. But Obregón's radical political rhetoric—and power as authoritarian president—won, and the school was closed in the middle of a semester.[40]

As the previous examples show, Vasconcelos's personal project was challenged and transformed at a multiplicity of levels, and it is therefore quite problematic to adjudicate everything that the ministry did to the coherent will of its official head. Even within the walls of his jealously guarded ministry in downtown Mexico City, the minister of education found opposition and reinterpretations of his carefully crafted plan. One particularly telling example is his relationship with the Mexican muralists. Today, Vasconcelos is remembered by many Mexicans as the man who gave his institution's walls to these painters to create on them an art that is internationally known as characteristically Mexican and particularly representative of the culture that emerged from the revolution. Paradoxically, however, the fact is that the minister had very important political and ideological conflicts with the muralists. David Alfaro Siqueiros, in his memoirs, *Me llamaban el Coronelazo,* identifies this peculiar aspect of their relationship:

> the more our work developed, the more it found roots in our tradition, the more it found the elements of our national idiosyncrasy, the more detestable it seemed to Vasconcelos. Throughout his whole life, in an astonishing paradox, the man who made the material apparition of our pictorial work possible, disdained it, and this disdain acquired an unprecedented scale in the last years of his existence.[41]

For his part, Vasconcelos shows his discontent with the muralists in *El desastre.* Talking about their insubordination, he complains that Diego Rivera's paintings broke the harmony of his decorative plan for the ministry. He is particularly upset at "some allegories [Rivera painted] in honor of Zapata and Felipe Carrillo [Puerto, governor of Yucatán and leader of the *Partido Socialista del Sureste*]"—images that sharply contrasted with the minister's tastes (*Desastre,* 1464–65). Contrary to Vasconcelos's expectations of a painting celebratory of Mexico's Hispanic heritage, the muralists painted a history of Mexico that exalted the Indian past and portrayed the colonial period as one of brutal exploitation. As was the case with the Cuauhtémoc monument and the homage to Zapata, Vasconcelos grudgingly accepted the muralists' *indigenista,* populist, and communist aesthetic. Vasconcelos wanted muses painted in the ministry; the muralists provided something else. The muralists found beauty and pride in an Indian culture; Vasconcelos saw this culture exclusively in folkloric terms and saw folklore only as an instrument to begin training aesthetic sensitivities to ultimately appreciate the "classics" (*Desastre,* 1272). The muralists conceived of themselves as workers and organized themselves in the Union of Revolutionary Painters, Sculptors, and Engravers of Mexico; Vasconcelos viewed their union with contempt and refused to deal with it (*Desastre,* 1465–67; Siqueiros, 190–93).

As the previous examples indicate, Vasconcelos represented but one among a multiplicity of agents and interests struggling to define the postrevolutionary nation. One must give credit to Vasconcelos for taking the initiative in the elaboration of such a complex and significant network. Nevertheless, one must remember that it was not his work alone. We should also realize that once uttered, or put in practice, ideas and attitudes take new meaning in the public domain. Concepts like that of the *raza cósmica* become signifiers of movements that overcome the authorial intent of their creator. In this regard, Cuauhtémoc Jerez Jiménez's assessment of Vasconcelos's legacy in Mexico's postrevolutionary cultural development is particularly appropriate, as he states that the minister achieved goals that did not necessarily match his mystical pedagogical ideas but did respond to the particular social needs of the country as a whole. Mexican pedagogy and the cultural production that now is identified with the Mexican Revolution received a great impulse, not necessarily from all of his ideas, but from the material actions—construction of schools, publishing of books, building of libraries, painting of murals, development of orchestras and choirs, and so on—that his tenure encouraged.[42] Indeed, after his three years of his leadership of the ministry of education, 722 *Casas del Pueblo* were in place, 62 missionary teachers traveled around the country, and 1,048 rural teachers staffed the new schools. Also, by the end of his tenure the country counted 50 to 70 percent—the figures range according to the sources—more official elementary schools, teachers, and students (Jiménez, 13; Skirius 1982a, 4). The approach that these official institutions took, however, became in the 1920s and 1930s much more actively anticlerical and anti-Spanish than the minister had hoped. These positions were oftentimes taken by invoking the image of the cosmic race that the minister had put forth.

Chapter Five

Civilian *Caudillo:*
The Presidential Campaign

In the early afternoon of 23 January 1924, two events shook the population of Mexico City. Francisco Field Jurado, the federal senator for the state of Campeche, was murdered in cold blood as he headed to his house for lunch. According to eyewitness reports, he had been followed from the Senate building by a group of five men in a Dodge car without license plates. As he prepared to enter his house he was shot eight times and the murderers calmly drove away in their vehicle. At approximately the same time, Senators Ildelfonso Vázquez, Francisco J. Trejo, and Enrique del Castillo were kidnapped.[1] The political situation in the Senate had been very tense in the days leading to the murder and kidnappings. As presidential elections approached, President Alvaro Obregón had put his support behind General Plutarco Elías Calles, alienating members of his political coalition including General Adolfo de la Huerta who, dissatisfied by the candidacy of Calles, led a rebellion against the government of Obregón. Obregón, for his part, needy of North American weapons and supplies to quell the rebellion, tried to push through Congress the Bucareli Treaties, necessary to win official U.S. recognition and, thus, military support.

In essence, the Bucareli Treaties, the result of secret negotiations between a small group of U.S. and Mexican officials—negotiations about which the Mexican Congress had not been informed—granted, in exchange for U.S. recognition of Obregón's government, two very important concessions: (1) they guaranteed the United States that the provisions of Article 27 of the Constitution, allowing the state to nationalize land and natural resources for the public good, could not be applied retroactively against U.S. oil and mining interests; and (2) they guaranteed that those U.S. citizens whose large landholdings were expropriated to distribute to landless peasants would be immediately compensated in cash, and not in government bonds used to pay Mexicans (Alessio Robles, 381–84). The agreement reached between the representatives of the presidents of both countries needed to be ratified by the Mexican Senate in order to take force. Obregón's supporters held a comfortable majority in the Senate, but the Treaties' opponents used a parliamentary delaying tactic to stop the vote. In order for the Senate to vote on a measure it needed a quorum of two-thirds of its members present and Field Jurado led an organized absenteeism campaign to insure that such a quorum was not present (Alessio Robles, 21). His assassination and the kidnapping of the three other senators was a successful measure to intimidate the Treaties' opponents, and shortly after these events they were approved by the Senate.

In response to the political violence prevalent in the country, on the 28th of that month Vasconcelos wrote his letter of resignation to Obregón. The actual letter is not available, but Mexico's National Archives contain a copy of a telegram in which Vasconcelos announces to Obregón that he will send him a letter explaining the reasons for his resignation, and a copy of a letter in which the president rejects his minister's resignation. Vasconcelos's telegram is extremely polite and diplomatic. On numerous occasions throughout the text the minister insists on his admiration, respect, and friendship toward the president, but he lists three factors that have turned his tenure into a "situation which offends my deeply rooted convictions": (1) his disagreement with certain (unnamed) people who have great influence within the administration; (2) the lack of funds for the ministry of education; and (3) the recent (unspecified) political violence "which you [Obregón] energetically condemn." After listing the reasons for his departure, the minister once again acknowledges his friendship toward the president and volunteers his help, as a private citizen, to search for a peaceful solution to the prevalent conflict, "as long as the rebels recognize the authority of the legitimate Government."[2] On the very day of Vasconcelos's resignation, the national newspapers ran stories announcing that he left the administration as a protest against Field Jurado's assassination. The minister, however, refused to publicize the content of his letter to the president until he had received a response from him.[3] Such publication never took place, but the *Heraldo de Cuba* in La Havana—a newspaper favorable to Mexico's exiled opposition to Obregón—published an apocryphal letter of resignation in which the purported author was much more specifically critical of Obregón (Alessio Robles, 53–54). In his autobiography Vasconcelos recalls the praises he received from Obregón's opponents upon the publication of the apocryphal letter and claims that he did not bother to deny its legitimacy.

Obregón rejected his minister's resignation in a letter sent from Celaya, Guanajuato, where he was conducting military operations against the de la Huerta uprising. In his autobiography, Vasconcelos refers to this letter as a "plea" on the part of the president (*Desastre*, 1433 – 40), but the letter itself reveals the text of an astute politician, who very politely, but firmly, intimidates the recipient back into the fold. He rejects one by one the reasons that Vasconcelos had given for his resignation. In a subtle, yet intimidating, gesture, Obregón questions his minister's disagreement with certain powerful members of his administration, asking him to be much more specific in his complaint in order for the president to "see the manner in which the people to which you refer decrease the morality of the public administration and constitute a motive of shame for my collaborators." As Vito Alessio Robles points out, Vasconcelos had been free between 1920 and 1923 to complain about any of Obregón's collaborators, and he had not done so; now it was too late (Alessio Robles, 52). Referring to the lack of funding for the ministry, Obregón claims that the Treasury had been experiencing problems and that such a financial crisis, rather than a resignation, deserves more solidarity from cabinet members. Finally, referring to the political violence, Obregón promises a full investigation of the events.[4] In response to the letter, Vasconcelos withdrew his resignation and contacted the newspapers announcing that he would continue working in the cabinet because the president had promised to investigate the "political violence that has taken place."[5]

Vasconcelos continued as minister of education for five more months. His political disagreements with the administration were kept aside and he continued working with a diminished budget, as he had been doing for a long time. In July 1924, however, he again presented a letter of resignation, which was accepted by Obregón.[6] This time the official excuse for leaving his post was not a political disagreement with the administration but his intention to run for the governor's post of his native state of Oaxaca, and, as Alessio Robles points out in his scathing critique of the minister, he did not mention at this time the fact that the assassination of Field Jurado remained unpunished (Alessio Robles, 55; *Desastre*, 1463 – 64). According to Vasconcelos's autobiography, his separation from Obregón's administration was cordial on the surface, but both men had become political enemies. The now former minister of education saw in his candidacy for the governorship of Oaxaca, and in the electoral fraud that he expected, an opportunity to publicly break with the Obregón regime (*Desastre*, 1467–70).

The Oaxacan's gubernatorial campaign was a dress rehearsal for the national presidential campaign he would run four years later. His appeal was to the middle classes, avoiding the collaboration of the rich elite. He opposed the political power that military leaders were accumulating in Mexico. The military, he argued, should keep themselves to the armed forces and leave public administration to civilians, in particular to intellectuals and professionals. In this spirit he promised that once governor his collaborators would emerge from the "Science Institute, not from the military headquarters or the political Mafia." According to his autobiography he did not receive financial support from political parties; the financing of events, according to him, was almost spontaneous, as people organized rallies in his support. Having just emerged from his prominent position in Obregón's cabinet, he enjoyed great prestige. Particularly useful to his campaign was the support of the national newspapers—specially *El universal,* where he had friends—which gave full coverage to his campaign. The central government, however, opposed his candidacy, organizing violent demonstrations against him with the aid of the labor unions led by Luis N. Morones, who had been closely involved in the murder of Field Jurado. Furthermore, Andrew Almazán, a friend of Vasconcelos, was removed from his post as head of the military in the state and replaced by an opponent of the candidate. Ultimately, through what the former minister claims was an intimidation campaign and electoral fraud, he was defeated in his bid for the governor's office (*Desastre,* 1470–95).

After his failed gubernatorial campaign, Vasconcelos returned to Mexico City, where he opened a magazine called *La antorcha* from which he criticized the Mexican regime and other military governments in Latin America. His publishing venture, however, did not last long. Ostracized by the government and unable to find sufficient advertising to finance the journal, he closed its offices after a few months (*Desastre,* 1495–502; *Indología,* 1069–72). After closing *La antorcha,* the former minister of education left the country for a long sojourn that took him through Europe, the United States, Puerto Rico, and the Middle East— Turkey, Syria, Palestine, and Egypt. It was during this period that he published his racial theories in *La raza cósmica* and *Indología.* An outspoken critic of the Calles regime, he did not feel safe enough to return to Mexico. Publishing articles and giving public lectures, Vasconcelos took advantage of his reputation as one of the foremost educators and thinkers of Latin America to make a modest living. He was particularly successful in the United States, where universities like that of Chicago and Stanford hired him as visiting professor. He also had a good reception among the Mexican exile population in the United States. For this community he published a weekly column in the Los Angeles based *La opinión* and the San Antonio based *La prensa*—a column that was also published weekly in Mexico's *El universal.* From these platforms he continued his critique of the Mexican regime and elaborated a project for what he understood as the redemption of Mexico, a country that he saw falling under the political violence of the revolutionary generals now entrenched in power. Particularly problematic for him were the anticlerical laws, which reached their maximum expression under the leadership of Calles and led to the *cristero* uprising. But from his self-imposed exile Vasconcelos did not have the political or cultural influence in Mexican affairs he once enjoyed. Another political assassination would change this situation, and change the destiny of both Vasconcelos and Mexico.

On 17 July 1928, as Vasconcelos was in the San Francisco Bay Area to teach a series of summer courses at Stanford University, in the Bombilla park in Mexico City where a luncheon was being held in honor of President-elect Obregón, José de León Toral, a Catholic opponent of the Calles regime's anticlerical policy, approached Obregón in the guise of a caricaturist and shot him point-blank, killing him. Although Madero's uprising in 1910 had as one of its basic demands the nonreelectability of the president, Obregón, with Calles's support, had been able to amend the 1917 Constitution in order to allow the reelection of a president, provided that he had been one term out of office. Obregón's assassination at a time when the federal government was waging war against Catholic rebels in Mexico's heartland intensified the sense of national crisis as members of the revolutionary elite struggled among themselves to determine who would succeed Calles in the presidency. In this context Calles made a political move that has shaped the arena of Mexican politics to this day. On 1 September 1928, in his last state of the union address, Calles announced that he would never again seek the presidency and called all revolutionary leaders to join in a political party in order to move the reins of the nation away from charismatic *caudillos* into the hands of an institutionalized political structure. Thus was founded the *Partido Nacional Revolucionario,* or PNR (national revolutionary party)—the original name of today's *Partido Revolucionario Institucional,* or PRI (revolutionary institutional party). Twenty-four days later Congress named Emilio Portes Gil—a civilian—provisional president, with a tenure from 1 December 1928 until 5 February 1930. It also set November 1929 as the date for new presidential elections. On 10 November 1928, Vasconcelos returned to Mexico to once again try his political fortunes, this time running for the highest office of the nation.

In the months prior to his return to Mexico Vasconcelos actively cam-
paigned in the United States, making the situation of exiled Mexicans a
central issue of his speeches and articles. It was actually in the United
States, among what he called *"El México de Afuera"* (the outside Mexico)—the Mexican émigré community—that he launched his presidential campaign, touring the Southwest in a series of paid conferences and
visits to organizations of Mexican exiles in order to garner support and
raise funds for his campaign. Prior to his presidential campaign the former minister of education was already part of the lecture circuit, but his
audiences were mainly universities and Anglo-American intellectuals.
With his sights set on the Mexican presidency Vasconcelos started
specifically addressing the Mexican population in the United States.[7] In
August and September 1928 he visited San Francisco, Los Angeles, San
Diego, Calexico, Santa Fe, Chicago, El Paso, San Antonio, Corpus
Christi, Laredo, McAllen, and Brownsville. He gave paid conferences to
raise funds for his campaign, and secured the support of rich Mexican
exiles who had much to gain with the defeat of the Sonoran regime in
Mexico.[8] Within the United States he enjoyed free press coverage from
the newspapers owned by Ignacio E. Lozano (*La opinión* and *La prensa*)
(*Desastre*, 1798). The support that he garnered from the Mexican exile
community was, however, very diverse. Groups, ranging from ex-
Villistas to ex-*Porfiristas,* that would otherwise be in conflict with each
other now joined hands with the hope of defeating Calles, securing an
amnesty to return to their homeland, or gaining religious freedom (Skirius 1982b, 58–59).

Vasconcelos's dialogue with the *México de Afuera,* while gaining him
the support of this population, was also an indictment of the Mexican
regime. It was, after all, the political repression, religious prosecution,
and economic failure of the Calles regime that Vasconcelos identified as
the principal cause of the Mexican exile. As he would draw a sharp contrast between the modern life of Eagle Pass and the stagnation in
Piedras Negras in the first part of his autobiography, now he drew a contrast between the destinies of people of Mexican descent on both sides of
the river. In an article published just a month before Obregón's assassination, Vasconcelos compared the two sides as follows: "On our side
everything is abandonment, misery, desolation; across, around South
Texas, there are regions almost completely inhabited by Mexicans and
these, nevertheless, are prosperous, pacific, joyful."[9] In his travels in the
United States, from Brownsville to Calexico he had seen expatriates
"who triumph in the cultivation of land, in commerce and in the rail-

roads," while they are still "careful to conserve their Hispanoamerican virtues." At a personal level, he claimed in an interview that even if he had been minister of education in Mexico, he had more economic success in the United States teaching and giving public conferences.[10] The economic progress and political liberties that he saw for many Mexicans living in the United States were an example of the potential that democratic reform held for Mexico. The great numbers of Mexican exiles—which he calculated to be between two and three million[11]—who left due to religious persecution, political abuses, and economic misery, represented a significant brain drain to Mexico. It was the strongest and smartest that dared to do the long journey to the United States, he reasoned, not the weak and apathetic. The goal of all Mexicans should be to bring their exiled brothers and sisters, with their enthusiasm and newly acquired knowledge, back to Mexico, guaranteeing to them the economic progress and civil liberties they experienced under North American democracy. "The day that this third of the Mexican population that now suffers in exile begins its return to our soil will be the happiest day of our history."[12] Vasconcelos's favorable assessment of the situation of Mexicans in the United States is not blindly celebratory. He notices the discrimination suffered by Mexicans at the hands of outwardly racist organizations like the Ku Klux Klan and even in supposedly progressive organizations, like the American Federation of Labor, which opposed Mexican immigration. He is also aware, as he would later write in *La tormenta,* that deprived of their land many Mexicans in states like Texas spent long hours working for their landlords, "prisoners of a situation which is the natural result of a conquest." Yet even the bad conditions that Mexicans had to face in the United States support his critique of the Mexican regime, since they must find a better situation in the United States than in their own country in order to decide to migrate north (*Tormenta,* 115–17; Skirius 1976, 487).

One particular aspect of life that attracts Vasconcelos's attention in the United States is what he identifies as a sort of pan-Latin consciousness developing within the northern country, as exiles from throughout the southern part of the continent encounter each other: "the Mexican who has never left Mexico rarely feels like anything other than Mexican; the Mexican of the United States immediately speaks about himself as 'Latino' " ("Afuera," 3).[13] Furthermore, when referring to the population of Mexican origin in California, Vasconcelos notices in many of them their self-identification as "Spanish" rather than "Mexican." This is justified in Vasconcelos's mind as a repudiation of Mexico's militaristic policies. According to him, the greatest developments in California took place during the period of Spanish colonial rule. Mexico's postindependence rule has simply destroyed most of those achievements, as the Mexican map has been reduced by half through lost wars, and as the country has been ruled by military dictatorships that have forced its inhabitants to seek refuge in the United States, a conquered but safer land. While official rhetoric in Mexico has rejected the Hispanic heritage, these Mexicans in the United States elevate the name of Spain with pride and honor.[14]

Vasconcelos's critique of the Mexican political system had been a staple of his writing during his exile years. However, there were two important changes in his positions following Obregón's assassination, as the former minister prepared to launch his presidential campaign from the United States. Concerning the *Cristero* War, Vasconcelos had been a vocal supporter of the rebellion, but as the possibility of a presidential campaign became clearer he proposed a peaceful solution to the conflict that would guarantee religious freedom. Concerning the institutionalization of power, Vasconcelos had been a vocal critic of *caudillismo,* opposing charismatic leaders in the name of properly set governmental institutions. Upon the death of Obregón he stated in an interview with *La opinión* that what the country needed were not *caudillos* or geniuses, but simply honest men.[15] As he prepared for his own campaign, however, his rhetoric changed, arguing for the necessity of a particularly virtuous individual to lead the country; one could assume that such an individual would be him. Such changes in positions, according to John Skirius, "revealed a supremely political attitude, not an ideological one. The new stance in each case was meant to improve his chance of becoming president" (Skirius 1976, 486).

In the United States Vasconcelos prepared to move his campaign to Mexico, but in order to do this he had to wait to obtain guarantees from the new government that he would not be prosecuted as a political enemy of Calles. On 6 October 1928 President Portes Gil announced that Vasconcelos was in voluntary exile and that his government would not impede his entrance to Mexico or prosecute him once in national territory (Taracena, 74–75). Thus, on 10 November 1928, with such guarantees, he entered Mexican territory through Nogales, Sonora, just in time to fulfill the one-year residency requirement to run in the elections of 1929. Once in Mexico, he developed a full platform that combined notions of economic nationalism with socialist tinges, cultural pan-Latinism, and a strong emphasis on the importance of a democratic civilian government to replace the military autocracy that had held power for almost two decades.[16]

Central to Vasconcelos's platform was a call for democratic reform at all levels. In his speeches he insisted upon a decentralization of power, by giving more autonomy to municipalities and by controlling the executive power through the legislative and judicial branches. He also insisted on an overhaul of the fiscal system, where real estate and income taxes would be collected at the state and municipal levels to decentralize the power that was enjoyed by the federal government. As he opposed the almost omnipotent power of the president, he also criticized local political bosses who through corruption and abuses of power enriched themselves at the expense of the majority of the population.[17] Concerning the military, he did not call for its outright dismantling since he believed that strong armed forces were necessary to defend the nation from foreign aggression. However, a major problem he saw with the professionalization of the army during the Calles regime was that it had become an instrument to fight the Mexican people. The armed forces should not be used to repress the Mexican people but instead its members should be put to work in the service of the nation. With such an approach, the military would gradually become a sort of ministry of public works. It would both help Mexico's economic development and, by keeping soldiers busy, move them away from governmental activity. He also insisted on the importance of education of the armed forces, expressing an admiration for programs like the ROTC in the United States (Pineda, 44–45; Skirius 1982b, 72–73).

Concerning economic questions, Vasconcelos proposed a much more active intervention of the government. He critiqued the Calles regime for falling under the influence of U.S. Ambassador Dwight Morrow, who insisted on a reduction of public expenditures in order to maintain a balanced budget and facilitate the payment of Mexico's public debt. Vasconcelos argued that the government should increase its public investment to develop the national economy free of the greater influence that foreign capital was garnering. Also in defense of the national sovereignty, he proposed the nationalization of the mining and oil industries and of the industries that provided key services, such as railroads and telegraphs. Such nationalized industries should be managed by technical personnel, free of political bureaucracies, and administered as autonomous businesses, but they should coordinate their activities with the state to benefit the public interest. Rather than expanding Mexico's economic ties to the United States, the candidate proposed an economic integration of Latin American (Pineda, 52–55).

Regarding the working classes, throughout his campaign Vasconcelos showed great admiration for Mexican workers. He strongly supported labor unions, finding in syndicalism one very important element of democracy. Unions, however, should be independent and not co-opted by the regime in power as was the case of the CROM (*Confederación Regional de Obreros Mexicanos:* Regional Confederation of Mexican Workers) under Morones's leadership. He also advocated for the formation of national centers to help workers find employment and for the creation of a national insurance system to provide for the necessities of injured or sick workers (Pineda, 43–44). His call for the defense of workers' rights was not exclusively guided by economic considerations but also by what he regarded as a moral imperative. While he was influenced by the socialist thought of his times, his final goal was not the creation of a proletarian state but one of a cultured middle class (Skirius 1982b, 25–26). Concerning agrarian reform, he was not satisfied by the simple redistribution of land. In order for a reform to actually work, Vasconcelos believed in the necessity of government participation in training Mexico's peasants and providing them with the necessary technical and financial backing to modernize their methods of production (Skirius 1982b, 89–91; Pineda, 57–59). According to him, Mexico needed machines to redeem it from its primitive Indian past:

> What is the use of many small landowners cultivating the land in the Aztec way and producing corn, if it is more expensive than the corn imported from the United States and produced with machines? The peasant needs machines, he should work with machines, we need the redemption of machines. (Skirius 1982b, 113)

Furthermore, he strongly criticized what he conceived as an unequal application of the laws that provided for the redistribution of large landholdings. While U.S. citizens controlled 51.7 percent of all the acreage in foreign hands and Spaniards controlled 19.7 percent, 53 percent of the land expropriated from foreigners had belonged to Spaniards and only 27 percent had belonged to North Americans. In addition to this, the central government had been returning some of the lands it had taken from U.S. citizens. Such an agrarian policy was for Vasconcelos one further example of the anti-Latin and pro-Anglo-Saxon policies of the revolutionary regime (Skirius 1982b, 75).

The candidate's belief in the redemptive qualities of modern technology was also evident in his position on education. The former minister of education did not propose specific pedagogical systems but insisted time and again on the importance of technical and industrial education for both workers and peasants. Education, he argued, was not a luxury but a necessity for the nation's development. Beyond the strictly technical concerns, the former minister was very critical of the Calles regime's educational policy. He condemned the reduction of the SEP's budget and the administration's harassment of private schools for political reasons. He was particularly bothered by the unequal application of the 1917 Constitution's anticlerical provisions, which were targeted against Catholic schools and churches, while Protestant schools and churches gained importance throughout the republic. Vasconcelos's critique of Protestant schooling went hand in hand with a critique of the growing influence of North American educational methods. This attack was welcomed by many students and teachers, dissatisfied by the introduction of new policies such as the undressing of students for medical exams and the implementation of IQ and other psychological tests (Skirius 1982b, 45–46, 110; Pineda, 38–39). Vasconcelos's critique of U.S. influence on Mexico's educational system is part of a broader concern about the growing influence of the more powerful northern nation in Mexico's domestic affairs. He was also appalled by the United States's open support of the *Callista* regime.

In March 1929, in the middle of the presidential campaign, the PNR surprised most people by nominating the relatively unknown Pascual Ortíz Rubio—who had been serving as ambassador in Brazil—as its candidate, in place of the favorite Aarón Sáenz. The reasons for this nomination were many and are still debated, but the fact of the matter is that there was a fracture among the ruling elite, leading to a military uprising led by General José Gonzalo Escobar. Vasconcelos strongly criticized the uprising as a violent interference in the democratic process and gave his support to provisional President Portes Gil (Pineda, 87–89). The U.S. government ignored its official weapons embargo toward Mexico and sold the government $1,500,000 worth of weapons and airplanes to quell the rebellion. Vasconcelos was extremely critical of a fratricidal war sanctioned and actively supported by the U.S. government (Skirius 1982b, 106–7). Nevertheless, he did not put all the blame on the northern arms dealers. Mexicans were also responsible for their own problems. The despotic rule by a military leader was greatly responsible for the violence in Mexico and other Latin American countries. In his first conference in Los Angeles in preparation for the presidential campaign, Vasconcelos declared that all of the Americas, with the exception of the United States, Colombia, and Brazil, suffered from either *"cesarismo"*—military dictatorship—or anarchy. In the case of Mexico, only Madero's regime, and the first three years of Obregón's, presented an alternative to these two extremes. "And the gravest thing for those peoples is that the anarchy which each revolution provokes in their midst is one step towards a loss of their sovereignty, towards their Nicaraguization *{nicaragüización}*." By "Nicaraguization" Vasconcelos referred to the situation of Nicaragua, which since the 1910s had been occupied by U.S. marines and whose elections had to be held under U.S. supervision.[18]

Yet, in spite of his criticisms toward the United States, Vasconcelos still maintained a certain admiration for the country. I have already discussed the way he placed it as a contrasting example of democracy and economic opportunity in relation to Mexico. In a talk given at the Los Angeles Knights of Columbus Hall on 14 August 1928, he praised the technological advancements of North American engineers, saying that North American capitalism will help Latin America conquer nature. The engineers will not be able to impose a cultural model on the Latin part of the continent, but their technology is important. In an ironic turn, the minister who had always praised the Latin heritage now, according to *La opinión*, "concluded that North Americans should not be feared by us. On the contrary, they should be esteemed, because they are not the Roman conquerors of ancient times, who enslaved those they defeated, instead they are collaborators who desire to achieve the happiness of their neighbors"!!!![19] Skirius notices this drastic change of positions and credits it to Vasconcelos's cozy relationship with Stanford, where he had taught. At the time of Vasconcelos's presidential campaign, Herbert Hoover—an engineer from Stanford—was becoming a candidate for the presidency of the United States, and, according to Skirius, it was convenient for the Mexican candidate to maintain good relations with people he already knew. Thus, Skirius interprets Vasconcelos's celebration of North American engineers as a veiled flirtation with one specific engineer, Herbert Hoover. Particularly significant for Skirius is the fact that with Hoover's candidacy Vasconcelos seemed to forget the previous support he had given to Al Smith, a Catholic candidate for the nomination of the Democratic Party (Skirius 1976, 484–86). Political positioning or not, there were aspects of the United States that Vasconcelos admired and respected.

Vasconcelos was the official candidate of the *Partido Nacional Antireeleccionista,* or PNA (national anti-re-electionist party), the same political organization that had postulated Francisco I. Madero almost two decades earlier. Yet, as Alessio Robles—PNA's president during Vasconcelos's campaign—insists throughout his highly critical assessment of the candidate, *Mis andanzas con nuestro Ulises,* Vasconcelos was very personalist and undisciplined throughout the campaign. In a letter sent to the *Frente Nacional Renovador* (national renewing front)—a group of youthful supporters of his candidacy—Vasconcelos wrote in December 1928, "My compromises with the Anti-re-electionist [Party] are limited to the fact that a group of supporters has registered my candidacy; but I do not owe anything to the party; it has not done anything to help me" (Magdaleno, 39). Even Salvador Azuela, a supporter of Vasconcelos who does not share Alessio Robles's virulent antagonism toward the presidential candidate, qualifies his character during the period as "irregular and capricious" (Azuela, 94). The candidate would set his own terms for the campaign and any disagreement the postulating party had with him would be the party's problem, not his. In this spirit, Vasconcelos in his memoirs remembers the candidacy as "a plebiscite and not a party designation of any [particular] group." He continues by stating that a variety of parties—including the Democratic, Anti-re-electionist, Socialist, and Catholic—lined up behind *him.*[20]

The PNA gave Vasconcelos's candidacy the name of a national organization with roots in the 1910 revolutionary movement, but beyond this party a whole network of specifically pro-Vasconcelos groups formed throughout the republic. These groups were loosely coordinated under the umbrella of the *Comité Orientador pro-Vasconcelos* (pro-Vasconcelos guiding committee), directed by Octavio Medellín Ostos. Particularly enthusiastic was the support received by Vasconcelos from the youth, many of them students, who had received their formation in the schools the former minister had sponsored. They now saw a chance to participate in the nation's renovation. It was, according to Hugo Pineda, "the first time that Mexico's youth actively participated in politics" (Pineda, 65). Members of the National Federation of Students declared their intention to mobilize the nation's youth in support of his candidacy.[21] Especially active was the previously mentioned *Frente Nacional Renovador,* which grouped many of these youthful enthusiasts, including even teenagers. The *Centro Revolucionario de Principios* (revolutionary center of principles), a group of former Madero supporters, also put its efforts into Vasconcelos's campaign. He also received active support of several Catholic organizations. Beyond the Mexican exile community in the United States, whose support for Vasconcelos we have already mentioned, the "Non Partisan Mexican Election Committee (Endorsing Señor Vasconcelos)" was formed in New York in order to influence public opinion in the United States. It distributed an eight-page pamphlet that explained Mexico's political situation and provided a bibliography for further reference (*El proconsulado,* 172; Azuela, 92–99; Magdaleno, 24–41; Pineda, 65–68).[22]

Beyond this alliance of various organizations, Vasconcelos's presidential campaign received the support of a broad array of individuals who sympathized with his cause for a variety of reasons. Some conservative members of the Porfirian elite saw in his campaign an opposition to the revolutionary regime and by implication a possibility to regain their lost properties (Magdaleno, 32). Catholics saw in Vasconcelos the return of religious peace to the country. Even "astromentalists *{astromentalistas}*, occultists and theosophists" gave their support to the author of *La raza cósmica* (Magdaleno, 46). Intellectuals saw in the former education minister the return of the cultural policies of the 1920s. Railroad workers gave their broad support to the candidate and aided him on his travels (Skirius 1982b, 70). Women, who did not have the right to vote, participated very actively in the campaign, as the PNA's platform advocated granting them this right. Many of Vasconcelos's female supporters were teachers who had served during his ministry and others were Catholic feminists who saw their faith challenged by the Calles regime (Skirius 1982b, 123–25; Azuela, 101–4; Magdaleno, 42–46).

One particularly active woman was Antonieta Rivas Mercado— "Valeria" in Vasconcelos's autobiography—a prominent supporter of the Mexican cultural avant-garde. The daughter of the famous architect Antonio Rivas Mercado, designer of *"El ángel"*—the renowned column on the *Paseo de la Reforma* to commemorate the centenary of Mexico's independence—she possessed a great financial fortune, which she put at the disposition of the candidate. She met Vasconcelos for the first time in Toluca, when she lent him her luxurious Cadillac for his triumphal arrival in Mexico City on Palm Sunday of 1929. Shortly thereafter, at Vasconcelos's request, she organized women around the campaign to gain their voting rights.[23] She became a close collaborator of the candidate, helping him write many of his speeches (Blair, 476–80), and within a short period they became lovers. Among some of her connections was U.S. Ambassador Morrow, with whose wife she was on very familiar terms. She even organized a dinner in her house for Vasconcelos to personally meet the ambassador he so much despised in order to diminish the tensions between the two (Blair, 420, 492–96). She was considered a rich dilettante by many of the members of the *Comité Orientador,* who disliked the influence she was gaining over their candidate,[24] but despite this opposition she remained a faithful companion of the candidate throughout his campaign and in his postelectoral exile, until her tragic suicide with Vasconcelos's own gun in front of the altar of Notre Dame Cathedral in Paris on 11 February 1931 (Blair, 11–13; *El proconsulado,* 484–91). *El proconsulado,* the fourth volume of Vasconcelos's autobiography, which covers the presidential campaign, is dedicated to her memory—or rather to the memory of "doña A.R.M. and all those who fell for the ideal of a regenerated Mexico," as her real name is concealed throughout the book by the pseudonym of "Valeria." Just prior to her death she had given the former candidate her own chronology of the presidential campaign, much of which Vasconcelos cites extensively in his own narration of the events both in *El proconsulado* and *La flama.*

Rivas Mercado was not the only prominent financial contributor to the campaign. Among those who gave important monetary support to his campaign were Luis Cabrera, Emilio and Alfonso Madero, Federico González Garza, Ramón P. De Negri, Jesús González Soto, a man identified simply as Rodríguez and, particularly, Manuel Gómez Morín, who with Raúl Pous Ortiz was very successful in fund-raising. The contribution of such donors added to the money gathered at the well-attended paid conferences and a variety of fund-raising activities organized by volunteers, whose free labor of all sorts greatly helped the campaign (*El proconsulado,* 175–78; Azuela, 96; Skirius 1982b, 197; Pineda, 67). One particularly intriguing contribution came from Valentín Garfias who, as Vasconcelos recalls in his autobiography, sent $300 a month to his family in California while the candidate was away (*Desastre,* 1798). Garfias was a petroleum engineer who managed the "Foreign Oil Department for Cities Services, a billion-dollar utility, oil, natural gas, and real estate company with headquarters on Wall Street." He was also a personal friend of Stanford president Ray Lyman Wilbur, who became Secretary of Interior of the Wilson administration. His contribution, which ultimately totaled $3,300, is quite interesting for a campaign that made a big issue of opposing the growing influence of North American capital in the Mexican economy (Skirius 1976, 492–93).

The evidence gathered by historians who have addressed the presidential campaign of 1929 leads one to believe that Vasconcelos's candidacy received wide popular support. In Querétaro on 27 July 1929, for example, *El universal* reported that members of all social classes went to

the railway station to receive the candidate despite the rain that fell on
that day. The people did not fit on the railway platform. After his reception great crowds gathered to listen to the candidate's speech (Pineda,
69). In a communication to the State Department on 13 November
1929, the U.S. consul in Ciudad Juárez, Chihuahua, estimated that an
overwhelming majority of that state's population was behind Vasconcelos. Just a week earlier the same consul had reported in a confidential
message to the secretary of state that:

> In the State of Chihuahua, as well as along the West Coast of Mexico, I
> believe that it can be frankly stated that excluding those directly or indi-
> rectly connected with Federal, State or Municipal Governments, the sen-
> timent is entirely in favor of Vasconcelos, especially outside of the larger
> towns. On the West Coast of Mexico I would judge that the whole of
> Sonora, Sinaloa and Nayarit, eighty per cent of the population is Vascon-
> celos [sic], thirty per cent active and the rest inactive, but with these sen-
> timents. Just before leaving Mazatlán [Sinaloa] I personally noticed that
> seventy five per cent of the houses of that city were placarded over the
> entrance doors with Vasconcelos posters. Here in Juárez the Rubio party
> [PNR] seems to predominate outwardly but information tends to indi-
> cate that the population is *Vasconcelista,* but fears Federal reprisals if too
> active. (Pineda, 69–70)

Similar assessments of the popularity of Vasconcelos and of political
manipulation by the PNR campaign came from U.S. consuls in Tampico
(Tamaulipas), Acapulco (Guerrero), Durango, and Yucatán (Pineda,
70–71). Vasconcelos received a massive reception in Tampico when he
arrived on a rainy day, 1 September 1929. Skirius estimates that after
Mexico City, it was in Tampico where Vasconcelos was the most popular.
According to estimates of the U.S. consul in that city, he commanded the
sympathies of 90 percent of the city's population. He was particularly
popular among the oil workers of the region (Skirius 1982b, 149–53).
   Despite Vasconcelos's enormous popularity, the official results indicated an overwhelming defeat. According to these results, Ortiz Rubio,
of the official PNR, received 1,825,732 votes, or 93.58 percent of
the total; Vasconcelos received 105,655 or 5.42 percent; and Pedro
Rodríguez Triana, candidate for the Communist Party, received 19,665
or 1.01 percent (Skirius 1982b, 166). Such results did not reflect the
support Vasconcelos had received throughout the campaign trail and
represent the first of a long history of adulterations of electoral results
that have characterized the PRI's long stay at the reins of Mexico's polit-

ical institutions. The days leading to and including the election were filled with increased political violence and intimidation, including assassinations (Magdaleno, 157–65). PNR sympathizers controlled most polling stations and the 30 members of the electoral commission, in charge of supervising the process, belonged to the same party. Throughout the country ballots were lost, and *Vasconcelistas'* names mysteriously disappeared from voter registries and many of them were intimidated and harassed as they tried to vote. Furthermore, as has been the tradition ever since, the PNR's ballot consisted of the red, white, and green of the Mexican flag, identifying a vote for that party as a vote for the nation. The air of intimidation was increased by the large military presence on election day. In Mexico City alone, a *Vasconcelista* bastion, 12,000 soldiers patrolled the streets, while Tampico, another *Vasconcelista* stronghold, was under martial law, and many oil workers who supported Vasconcelos were not allowed to reach the polling booths. Such an atmosphere certainly kept many voters away from the polls. Beyond this intimidation, there is strong evidence that the results were manipulated to a degree that is absurd. In Tampico, for example, where thousands had received the candidate on a rainy day, official results indicated 6,000 votes for Ortiz Rubio and *only one* for Vasconcelos. In Mexico City, where over 100,000 people had received Vasconcelos on Palm Sunday, the official results only granted him 1,517 votes (Pineda, 105–7; Skirius 1982b, 161–68). The PNR was not satisfied with just a majority; it wanted the official results to reflect a complete and overwhelming victory.

The atmosphere of violence and intimidation, which included beatings and assassinations during the campaign, did not limit itself to the repression of *Vasconcelistas* in the streets. An important factor in Ortiz Rubio's campaign was the censorship that the official regime exercised over the press. Vasconcelos's campaign put a great emphasis on the spoken and written word. Beginning with the campaign in California, Vasconcelos had counted on the support of the Lozano newspapers, which regularly and favorably covered his activities and published his editorials and transcriptions or summaries of his speeches. In Mexico, Vasconcelos recognized that he received important support from a variety of newspapers, particularly small regional ones. He specifically mentions *La gaceta* from Guaymas, *El pueblo* from Hermosillo, *El demócrata sinaloense* from Mazatlán, *La palabra* from Tuxpan, the Zazueta newspaper from Culiacán, and *El hombre libre* and *Omega* from Mexico City. These newspapers, among others, the autobiographer recalls, supported his campaign and remained faithful to him after his defeat (*El proconsulado,* 118–19). However, the larger national newspapers distanced themselves from *Vasconcelismo.* They often characterized the candidate as an idealist who would be unable to fulfill the practical requirements of running a country (Taracena, 76). The one notable exception was *El universal,* in whose pages Vasconcelos had regularly published a weekly editorial since 1925. Yet even this newspaper was forced to cancel Vasconcelos's column after 8 August 1929 due to political pressure (Pineda, 92).

On the night of 20 September 1929, a *Vasconcelista* demonstration of workers, students, and peasants had a run-in with a gang of PNR thugs who murdered three of the demonstrators—Germán del Campo, Alfonso Martínez, and Eulalio Olguín.[25] This act marked an escalation in the political violence, which would continue increasing until well after the elections. The morning after the assassinations, *El universal*— which no longer carried Vasconcelos's column, but continued informing about his campaign—reported the assassinations. The newspapers, however, were confiscated by government supporters. Despite public appeals by its editor, Miguel Lanz Duret, a campaign of intimidation continued against the paper. The government applied a "national boy-cott" against it, making it impossible to transport it on the railroads. Gradually the newspaper was forced to stop covering Vasconcelos's cam-paign. Another major newspaper, *Excélsior,* had tried to keep a neutral stance, but state coercion forced it to take a position favorable to Ortiz Rubio. Autumn, "The period marked by the bloodiest repression was the one which had the least information" (Skirius 1982b, 145–47). Thus, in the last three months of the campaign the newspaper headlines were dominated by information about airplane races and intercontinen-tal flights, rather than by information about national politics. Vasconce-los had to rely on speeches that did not enjoy the national distribution of the major newspapers (Pineda, 94–95). To make matters worse for him, the official candidate had at his disposition a whole array of the latest technologies to spread his propaganda. Thus, he could rely on the radio, controlled by the government, on airplanes, which could distribute leaflets even in hostile *cristero* territory, and on the cinema to produce favorable political movies (Skirius 1982b, 145).

The extreme violence and intimidation that marked the last three months of the presidential campaign differed from the political atmos-phere prevalent in Mexico during the spring of 1929, which Skirius calls a "spring of tolerance." According to his interpretation, this freer moment during the campaign—which was by no means exempt of violence perpetrated by government-supported thugs—was not necessarily due to an enlightened and democratic spirit of the regime in power, but because the government was too busy fighting the *cristero* rebels on one front and the *Escobarista* rebels on another one. The government simply had too much on its hands to start another front of confrontation against the *Vasconcelistas* (Skirius 1982b, 97). In this regard, it is very important to realize that throughout his campaign Vasconcelos opposed violence on the side of his partisans. He had an opportunity to join his forces with those of the *cristeros* or the *Escobaristas*, but instead he condemned violence from all sides, advocating for the solution of Mexico's political problems through the electoral ballot. In the spirit of Madero, he believed that violence should only be an instrument of last resort, used after the confirmation of an electoral fraud, not as an instrument to bypass a democratic electoral process.

In January 1929, while campaigning in Guadalajara, Jalisco, Vasconcelos was visited by two men who identified themselves as representatives of *cristero* general Enrique Gorostieta, who had 25,000 armed men at his disposition. The envoys invited the presidential candidate to join forces with them. Although Gorostieta had a large and organized army, he did not have the armament or financial support that the government had. He realized that his army could survive with its guerrilla tactics, but envisioned a long stalemate. The political support of the prestigious Vasconcelos could give his movement a crucial infusion, particularly in the urban centers. For the presidential candidate, an alliance with the armed, mainly peasant, rebels could provide his campaign with crucial military backing to counterbalance the government's forces. He willingly welcomed Gorostieta's envoys and listened to them, asking them how long they could continue fighting in the mountains, to which they responded that they could continue their struggle for the next two years. Hearing this forecast Vasconcelos explained that he wanted to take the political campaign to its conclusion through peaceful means, but set up an appointment with the rebellious general for the day after the elections. He counted on this support only as an instrument to assert his victory, not as an instrument to take him into power. "I have come for the elections," he said, "not for a rebellion. . . . We will go to the elections and if there is an infringement of the vote, as I have already said in Nogales, I will not accept the result of intrigue and imposition."[26]

With his tacit agreement with Gorostieta, Vasconcelos was certain of armed support after an electoral fraud. However, this armed support would never come through. On 21 June 1929 an agreement was reached between the government and the Catholic Church hierarchy to put an end to the religious conflict. Shortly after the agreement the *cristero* troops were demobilized and they returned their weapons. Only oral guarantees were given to the demobilized rebels and many of their leaders, including Gorostieta, were killed as they surrendered. The agreement was, according to Vasconcelos, "a low blow which was completely unexpected" (*El proconsulado*, 160–62). This strategic political move on the part of the government is characterized by the former candidate as his "first defeat." Prior to the solution of the conflict Vasconcelos had counted on the support of a Catholic political party in the cities to watch over the proper elaboration of electoral lists. In the countryside the threat of increased violence functioned in his favor as well. "All this came tumbling down with the secret pact which forced the surrender of the rebels" (*Flama*, 195–96). Although the presidential candidate realized the damaging effects of this resolution to his strategic goals, he could not publicly oppose the agreements after having put so much emphasis during the campaign trail on the necessity of a peaceful solution to the conflict (Skirius 1982b, 121).

Vasconcelos saw in the conflict's solution "the hand of [U.S. Ambassador Dwight W.] Morrow" (*El proconsulado*, 162–63), and later evidence points in that direction. Since his arrival in Mexico in the fall of 1927, the ambassador proved to be a conciliatory pragmatist. While the departing ambassador, James Sheffield, had defended U.S. oil interests in Mexico with a "racist arrogance which only turned him into an enemy of Mexico's rulers and intensified their nationalism," Morrow, who had close links with the banking industry after working 13 years as a lawyer for J. P. Morgan, had a much more diplomatic approach toward the Mexican government. "[H]e became such a friend of the Calles government . . . that he could be qualified as confidant and principal advisor of President Calles." Since the beginning of the revolution, the U.S. oil industry had seen in Mexico's political instability an opportunity to continue their exploitation of the country's oil fields without government interference. The banking industry, on the other hand, was more interested in a stable government to guarantee the timely payment of the foreign debt. Morrow took sides with the bankers (Skirius 1982b, 28–29). In this spirit, the *cristero* rebellion constituted an obstacle to the pacification and stability of Mexico's government. He took a personal interest in the religious conflict, convincing both the government and the church to establish a dialogue. Jean Meyer reports in his voluminous study of this conflict that the ambassador was personally involved in the writing of the correspondence between the parties and actually drafted the final agreements himself (Meyer, 316–18, 339–40).

But Morrow and the U.S. bankers were not the only foreign parties interested in solving the religious conflict. Throughout the three years of bloody war, which took the lives of tens of thousands of Mexicans, the highest church authorities from the Vatican had expressed an interest in a peaceful solution. It was actually the Roman authorities, not the peasant Mexican militants, who reached an agreement with the Mexican government, leaving those who had taken the risk to fight the anticlerical authorities—and also the *Vasconcelistas*—out on a limb. They were not even present at the negotiations and were only instructed to disarm after the fact.[27] The good faith of the Mexican government in the "solution" to the religious conflict is questionable as "the truce of 1929 did not last more than a few months, the necessary time to arrange the *Vasconcelista* issue" (Meyer, 374). It was politically expedient to take one tool away from Vasconcelos's presidential ambitions, and the strategy worked. Without diffusing this problem the federal government would have had to face a broad alliance between rural Catholic peasants—the *cristeros*—and urban, young middle classes and intellectuals—the *Vasconcelistas* (Meyer, 367–68). The truce with the *cristero* rebels—with or without the assistance of Dwight W. Morrow—was a very useful strategic move on the part of interim President Portes Gil to facilitate the triumph of Ortiz Rubio.

Another very practical strategic move of Portes Gil to diffuse *Vasconcelista* support was his granting of autonomy to the National University. The idea of making the university an autonomous entity, independent of the political and economic imperatives of the state, dates back to 1881, when then federal representative Justo Sierra included this idea in a bill referring to federal education. His project was not approved, but in his September 1910 speech at the inauguration of the newly organized National University Sierra once again insisted on the importance of granting such autonomy to the institution. From that moment the proposition for an autonomous educational entity was taken on by different administrations and student groups, without success. Even during Vasconcelos's ministry—in 1923—a student strike included among its demands such autonomy. This strike did not succeed either (Azuela, 110–17). In 1929, in the middle of the presidential campaign, the issue would once again come to the fore. As the school year began, Narciso Bassols, director of the Law School, insisted upon the establishment of new periodic written exams to track the students' progress. At the same time, Antonio Caso, director of the National High School *(Escuela Nacional Preparatoria)*—dependent on the university—proposed the addition of one more year to the two-year curriculum of this institution. The two changes were considered arrogant and undemocratic by the students, who had been formed by teachers who, in the spirit of the revolution, encouraged civic participation and activism. Law and high school students declared a strike and Portes Gil closed their schools. During the month of May many student demonstrations, at times reaching as many as 30,000 participants, paraded in the streets of Mexico City. These were met by repression on the part of the police and fire departments. As the protests grew, so did the students' demands, which now not only called for an elimination of the two new curriculum changes but also called for administrative and economic autonomy for the university and for student participation in its governing bodies. They also called for the resignation of the school and city authorities responsible for the violent repression of the demonstrations. From Córdoba, Veracruz, Vasconcelos saw the political advantage of student discontent and encouraged the demonstrations, labeling the school reforms as evidence of Protestant influence in the country's educational system. By early June Portes Gil ceded, granting the university its autonomy, thus diffusing once again possible larger problems and taking the initiative away from Vasconcelos, who had to concede and recognize that the provisional president had acted as a "civilized gentleman" in choosing dialogue over bullets (Azuela, 116–23; Skirius 1982b, 115–17). A decade after the campaign, in the pages of *El proconsulado*, Vasconcelos cynically and bitterly recalls the political cost to his campaign of this political decision by Portes Gil, "The students, entertained with their new toy of a University, in which exams were eliminated and students named their professors and could remove them at will, deserted the electoral activities to a large degree" *(El proconsulado*, 254–56).

With decisions like the truce with the *cristeros* and the granting of autonomy to the university, Portes Gil proved to have very good political skills to complement the organizational and repressive forces on which the official faction could count to secure the presidency of Ortiz Rubio. Political violence perpetrated by supporters of the official party was a reality throughout the presidential campaign of 1929. But this violence, as Pineda insists, was the task of second- or third-rate obscure characters from the official structure. Interim President Portes Gil always declared himself an enemy of such violence and distanced himself from such actions. This attitude gained him prestige and legitimacy, celebrated by the press and even by Vasconcelos himself (Pineda, 97–101). On 13 August 1929, *El universal* published an article listing the achievements of a provisional administration in power for less than a year. Among them the newspaper included the pacification of the country, the solution of the religious conflict, the creation of a labor code and the autonomy of the university. Such achievements gave prestige to an administration, the continuity of which was represented by Ortiz Rubio. The official candidate, for his part, also gave a rather conciliatory tone to his electoral campaign, promising to accept ideas from the opposition and insisting upon the necessity of uniting the "Mexican family" (Pineda, 85). In the meantime, Calles—the outgoing president who, as the historical record has shown, remained behind the reins of political power—gave the impression of opening up the political arena by voluntarily giving up power, calling for elections, and even leaving the country for Europe "for health reasons" in July 1929 (Pineda, 81–82). In front of the violence targeted against the *Vasconcelistas* lay a veneer of political tolerance, civility, and political achievement. Furthermore, and perhaps much more important in the real struggle for power, Ortiz Rubio's campaign, with its linkage to the established political structures, enjoyed the support of key leaders of the church, the bureaucracy, the armed forces, business, and the United States (Skirius 1982b, 174–80).

Despite the PNR's political ability, great organizational strength, and support of key political actors, one cannot underestimate the importance of violence and intimidation in its securing of its first "electoral" triumph. Throughout his campaign, Vasconcelos had counted on the use of violence to challenge an electoral fraud after it had taken place. Yet the Mexican people were intimidated and tired of two decades of violence and were apparently willing to accept the imposition of the PNR's candidate instead of launching themselves into a continuation of a civil war that had already taken too many lives (Pineda, 103–5). The section of Vasconcelos's autobiography dedicated to the last month of his campaign, the election itself, and its aftermath, reveals the bitterness of a man who feels betrayed by the people on whom he had counted. According to him, by October 1929 the violence had taken unprecedented proportions. *Vasconcelista* leaders, sympathizers, students, and workers were assassinated throughout the republic, and supporters, fearful for their lives, disbanded. While some of his partisans encouraged the taking up of arms at this point, Vasconcelos and his key advisors insisted upon remaining calm, fearful of giving the government an excuse for much more open repression and the cancellation of the elections, which he intended to use as a legitimizing element for his later violent uprising. In preparation, some of his supporters, like Alessio Robles, were in charge of feeling out the armed forces and trying to win possible supporters from within their ranks (*El proconsulado*, 246–48). While the presidential candidate did not want to call for an uprising prior to the November elections, he attempted to prepare the atmosphere for the postelectoral uprising. His strategy, however, showed a great level of political and strategic naïveté. Supporters like Miguel Palacios Macedo encouraged the former minister to organize a plan for the future uprising. He, however, resisted, insisting that the uprising would be a spontaneous expression of the people's rage after the imposition. He had in mind the 1910 Revolution, when people from all walks of life rose up in support of Francisco I. Madero, without him having personally organize each one of the contingents. Thus, rather than elaborating a specific strategy of resistance, Vasconcelos limited himself to spreading the word that people should rise up and oppose the PNR candidate after the election.

During the last days of the presidential campaign Vasconcelos was literally on the run. He did not stay in Mexico City to vote or wait for the final results. Rather, he went on train to Mazatlán, Sinaloa, and then to Guaymas, Sonora, on the west coast of Mexico, where he felt he had more supporters and the possibility of leaving the country if it were necessary. In both cities he was surrounded by police and soldiers who were supposedly provided for his security by the government, but who actually intimidated those who wanted to come in close contact with him and greatly limited his freedom of movement. To make his situation more precarious, the government controlled the means of communication—telegraphs, telephones, mail, and the media—making it impossible for the sieged candidate to communicate with his constituents, and, furthermore, giving the PNR-supporting authorities the possibility to shape not only their own message, but also information about Vasconcelos and his supporters. Surrounded and unable to communicate with the Mexican people, the candidate had two options: he could hide in Mexico and lead a rebellion that had not actually started, or he could go into exile where he figured he would at least have more freedom to speak out (*El proconsulado*, 248–53, 265–69).

As the impossibility of winning in clean and transparent elections became more and more evident, some of Vasconcelos's supporters, particularly Gómez Morín, recommended that he accept the electoral fraud, remain in Mexico, and continue working with the party in the opposition. Vasconcelos saw this alternative as immoral. He could not accept the imposition. He could not accept a position offered to him as a consolation prize by those in power, those whose hands were full of blood. Such an acceptance could be interpreted by the people as if he had "lent [himself] to make a comedy of elections in order to consolidate *Callismo* in exchange for a position that they would later throw at [his] face" (*El proconsulado,* 250–51).[28] Once in exile in the United States, Gómez Morín and Garfias again proposed the idea of returning to Mexico and heading the opposition, something which Vasconcelos again refused (*El proconsulado,* 291–92). Similar conciliatory proposals were given to him at least twice by Ambassador Morrow. During the presidential campaign, Morrow had met with the candidate in Cuernavaca, Morelos. He had proposed that if Vasconcelos accepted an electoral defeat, his supporters would be guaranteed three positions in Ortiz Rubio's cabinet—excluding the strategic posts of minister of interior, of war, or of the treasury. After the election, when Vasconcelos was surrounded by the military in Guaymas, Morrow sent John Lloyd—head of United Press International's office in Mexico City—with a message for him. If he would publicly recognize that Ortiz Rubio was Mexico's official president, Vasconcelos would be named president of the National University. On both occasions Vasconcelos was deeply insulted and refused the ambassador's tokens (*El proconsulado,* 283–84; Skirius 1982b, 132–34, 169).

Isolated and surrounded by a military guard that supposedly was kindly provided for his protection, Vasconcelos remained in Guaymas for approximately two weeks after the elections. He finally decided to leave the country and did so by train, always accompanied by a military escort of 40 men who followed him until the border at Nogales (*El proconsulado,* 284–85). Once in the United States he published his "*Plan de Guaymas,*" dated 1 December 1929, which, in the spirit of Madero's "*Plan de San Luis,*" called on the Mexican people to rise up against an illegitimate government. It declared that Vasconcelos was the country's legitimate president and did not recognize any of Mexico's established authorities, calling instead for new elections at the municipal level once the established authorities were defeated. The plan also told the Mexican people that "The President Elect is now leaving the country, but will return to take direct charge as soon as there is a group of armed free men who are able to make me be respected." The plan was published by *La prensa* in San Antonio and by several minor newspapers in Mexico. It was also circulated in typed copies throughout the country (*El procon-sulado*, 290).[29]

The armed uprising never came through. There were sporadic upris-ings, but the massive rebellion that Vasconcelos had expected never hap-pened. Possible *Vasconcelistas* were terrorized by months of brutal repres-sion that followed the electoral campaign, and the Mexican media reported that Vasconcelos did not want an uprising (Pineda, 112; Skirius 1982b, 169–74, 180–83). To make matters worse for the *Vasconcelistas*, on 5 February 1930 Ortiz Rubio was shot shortly after he was sworn in as president. The perpetrator of this assassination attempt was Daniel Flores who, according to Mauricio Magdaleno, one of *Vasconcelismo's* principal leaders, was not known to him, but who, Magdaleno specu-lates, could very well have been on the fringes of the movement (Mag-daleno, 205). The following weeks were marked by disappearances and executions of *Vasconcelistas*. Particularly gruesome was the discovery by a dog of the mutilated bodies of about 12 *Vasconcelistas* close to Topilejo on the outskirts of Mexico City. These partisans of Vasconcelos were taken from prison, forced to dig their own graves, and then strangled and bru-tally mutilated. Although generals Maximino Avila Camacho and Eulo-gio Ortiz were implicated in this massacre, they were not punished for their crimes. Vasconcelos paid tribute to these victims and indicted their assassins in his 1933 short story "Topilejo."[30]

Thus Vasconcelos remained in exile waiting for an uprising that never happened, calling himself Mexico's president-elect. What he perceived as lack of popular support at a crucial moment in his personal—and the nation's—history turned into a bitter obsession. He had carried on the campaign as a personal mission, not submitting to the discipline of any party and instead presenting his political agenda as his own. It was he, Vasconcelos, who would redeem the Mexican nation, and when the Mexican nation did not rise up in support of him the former candidate took this as a personal affront. As Skirius puts it, "His resentment became a general hatred towards the nation which he considered had failed him. He disdained Mexico and said that it was a sick country" (Skirius 1982b, 200–201). The nation was not ready for him and his ideals, he figured. Mexico was, in his opinion, a country of subservient people who got the bloody dictatorships they deserved. Modern Mexi-cans were very different from the conquerors like Hernán Cortés whom Vasconcelos so much admired; men who fought for their convictions against all odds and against all authority. Mexico was a country that now disgusted him *("El asco que tengo por México")* (*Cartas*, 258). During his California stay, prior to the electoral campaign, he had already developed a dichotomy that identified the glories of Mexico with its Hispanic colonial past and blamed most of its problems on the militarism that followed its independence. With his failed presidential campaign and the feelings of abandonment it elicited, Vasconcelos's rhetoric would more and more identify the militaristic regimes with what he saw as an Aztec bloodthirsty heritage. No longer would he attempt to redeem the Indian past. Only the figure of Quetzalcóatl—the wise god who was expelled by the warring Huitzilopochtli; the god that *criollo* nationalists like Fray Servando Teresa de Mier had identified with an American Christianity—would remain from the pre-Columbian past as a symbol for Vasconcelos's cause.[31]

Throughout the rest of his life, the former presidential candidate would blame his defeat on military repression and U.S. intervention. These were, indeed, important factors in his defeat. One cannot deny the level of violence that preceded and followed the elections. One cannot deny either that the United States had developed close economic and political ties with the Calles regime, particularly since the arrival of Ambassador Morrow. In 1929 U.S. capitalists had invested $1,323,000,000 in the Mexican economy—a 40 percent increase over the $800,000,000 invested in 1912. Furthermore, Mexico's debt to its northern neighbor amounted to $872,900,000 in 1930. The United States had very important economic reasons for maintaining stability in Mexico. It had to protect its financial interests, particularly at the time of the stock exchange crash. It had courted Calles and found a reliable partner in him, while Vasconcelos throughout the campaign called for economic independence from the United States. Under these circumstances, the North American government gave all its political and economic support to Calles, helping his regime reach a truce with the *cristeros* and aiding in the suppression of the *Escobarista* uprising by postponing payments on Mexico's debt and ignoring the arms embargo against the country (Skirius 1982b, 196–97). In this regard, Vasconcelos's personal hatred toward Ambassador Morrow definitely did not help (Pineda, 71–72).

Beyond the overwhelming military and communicational advantages that the PNR candidate had at his disposition, there were a series of factors within Vasconcelos's own campaign that damaged his chances of winning. Particularly significant was the candidate's own character, intransigent and personalist. Just as he was unwilling to dialogue with Ambassador Morrow, Vasconcelos held on to certain principles that worked to his disadvantage. A vocal critic of militarism and of professional politicians, he made enemies for himself who could have otherwise given him crucial support. His public condemnation of the *Escobarista* rebellion and vocal support of interim President Portes Gil in this instance, for example, alienated many who shared his goals to change the governing system. Within the PNA he distanced many as he refused to follow party discipline. He wanted the party's name and tradition, but insisted on setting his own rules. He was particularly critical of any association the party had with military leaders. Alessio Robles, who was party president at the time, has written a tendentious and very critical book on Vasconcelos's personalism and lack of discipline, *Mis andanzas con nuestro Ulises* (My adventures with our Ulysses). As Vasconcelos did not follow his nominating party's line, he counted on a broad array of organizations to support not the PNA's agenda but *Vasconcelismo*. There were many tensions and conflicts between his young enthusiastic supporters and the older generation of PNA activists. Oftentimes the young volunteers did not even follow Vasconcelos's orders. Furthermore, Vasconcelos would often pay more attention to his personal friends, like Rivas Mercado, than to the more experienced politicians of the party. The campaign was thus marked by a lack of organization that could not compare with the forces of the newly formed PNR. Finally, Vasconcelos's supporters did not necessarily have a coherent ideology, as many joined his movement not necessarily because of ideological affinities toward him, but because they repudiated *Callismo*. In this regard, his supporters ranged from young radical students to reactionary *Porfiristas* who saw in his campaign a possibility to gain back the positions of power they had lost (Pineda, 71–72; Skirius 1982b, 199–205).

Chapter Six

Epilogue: At Life's Dusk— The Final Years

In 1957 a small 289-page paperback was published in Mexico City by the publishing house *La Prensa*, as part of its *Populibros* collection. For Mexico's standards it had a large run: 25,000 copies. Its cover has a printed price in Mexican pesos and U.S. dollars for sales "abroad." It is a relatively inexpensive book—at 5 Mexican pesos or 50 U.S. cents— intended for a large circulation. Its golden and orange cover includes a colorful portrait of an older Vasconcelos. Over his white hair is the seal of the National University, with its map of Latin America and its slogan *"Por mi raza hablará el espíritu."* Directly in front of his pensive face is a brass oil lamp with its flame shining. The anthology is titled *En el ocaso de mi vida* (At my life's dusk). The book's cover announces, "The Continent's most discussed voice speaks about everything and everyone from his luminous maturity." Its price and presentation imply a popular reading audience, not necessarily the intellectual circles accustomed to discussing Vasconcelos's early legacy. It is a publication with no recognized editor, other than Vasconcelos himself, who writes the book's *"Advertencia"* (warning preface). The volume's introductory pages, numbered with roman numerals, contain this "Advertencia" and two other sections. One is titled *"Mi código es el Evangelio"* (My code is the gospel") and consists of a commented interview given by Vasconcelos to the Spanish magazine *El español* in November 1954. The other one is a speech given at an undated meeting of the National Student Confederation titled *"Los motivos del escudo"* (The seal's motives [or motifs]),[1] explaining Vasconcelos's understanding of the National University's seal that he himself had created. The book is then divided into ten sections, grouping articles under broad subjects such as death, religion, truth, politics, nuclear war, and art.

The small paperback appears as an authorized last testament of a man who would die less than two years later. The image he presents of himself is clear: he is a devout Catholic who sees in Catholicism and the Spanish language the unifying principle of his country and all of Latin

America. The man who claims in the introductory interview that if he had to do it all over again he would like to become a philosopher—a theologian, more precisely—chooses to present himself not as such but rather as journalist and commentator. It is through journalism, he claims, that a contemporary thinker can quickly and clearly address the vast amount of "moral, political, scientific, [and] economic" concerns that compete for a modern person's attention. Furthermore, journalism pays a regular salary, something longer philosophical books do not necessarily do.[2] He continues to combine his philosophical curiosity about origins, human destiny, truth, and morality with his ever-pressing concern about the quotidian, the political, and the economic. He is still a man that fuses ethereal philosophical preoccupations with the very prosaic activity of journalistic political agitation.

In these introductory pages the former minister of education, now in his mid-seventies, recognizes that he has been "filed" (archivado) as director of the México Library, a position that keeps him away from the higher political echelons, but which has allowed him to "comfortably receive [his] friends" (Vida, xix). It was here that G. Nicotra di Leopoldo met him, "In that almost empty hall, with a book shelf, a sofa and two armchairs, sitting at his table, every morning invariably from ten on, he received everyone without exception, and read the newspapers."[3] He was kept in an anonymous office, in a third-rate bureaucratic position, but even here his admirers visited him, and he had a very active life giving lectures, attending conferences and honors, publishing in magazines and newspapers. He kept abreast of current events and maintained strong opinions, which he still made public.

He had returned to Mexico almost a decade after the electoral campaign, after his U.S. visa expired and he was forced to leave the country in order to apply for a new one. The political climate in Mexico had changed. General Lázaro Cárdenas was in power and he had forced General Calles into exile. In California Calles and Vasconcelos met. Now that Calles was not in power, they both met "as men" and not as enemies. According to Vasconcelos, Calles recognized that he had won the 1929 election when it came to popularity, but that he had not amassed enough power to take over the presidency. Now that they found themselves in similar positions, Calles told Vasconcelos that he did not want power but simply to take revenge on Cárdenas for the humiliation of exile. The former president said he would support a military uprising against Cárdenas. Then new elections could be held and Vasconcelos would certainly win. Vasconcelos claims he agreed with the proposal and even received some money from Calles, but the rebellion never happened. The two men remained in contact, and once Vasconcelos was settled in Mexico City he interceded with President Avila Camacho in favor of Calles's return to Mexico. They remained in communication until the general's death. At the former president's funeral, Vasconcelos participated in an honor guard around his casket, sharing this duty with General Joaquín Amaro, his former declared enemy. Amaro himself, the radical minister of the army who during the *Cristero* War had a party celebrated in his honor in the church of his patron saint, had become an observant Catholic.[4]

The former presidential candidate had returned slowly and discreetly. In August 1938 he was informed that his U.S. visa would expire. He was not actually deported; he just needed to cross back into Mexico to fulfill a bureaucratic requirement. His return to the homeland, however, would put his status in Mexico to the test. Vasconcelos had last been in the country in 1929, when after the presidential election he was escorted by a military convoy to the Nogales border. Shortly thereafter provisional President Portes Gil had made public an order for border authorities to impede the rebellious defeated candidate's return. As Lázaro Cárdenas—president between 1934 and 1940—consolidated his power, after having forced Calles into exile, he declared a political amnesty. This Vasconcelos refused to recognize, claiming that he was not a criminal and he did not need to be pardoned. Cárdenas replied to Vasconcelos's concerns in the newspapers, clarifying that the former minister was in voluntary exile and not a criminal, and he was free to return at his own will. It was a convenient opportunity, Vasconcelos recalls. By this time he had lost any hope for an armed rebellion to instate him as president. This bureaucratic requirement of the U.S. government gave him "a magnificent excuse to put an end to my exile and return honorably to my country" (*Flama,* 488–89). By 21 September 1938 he was quietly settled in the western city of Hermosillo, Sonora, after having entered the country through Nogales. General Yucupicio, the state governor, made Vasconcelos welcome, and soon after his arrival he was named president of Sonora University. Political intrigues spread around him, accusing him of being a reactionary, and by August 1939 he left Sonora for Mexico City, where he tried to return to the legal practice.[5] His career in law did not prove the success he had expected. Yet, despite his still marked oppositional stance, Vasconcelos had friends and sympathizers both in civil society and the administration. By the presidency of Manuel Avila Camacho (1940–1946), Vasconcelos was appointed head of the National Library, and in 1946 he was transferred to the less prestigious but better paying position of director of the México Library, next to the Ciudadela in Mexico City (Taracena, 131–34).

From his office at the México Library, Vasconcelos continued meeting his supporters and writing. He also traveled very much during this period and was engaged in a variety of forums including his short participation in a television program, *"Charlas mexicanas"* (Mexican conversations), where three panelists discussed topics usually related to Mexican history (Cárdenas Noriega, 247–52). From Mexico he maintained close contact with Spain; he was invited to the country by Francisco Franco and also honored with the Spanish *Gran Cruz de Alfonso el Sabio*. Such acts served as proof to his detractors of his fascist sympathies, and they were quick to point it out (Taracena, 135–36, 140). Indeed, during the Second World War, he expressed sympathies toward the fascists, particularly the Italians and Spanish, who in his opinion posed an alternative to North American and British power. He was "anti-Yankee," Alfonso Taracena remembers. "One day I found him in the National Library concerned because Mussolini had allowed Yankees to land on a small Mediterranean island to prepare a leap unto the [Italian] peninsula" (Taracena, 132). Any blow the Axis powers gave the Anglo-American alliance implied a blow against Vasconcelos's enemies. Furthermore, Italian fascism was often perceived in Latin America as distinct from its German variety inasmuch as in the definition of its constituting identity it placed more emphasis on the Roman and Catholic cultural tradition than on biology and the Aryan race, as its German counterpart did (Leys Stepan, 140–41). In this regard, Italian victory represented victory of Latin Catholicism over Anglo-Saxon Protestantism. In the journal *Timón* he claimed that an allied victory in the war "would be the worst calamity for this continent's inhabitants. IT WOULD SIMPLY SINK US INTO A DESPICABLE AND ENSLAVING COLONIALISM" (Taracena, 129, emphasis in original). At a celebration marking the inauguration of courses at the Institute of Italian Culture in Mexico, Vasconcelos praised the role of Italy in the discovery and spiritual formation of the New World, pointing at the role of Columbus, Americo Vespucio, the Franciscan order, and countless other Italians on the American continent (Taracena, 129).

By the end of the war his positions on the Axis powers had definitely changed as he understood the scope of the war's horrors, but he still maintained many ideas linking him to the conservative right wing. His Catholic orthodoxy remained throughout his last years. So did his sympathy toward the Franco regime. His religious pronouncements often refer to church authorities and traditions for guidance, "the Gospel's strict norms as interpreted by the Encyclicals" (*Vida,* xxvii), but oftentimes his thoughts on religion are highly charged by the totalizing philosophical spiritualism that had characterized him from his youth. God in these cases is the totalizing principle toward which matter must move through a process of depuration. God represents a unifying force that gives sense to a repulsive material reality, full of grotesque secretions and violence. It is both a redemptive goal and ordering principle. Seen under this light, his notion of God is similar to that of the spirit included in the National University's motto. This is a point upon which he insists in a talk given to the National Confederation of Students in 1942, *"Los motivos del escudo."* Referring to the origins of what is the most ubiquitous slogan of his legacy, *"Por mi raza hablará el espíritu,"* still reproduced today in any official document of the university, Vasconcelos insists that he has maintained a constant position throughout his life. The slogan, he told the students, was "a protest" against the "altar of the Jacobin homeland. Altar without God or saints." The mention of the spirit in the slogan of such an influential cultural institution at the service of an anticlerical rational regime is indeed the paradox, not the changing in the positions of its author. Viewed from his declared Catholic perspective he asked the students: What else could the spirit represent if not God, or at least the Holy Spirit? But stating it as such would imply the use of words forbidden by the Jacobin state (*Vida,* xxii–iv). Vasconcelos did work for the "Jacobin state" and he recognizes it, but he qualifies his participation by pointing at his actions. He included the term "spirit" in the University's slogan. Challenging what one would expect from an anticlerical state he regularly published Tolstoy, whose Christian socialism he admired, in the SEP's journal, *El maestro.* He also published a Spanish edition of the Gospels, followed by a 70-page essay by Tolstoy titled "What is the Gospel?" as part of the ministry's series of "classics."

Now a fervent Catholic, he did not spend his time in calm religious contemplation. He was always preoccupied by political concerns. Vasconcelos proposed a Christian socialism, inspired on the vision of Tolstoy and Dostoevsky, which demands "social justice." This is the position he claims was shared by the early *Maderistas,* who had launched a spiritual critique of the excesses of Porfirian bourgeois liberalism—for him *Juarismo* by association—which in the name of science and progress justified gross inequalities under the slogan of "the survival of the fittest," denied humanity's spiritual element, and hindered the educational and cultural traditional role of the church by nationalizing its possessions. Vasconcelos claims that the Christian socialism of the *Maderista* revolution was unorthodox inasmuch as "the encyclicals' doctrines about social justice had not yet taken the shape of political parties." At the time of his statements he claims that such doctrines had already gelled into political parties. Such a Christian socialism should not be confused with "Marxist socialism," which he identifies with materialism, party dictatorship, and the suffocation of dissidence. A socialism infused by the Christian values of charity and neighborly concern, as he had claimed since the early revolutionary years, held the only solution to contemporary economic questions. On this matter there is a definite continuity in his thought and concern for social justice. But now he marks a clear distinction between Marxist and Christian socialisms. He characterizes them as "the Antichrist" and "Christ"; evil and good (*Vida,* 255–57). Morality and religion have taken the place of aesthetics.

As older age stepped in, Vasconcelos saw his utopia in a place very different from the tropical Amazon of his youth. He looked forward to redemption in the afterlife, where his spirit would be freed from the burden of a material body. His *Letanías del atardecer* (Dusk's litanies), a posthumously published collection of verse, is a song of denial of the body's needs and passions in thirsty expectation of spiritual eternity.[6] As counterpoint to these philosophical preoccupations he maintained an avid curiosity and was eager to read about the latest events or inventions. *En el ocaso de mi vida* includes an article titled *"Casa, tierra y auto"* (House, land and car). The article's title and central thesis is a reaction to Ford Motor Company, which had recently announced an increase in its employees salaries, already, according to Vasconcelos, the highest in the field. It was Henry Ford who proposed that every man must own a house, a plot of land, and a car, and Vasconcelos agrees with the champion of modern North American capitalism. While the house provides, according to the Mexican, for the family's sovereignty and the land might be harvested in times of economic need, the car "is a necessity of the soul. Not just for transportation." He goes on to explain the way a car can be used to explore the world that surrounds us and to meet different people. It could be used in this way as an instrument of peace, through the encouragement of international understanding. In the tone of the former minister who wanted to regulate even the usage of leisure time, the article claims that by allowing their owners to visit the grandeur of the countryside automobiles will keep people away from vices such as alcohol, movies, and bullfights. As the necessities of war had helped to develop the jeep, the author now expected the factories of peace to produce a vehicle capable of dealing with the dangers and pests of the tropics. In a future time any person should be able to own a home, land, and an automobile with the proceeds of their honestly earned wages, without the intervention of "parties" that use homes, lands, and cars as instruments of manipulation and discipline, rewards and punishments (*Vida*, 134–37). Its scope is not as grandiose or cosmic, but the future tropical civilization with driver-civilians echoes in some way the bustling Amazonian Universópolis. It is just less spectacular and terminal, more prosaic; Ford is its model, not Plotinus.

Through figures like that of Ford, the United States is still a model for Mexico and the world to follow. In his continuous love-hate relationship with the United States, Vasconcelos is still as impressed by U.S. technical capabilities as he was during his early days at Eagle Pass. The car is one such invention, so ubiquitous in the United States of the mid-century, he notices, that some houses even reserved a special place on their land to house the vehicles. New suburbs were emerging as transportation was facilitated through these motorized self-contained vehicles. It was in the United States that he, a simple lecturer and visiting professor, could purchase a car, something he had enjoyed in Mexico, but only as a privilege of his ministerial post. As he returned to Mexico in 1938 he did so in a brand new Oldsmobile, purchased with the proceeds of his *Philosophy Manual* and of his regular contributions to the journal *Hoy* (*Flama*, 487–88). Now, at the dusk of his life, his vision of a good life on earth still required technology produced elsewhere. His vision was no longer that of permanent aesthetic contemplation and fantasy. This is a much more quotidian vision of middle-class homeowners able to travel with their cars. His grandiose visions are now reserved for the world of the heavens that await us after death. It is indeed paradoxical, but perhaps characteristic of his times, that he felt such admiration for the man who rationalized the production line, subtracting from the artisans the last vestige of individual creativity and turning them into cogs of a precise technology in the name of scientific mechanization. But then again, like Rodó, Martí, Sierra, and Sarmiento, Vasconcelos was fascinated by the productive might of the industrialized north, even if it was a rapacious Caliban, dehumanized and brutal in its cold efficacy.

As his utopian vision of the conquest of the Amazon gives way to that of suburban homeowners, his triumphant vision of the Latin race becomes somewhat subdued. He is still a proud Hispanic Catholic and insists on the significance of Hispanic civilization in the past, present, and future. He remains an ardent opponent of liberal *Juarismo* as an attack on the national sovereignty and character. Nevertheless, he realizes the new imperial role acquired by the United States in the twentieth century. In an article titled *"Crisis del nacionalismo"* (Nationalism's crisis), Vasconcelos, like in older times, criticizes petty nationalisms in favor of larger conglomerates. At the time of *La raza cósmica* he had predicted a miscegenated cosmic humanity, coalescing around a Hispano-Catholic cultural paradigm spread around the world by the Spanish empire. By the 1950s the United States had acquired imperial status. It was no longer the admired antagonist against whom the destiny of America— and the world—would be decided. The United States was now the ruling empire, which could assert its sovereignty and will by the force of arms. He saw an empire that emerged from a well-defined, race-based nationalism, but now, with its world reach, had to adapt itself to its more cosmopolitan reality. "In an imperial people, any nationalism has something of narrow and petty." An empire, he reasoned, like the Spanish or now the North American includes many more peoples than a simple nation-state. Its international trade and military endeavors put it in contact with the entire world. There are migrations to and from the metropolis. At this point in his life Vasconcelos is willing to recognize that the U.S. empire is poising itself to be stronger and longer than the British was. In his assessment, the British Empire has been one of the shortest lived in history because it was "too English." Unlike its British counterpart, the North American empire, like that of the ancient Romans, "has managed to incorporate into its ranks some of the most diverse racial groups." It seems that the United States has taken over the mission once destined for the Latin regions of the continent. As an example of the expansive nature of North American identity, which in its origins had been determined by an English Protestant worldview, Vasconcelos points at the importance of the Catholic Irish, nemesis of British hegemony on the isles, in U.S. politics. President Roosevelt had to court the Irish Catholic vote, like that of the Poles, Italians, and "Hispano-Yankees," including "the seven million Mexicans who vote with the Catholics" (*Vida,* 249–51). As usual, his observations are Eurocentric. He poses the representation of European Catholics as an otherness within an Anglo-Saxon Protestant hegemony. As in *La raza cósmica* the world remains the forum for a particularly European conflict. He does not consider the Native American, African, or Asian presence within the United States. Did they not count? Was he not aware of them? Did he consider them unimportant?

What is particularly revealing about Vasconcelos's assessment of the North American empire is the weight he gives to the factor of force. The imperial stage was the conclusion of an evolution from a strong national stage, and such can only be achieved when a people enjoy sovereignty. "[N]ationalism supposes sovereignty and sovereignty depends on the reach of the cannons and the bombs of a sovereign people." Without such sovereignty, or the instruments to defend it, "[w]e, in the Spanish America," he writes, "spent the first century and a half of our independence formulating rhetorical declarations about our national sovereignty, while we arranged our economy and our institutions to the demands of Anglo-Saxon nationalism." It was this nationalism, with its cohesiveness, vast natural resources, and overwhelming military force, that was able to assert itself as the ruling empire and the paradigm for the future. Comparing favorably the United States with its Latin American counterparts he writes:

> This is an empire and this is the future. Meanwhile, the nationalisms of the encyclopedia or revolution type continue accommodating themselves to the empire, despite the fact that to distract their prejudices they entertain themselves with the fantasies of the nationalism and sovereignty of peoples without squadrons or airplanes. (*Vida*, 250–51)

His earlier model in *La raza cósmica* considered military might. It was a superior technology—reflected in but not limited to military power— that to a great degree facilitated the formation of the Spanish overseas empire. But in the 1920s Vasconcelos placed a far greater emphasis on cultural character and aesthetics in defining the future cosmic race. Squadrons of airplanes appeared in the earlier utopia, but as bearers of good news, not enforcers of a national sovereignty. Now he understood the power of weapons. Weapons that the United States had at its disposal and provided to "friends" for a fee. It was the U.S. unilateral weapons embargo against Pancho Villa that set the revolutionary conflict in Carranza's favor. It was U.S. weapons that quelled the *cristero* rebellion and the various military uprisings in Mexico. It was U.S. weapons that were used to impose his electoral defeat.

Vasconcelos continued to insist on the importance of the Hispano-Catholic heritage in Latin America and its growing presence within the United States, but his cosmic dream of a fifth race utopia, while invoked at times, lost its centrality in his thought. Religious faith took its place. This faith, however, did not preclude him from participating in the current political debates; on the contrary, it encouraged him. He continued to criticize the liberal project of the *Reforma* and the postrevolutionary regimes as Protestantizing and Anglo-Saxonizing. He defended the role of the church in the development of Latin American culture and civilization and condemned liberal anticlericalism that destroyed the nation's cultural networks, opening up space for Protestant North American influence. He identified in the regime the rhetoric of radical *indigenista* scientific socialism, while in practice the political bosses enriched themselves at the expense of the people. Within a radical discourse of national sovereignty, Vasconcelos sees the nation more and more entangled with the United States. In his conspiratorial sort of analysis he sees even in Lázaro Cárdenas's 1938 nationalization of the oil industry—a landmark of Mexican nationalism, signifying economic independence—the advancement of U.S. industrial interests. He characterizes this action, long considered an affront to North American interests that coincidentally took place precisely in the year of Vasconcelos's return to Mexico, "the Roosevelt-Cárdenas accords to expel English companies" from the Mexican petroleum industry (*Flama*, 486). He claims that his friend, petroleum engineer Valentín Garfias, told him just before his return to Mexico in 1938:

> what the Yankee government is looking for is for Cárdenas to expel the English from the Poza Rica zone, potentially one of the best in the world. For their part, the North American companies, tired of strikes and all sorts of difficulties, will be glad to see the [Mexican] government become the administrator. . . . Later, everything related to exports will have to remain in the hands of the companies which have the ships for the transportation. The price of each export barrel will be imposed by the same consortiums at the port's mouth without having to take the responsibilities of production or workers' administration. (*Flama,* 476)

The fleets that four centuries ago left Mexico to travel the seven seas no longer belonged to Mexicans. One can only wonder what Vasconcelos would today say about the "rescue package" put in place to support the peso, which sharply devalued shortly after NAFTA's implementation. As collateral Mexico gave up the future proceeds of its oil exports.

In the years after the presidential campaign Vasconcelos also published the majority of his philosophical works, as he had the time to pursue his long-term life interest. His calmer life in the library did not, however, bend his ultimate opposition to the regime, which would follow him even to his death. In an example of both this opposition and the arro-

gance that characterized him, in 1952, when he started to feel his health
falter, he had written a letter to his son in law, Herminio Ahumada,
informing him that he did not want to be buried in the *Rotonda de los
Hombres Ilustres,* a section of a national cemetery where prominent Mexicans honored by the state are buried. He strongly believed that "our
country's citizens do not have the right to honor me as a writer while
they do not recognize me as a politician." Such a recognition could only
come by accepting the electoral fraud of 1929. He also figured that he
would not be in good company were he buried there, as his neighbors
would be heroes of the Liberal *Reforma* pantheon (Bar-Lewaw Mulstock,
214–15; Cárdenas Noriega, 256–57). On 20 June 1959 he passed
away after a series of heart attacks. He was put to rest in the *Jardín*
graveyard and President Adolfo López Mateos—a *Vasconcelista* during his
youth—was part of an honor guard around the coffin, as were representatives of the legislative and judicial powers. His funeral was attended
by over 2,000 people (Cárdenas Noriega, 257; Taracena, 148).

On his death Vasconcelos received some of the official recognition he
was certain he deserved but claimed he did not want. What he did not
get was a recognition of the continuity of his legacy. In the speech
explaining the university seal's motives he insisted upon the continuity
of his thought. One must certainly recognize that in over 70 years of
development a person's ideas are bound to change. There is nothing sur-
prising in that. Vasconcelos did change. He became much more reli-
giously orthodox and much more suspicious of the United States, the
Soviet Union, masons, Protestants, and Jews. He also flirted with Spanish and Italian fascism as an alternative to reinstate the grandeur of a
Latin past. Some of his pronouncements indeed went to extremes that
have discredited their author. However, a too easy and clear-cut distinction between the early and later Vasconcelos is very problematic. As I
have argued throughout my study, one finds preoccupations that
accompany Vasconcelos's thought throughout his life, undergoing just a
variety of mutations in changing contexts—a nostalgic and prophetic
view of Spanish culture, its language and religion; the search for a totalizing spiritual and aesthetic dimension; admiration and repulsion for the
United States; a fascination with modern technology; a rejection of
political violence and advocacy of democratic institutions; a self-
construction as redeemer.

The early Vasconcelos who participated in the *Maderista* revolution
and headed the institutionalization of an educational system during
Obregón's regime is easily assimilable into the official historical canon.

Similarly, the bitter fascist-leaning Vasconcelos of the 1930s is easily dismissible. There is, however, a much more problematic Vasconcelos as a bridge between the two extremes—the presidential candidate. During his presidential campaign Vasconcelos attempted to rekindle the democratic spirit of Madero. It was a movement of protest against the extreme political violence of a new revolutionary elite. It was a call for the respect of civility, civil procedure, and civil rights. His campaign proposed a modernizing yet nationalist model of education and economic development. The demands of his campaign were consistent with those put forth by the revolution's ideologues, and it was carried out with a spirit of dignity and respect of legal procedures. In this regard, his presidential campaign is a high moment in his career. His campaign, however, was carried out against overwhelming odds.

Today, at a time of transformations uncannily similar to the ones witnessed by Vasconcelos in 1929—both moments share the assassination of an official candidate, armed uprisings throughout the nation, the demands by civil society of democratic reform, a transformation toward greater integration with the United States—revisiting Vasconcelos's thought seems pertinent. His critique of violence is as valid today as it was seven decades ago, as is his demand for transparent democratic elections. The United States's ever-growing economic and cultural influence over Mexico, Latin America, and the world reminds us of Vasconcelos's concerns as well. In moments such as those when the U.S. Congress arrogantly and unilaterally debates whether to grant Mexico passage into NAFTA or "certification" as a partner in the war on drugs, Vasconcelos's indictment of North American insolence sounds again.

Vasconcelos's legacy is complex and contradictory, like the history of the nation where he happened to be born. It is far more fruitful to attempt to grasp the whole complexity of his thought, instead of limiting our understanding of him on the basis of a few popular slogans. In an essay called "Fariseos documentados" (Documented pharisees), Vasconcelos defends his version of history from those who criticize his lack of documentation. Documents, he reminds us, can be used to distort history, and documents, while useful, are not the only tools of the historian. He goes on to talk about Madero's assassination, which he says is well known to have been perpetrated by Victoriano Huerta. That is the historical truth, he tells his readers. However, any search for the explanation of his death in official documents, those prepared by the perpetrators of the crime, would reveal that Madero died in a skirmish as his supporters intended to rescue him. Such a version, while well documented, and precisely because it was documented by those who must hide the truth through documentation, is patently false. Documented histories, thus, can be very dangerous. But even more dangerous are those histories that are partially documented. This is the technique of the "most perverse" of historians, "who uses true documents, but loosely and incoherently. With them a coherent lie is not fully constructed, but they help to create doubts about the manifest truth" (*Vida,* 97–101). Such has been the selective rewriting of Vasconcelos's legacy. I believe that a more complete understanding of the contradictions that both synchronically and diachronically characterized Vasconcelos is necessary, although not for the moral obligation of saving the good from the perverse intervention of the selective official historian. The contradictions within Vasconcelos shed light on the contradictions present in the broader question of the definition of a coherent nation and a race in postcolonial Latin America—*post*colonial inasmuch as the Spanish flag no longer waves over the Indies, but also post*colonial* inasmuch as the region maintains the European "Latin" in its name, Spanish as its lingua franca, Catholicism as its dominant religion. It is the contradiction of a "postcolonial" settler nationalism—a nationalism espoused by the *criollo* and *mestizo* intellectual descendants of conquerors, missionaries, and settlers that bases its originality and reason for existence on its Americanness, but which links its ideals, and even the very notions of nation and race, to the European metropolis. It is the contradiction of the closeness to the United States, fascinating in its technological might and greater civilian freedom, feared in its expansionist impulse. The contradiction of the migrant or occupied Mexicans who must define their *raza* in the United States through linkages both to the Native American original occupants of the foundational Aztlán and to the Spanish conquerors, explorers, and settlers who discovered the region for the West and left a legacy of language, traditions, land grants, and names. Within Vasconcelos these contradictions took a very peculiar tinge, but these are contradictions not limited to him. They are actually constituent of all attempts to define a peculiar Latin/Ibero/Hispano/ Indo/South/*Nuestra* or plainly American experience.

Vasconcelos saw *mestizaje* as a synthesizing principle. *Mestizaje,* however, is in itself representative of rupture. Such is the interpretation that Octavio Paz gives it in *El laberinto de la soledad;* such is also the interpretation given to it by Chicano activist and poet Rodolfo "Corky" González in his epic poem "I am Joaquín." Vasconcelos's was not the one true theorization of *mestizaje.* What seems valuable in our understanding of his racial theory is an understanding of the tensions present in the broader theoretical debates and practical implementation of national identities in which it intervenes. Those tensions are still present today. The recent *Zapatista* uprising is but one example of the questioning of the revolution's understanding of the nature of national identity and its political representation. Brandishing the Mexican flag as a symbol of their membership in the larger national community, the *Zapatistas* demand, among other things, greater sovereignty and recognition for the native ethnic groups within the national context. Such actions question our understanding of *mestizaje* and bring forth many of the contradictions Vasconcelos tried to resolve. Furthermore, the predominant role of Latina/os in the United States gives new shades to the question of *mestizaje*. Today it is precisely in the United States that the notion of a pan-Latinism—in the general use of the term "Latina/o"—is gaining greater currency. Vasconcelos's notion of the cosmic race is as applicable to this broader understanding of "Latina/o"—and in many instances more closely applicable—as it was to the more *indigenista* nationalist deployment of the term "*raza*," invoking Vasconcelos, during the Chicano movement. And finally, Vasconcelos's sustained critique of liberalism, for its inhumane mechanization and its great dependency on the United States, may once again gain currency as the neoliberal policies of recent administrations have in a great way challenged the long-held understanding of the nationalist liberal tradition.

Notes and References

Chapter One

1. See Juan Hernández Luna, ed., *Conferencias del Ateneo de la Juventud* (Mexico: UNAM, Centro de Estudios Filosóficos, 1962). This anthology is of particular interest regarding the centennial, as it contains the talks given during the cycle of conferences and a useful introduction.

2. José Vasconcelos, *Ulises criollo* (1935), in *Obras completas* (Mexico: Libreros Mexicanos Unidos, 1957), 1:533; hereafter cited in text as *Ulises criollo*. This and other translations of the Spanish originals are mine.

3. Martín Luis Guzmán, *El águila y la serpiente* (1928), in *La novela de la Revolución Mexicana,* ed. Antonio Castro Leal (Mexico: Aguilar, 1971), 1:391; hereafter cited in text.

4. José Vasconcelos, *La tormenta* (1936), in *Obras completas* (Mexico: Libreros Mexicanos Unidos, 1957), 1:886; hereafter cited in text as *Tormenta*.

5. One should point out that Vasconcelos was not the first person to take on the mantle of Quetzalcóatl as symbol of Mexican salvation. This god has played an important role in *Criollo* nationalism since the seventeenth century. See J. Lafaye, *Quetzalcóatl y Guadalupe. La formación de la conciencia nacional en México* (Mexico: Fondo de Cultura Económica, 1985).

6. José Vasconcelos, "¿Qué es la Revolución?" in *Qué es la revolución* (Mexico: Botas, 1937), 91–92.

7. Guzmán, *El águila y la serpiente,* 289. "{L}ive stock-brokers," "Far West," and *"el embargo de armas"* in the original.

8. The term *indigenismo* is usually used, as Luis Villoro points out, to refer to "every cultural expression which manifests a special fascination with the Indian world." It is also, as Villoro insists, a movement created and led by *criollos* and *mestizos,* not necessarily by Indians. Under such a perspective, the authentic national origins lie not in the colonial period but in the pre-Columbian Indian past. Its rhetoric, in this regard, is usually anti-Spanish and anti-European. Ironically, however, as thinkers like García Canclini, Bonfil Batalla, and Villoro himself indicate, more often than not this fascination lies on an Indian *past.* The modern Indian, in order to be integrated into the present-day national culture, must, as Bonfil Batalla insists, "de-Indianize" him- or herself. See Luis Villoro, "De la función simbólica del mundo indígena," in *Fuentes de la cultura latinoamericana,* ed. Leopoldo Zea, vol. 2 (Mexico: Fondo de Cultura Económica, 1993); Luis Villoro, *Los grandes momentos del indigenismo en México* (1950; reprint, Mexico: La Casa Chata, 1979); and Guillermo Bonfil

Batalla, *México profundo. Una civilización negada* (Mexico: Grijalbo, 1994), hereafter cited in text.

9.   Alfonso Taracena, *José Vasconcelos* (Mexico: Porrúa, 1982), 122; hereafter cited in text.

10.   See, for example, Elizabeth Martínez, ed., *500 Años del Pueblo Chicano/500 Years of Chicano History in Pictures,* 2d ed. (Albuquerque: SouthWest Organizing Project, 1991), 1–13.

11.   See chapter 8 of Sandra Messinger Cypess, *La Malinche in Mexican Literature: From History to Myth* (Austin: University of Texas Press, 1991).

12.   See Gobierno del Estado de Tlaxcala, *Historia de un Pueblo, Tlaxcala* (Tlaxcala: Gobierno del Estado de Tlaxcala, 1994).

13.   Here, of course, I refer to the liberal tradition as understood in the nineteenth century, not as it is understood today in the United States. Liberalism in nineteenth-century Latin America was rich and complex, consisting of a great variety of competing tendencies. Nevertheless, for our general purposes it can be understood as very akin to what we today call neoliberalism; that is, putting forth a political, economic, and social policy in which modernization, capitalism, and globalization are encouraged and in which people are conceived of as individual citizens and economic agents in a democratic system of government.

14.   Michael Johns, *The City of Mexico in the Age of Díaz* (Austin: University of Texas Press, 1997), 32.

15.   For a very interesting article on this subject see Lourdes Arizpe, " 'Indio': Mito, profecía, prisión," in *América Latina en sus ideas,* ed. Leopoldo Zea (Mexico: Siglo XXI/UNESCO, 1986).

16.   See Rafael Bernal, *El gran océano* (Mexico: Banco de México, 1992), 71, 252–58.

17.   José Enrique Rodó, *Ariel* (1900; reprint, Mexico: Fondo de Cultura Económica, 1984), 73.

18.   Arturo Ardao, "Panamericanismo y latinoamericanismo," in *América Latina en sus ideas,* ed. Leopoldo Zea (Mexico: Siglo XXI/UNESCO, 1986), and John L. Phelan, "El origen de la idea de Latinoamérica," in *Fuentes de la cultura latinoamericana,* ed. Leopoldo Zea, vol. 1 (Mexico: Fondo de Cultura Económica, 1993).

19.   Passages like the following are revealing of a certain Eurocentrism in Martí: "The mute Indian moved around *us,* and went to the mountain, the summit of the mountain, to baptize his children. The observed black sang in the night the music of his heart, lonely and unknown, among the waves and the beasts" (my emphasis). In cases like this, by using the "us" (*nos*) he separates himself and, by implication, those like him, from their Indian and black others. This type of Eurocentrism is almost certainly unintentional, but nevertheless symptomatic of the ideology of his time. José Martí, "Nuestra América," in *Fuentes de la cultura latinoamericana,* ed. Leopoldo Zea (Mexico: Fondo de Cultura Económica, 1993), 1:125.

20. The pioneer is an image that Rodó also uses.

21. Stuart Hall, "On Postmodernism and Articulation: An Interview with Stuart Hall," *Journal of Communication Inquiry* 10 (1986): 53.

22. Hugo Achúgar, "The Book of Poems As a Social Act: Notes toward an Interpretation of Contemporary Hispanic American Poetry," in *Marxism and the Interpretation of Culture,* ed. Cary Nelson and Lawrence Grossberg (Urbana: University of Illinois Press, 1988); hereafter cited in text.

23. Sheila Fitzpatrick, *Education and Social Mobility in the Soviet Union, 1921–1934* (Cambridge: Cambridge University Press, 1979), 10.

24. Max Weber, "Bureaucracy and Revolution," in *Revolutions: Theoretical, Comparative and Historical Studies,* ed. Jack A. Goldstone (San Diego: Harcourt, Brace, Jovanovich, 1986), 36–37.

25. Alexis de Tocqueville, *The Old Regime and the French Revolution* (New York: Doubleday, 1955), 59.

26. Jean Meyer, *El conflicto entre la iglesia y el estado, 1926–1929,* vol. 2 of *La cristiada* (Mexico: Siglo Veintiuno, 1994), 148; hereafter cited in text.

27. Jean-Pierre Bastian, *Los disidentes. Sociedades protestantes y revolución en México* (Mexico: Fondo de Cultura Económica/El Colegio de México, 1989), 32–40.

28. Meyer, 43–62, and Alicia Olivera Sedano, *Aspectos del conflicto religioso de 1926 a 1929. Sus antecedentes y consecuencias* (Mexico: Secretaría de Educación Pública, 1987), 27–50, 75–82.

Chapter Two

1. José Vasconcelos, "Discurso en la Universidad" (1920), in *José Vasconcelos y la Universidad,* ed. Alvaro Matute (Mexico: UNAM/IPN, Textos de Humanidades, 1987); hereafter cited in text as "Discurso."

2. José Vasconcelos, "La campaña contra el analfabetismo" (1920), in *José Vasconcelos y la Universidad,* ed. Alvaro Matute (Mexico: UNAM/IPN, Textos de Humanidades, 1987); hereafter cited in text as "Campaña."

3. José Vasconcelos, "Instrucciones sobre aseo personal e higiene" (1920), in *José Vasconcelos y la Universidad,* ed. Alvaro Matute (Mexico: UNAM/IPN, Textos de Humanidades, 1987); hereafter cited in text as "Instrucciones."

4. José Vasconcelos, "Se convoca a las mujeres para la campaña contra el analfabetismo" (1920), in *José Vasconcelos y la Universidad,* ed. Alvaro Matute (Mexico: UNAM/IPN, Textos de Humanidades, 1987).

5. José Vasconcelos, "Libros que recomienda la Universidad Nacional" (1920), in *José Vasconcelos y la Universidad,* ed. Alvaro Matute (Mexico: UNAM/IPN, Textos de Humanidades, 1987).

6. Vasconcelos's proposal of breathing exercises reflects the interest he had at that time in South Asian religions.

7. E. J. Hobsbawm, *Nations and Nationalism Since 1780: Programme, Myth, Reality,* 2d ed. (Cambridge: Cambridge University Press, 1992), 95–96.

The close relationship between a common language, literacy, and nationalism is explored in Benedict Anderson, *Imagined Communities: Reflections on the Origin and Spread of Nationalism,* 2d ed. (London: Verso, 1991).

8. Manuel Gamio, *Forjando patria* (1916; reprint, Mexico: Porrúa, 1982), 9–10; hereafter cited in text.

9. Simón Bolívar, "Carta de Jamaica" (1815), in *Fuentes de la cultura latinoamericana,* ed. Leopoldo Zea (Mexico: Fondo de Cultura Económica, 1993), 1:22–24.

10. Andrés Bello, "El castellano en América" (1847), in *Conciencia intelectual de América. antología del ensayo hispanoamericano (1836–1959),* ed. Carlos Ripoll (New York: Las Américas, 1966), 55–57.

11. Antonio Tovar, "La incorporación del Nuevo Mundo a la cultura occidental," in *Lo medieval en la conquista y otros ensayos americanos* (Madrid: Seminarios y Ediciones, 1970); hereafter cited in text.

12. José Gálvez, *Proyecto para la organización de las Misiones Federales de Educación,* Cámara de Diputados al Congreso de la Unión, Primera Comisión de Educación Pública (Mexico: Imprenta de la Cámara de Diputados, 1923); hereafter cited in text.

13. Raymond Williams, *Keywords: A Vocabulary of Culture and Science* (New York: Oxford University Press, 1983), 270–74, emphasis in the original.

14. For a discussion of the transformation of this region from frontier to border, see Ana María Alonso, *Thread of Blood: Colonialism, Revolution, and Gender on Mexico's Northern Frontier* (Tucson: University of Arizona Press, 1995), 131–32. Here, referring to the work of Friedrich Katz, Alonso explains that "The 'transformation of the frontier into the border' . . ., that is, the incorporation of the periphery into the capitalist world market and its increased integration into the nation-state, was a long-term socio-historical process that spanned several decades." Interesting studies of the frontier/border in this period are Américo Paredes, *With His Pistol in His Hand: A Border Ballad and Its Hero* (Austin: University of Texas Press, 1958); David Montejano, *Anglos and Mexicans in the Making of Texas, 1836–1986* (Austin: University of Texas Press, 1987); Héctor Aguilar Camín, *La frontera nómada. Sonora y la Revolución Mexicana,* 2d ed. (Mexico: Cal y Arena, 1997); and James A. Sandos, *Rebellion in the Borderlands: Anarchism and the Plan of San Diego, 1904–1923* (Norman: University of Oklahoma Press, 1992). In a more literary vein and dealing with the broader Latin American context, novels known as *novelas de la tierra* (novels of the land), like Rómulo Gallegos's *Doña Bárbara* (1929) and José Eustaquio Rivera's *La vorágine* (1924), deal with these frontier environments at a time when urban intellectuals attempt to dominate and know them.

15. Barry Carr, *The Peculiarities of the Mexican North, 1880–1928: An Essay in Interpretation* (Glasgow: University of Glasgow, 1971), 1–4.

16. One must bear in mind that *Ulises criollo* was published in 1935 and, as I have already mentioned, by this point Vasconcelos's attitude had become that of an outspoken Hispanophile—something evident in his choice of

Criollo as opposed to *Mestizo* in his autobiography's title. Nevertheless, this construction of Indian "barbarism," particularly in the case of the Apaches, is perfectly consistent with his earlier ideology. Thus, in his 1926 *Indología* he expresses pride about his *mestizaje*, yet he calls "red skins" (referring particularly to the northern nomadic Indians) a "primitive" race, in contrast to the Indians of the tropics, which he characterizes as an "ancient and refined race" now in decadence. The former are frontier "savages," the latter descendants of "civilized" peoples who had once built great cities and dominated nature. José Vasconcelos, *Indología. Una interpretación de la cultura ibero-americana* (1926), in *Obras completas* (Mexico: Libreros Mexicanos Unidos, 1958), 2:1089, 1184–85; hereafter cited in text as *Indología*.

17. Vasconcelos's admiration of the United States was not limited to his formative experiences viewing the contrasts between Piedras Negras and Eagle Pass. Emerging from his adult life experience, the Mexican Ulises's descriptions of New York City in *Indología* are full of awe. He is overwhelmed by the dynamic might of the modern city; he is fascinated by the power of its skyscrapers, its electric lights, and its wealth. The city causes such an impression on him that he momentarily forgets his resentment toward the United States. The modern metropolis comes to symbolize his utopian vision of the future: "New York, the port of the New World, imposes its vitality on us; we wake up from the semi-dream left in us by Europe, the continent where all things have already been done, and we are reinvigorated by the aura of the continent where things are being done." The Mexican traveler on this occasion has but one complaint about the city: the coldness of its churches and banks (*Indología*, 1077–78). He was also struck by the libraries and schools of the United States, dedicating long praising passages to the New York City Library and those endowed by Carnegie (*Tormenta*, 993–94, and *Indología*, 1091–92). The Mexican's admiration for the North American educational system is also present in his article *"Universidad y capitolio"* (University and capitol), dedicated to Austin, Texas. Here he celebrates what he sees as a harmonic and mutually respectful coexistence of governmental and educational institutions within the city. This he finds very different from his own country's situation, where he feels that the state does not appreciate the value of schooling. Vasconcelos's admiration for Austin apparently did not allow him to see the racist segregation in the city and the exclusion of ethnic minorities, including Mexicans, from the university he so much respected. José Vasconcelos, "Universidad y capitolio," in *Qué es la revolución* (Mexico: Botas, 1937).

18. Vasconcelos's construction of a biological linkage through blood is one of the many contradictions in his racial theory. Vasconcelos's *Raza cósmica,* as is discussed in the next chapter, claims to be an intervention against essentialist biological theories of race. He denies biological racial determinism, but uses race as the central category of his system. He attempts a cultural discussion of race, but the biological underpinnings of the concept are a heavy ballast. One could argue that in the particular instance of the autobiography, "blood" is

used in a metaphorical way. It almost certainly is. Nevertheless, Vasconcelos chooses blood, an overused biological metaphor, from the many possibilities his rich vocabulary affords him.

19. See Juan Bruce-Novoa, "Chicanos in Mexican Literature," in *Retrospace* (Houston: Arte Público, 1990), 65–66.

20. See chapter 1, "El pachuco y otros extremos," of Octavio Paz, *El laberinto de la soledad* (1950; reprint, Mexico: Fondo de Cultura Económica, 1990).

21. José Vasconcelos, "México en 1950," in *Qué es la revolución* (Mexico: Botas, 1937), 131–39.

22. Pierre Broué and Emile Témime, *La revolución y la guerra de España* (Mexico: Fondo de Cultura Económica, 1979), 1:138–39.

23. José Vasconcelos, "También Francia," in *Qué es la revolución* (Mexico: Botas, 1937), 185–86; hereafter cited in text as "También Francia."

24. Ricardo Pérez Montfort, *Hispanismo y Falange. Los sueños imperiales de la derecha española* (Mexico: Fondo de Cultura Económica, 1992), 74–75.

25. José Vasconcelos, "El amargado," in *Qué es la revolución* (Mexico: Botas, 1937), 84; hereafter cited in text as "El amargado."

26. Martha Robles, *Entre el poder y las letras. Vasconcelos en sus memorias* (Mexico: Fondo de Cultura Económica, 1989), 53–55; hereafter cited in text. The image of Vasconcelos as martyr, prophet, messiah, and teacher is one that the author constructs himself in his own texts, as Martha Robles points out. Such a construction of Vasconcelos is also apparent in biographies, histories, and assessments of the author by many of his associates and followers. See, for example, Fedro Guillén, *Vasconcelos, "Apresurado de Dios"* (Mexico: Novaro, 1975); Oscar Monroy Rivera, *México y su vivencia dramática en el pensamiento vasconcelista* (Mexico: Costa-Amic, 1972); Mauricio Magdaleno, *Las palabras perdidas* (1956; reprint, México: Porrúa, 1976), hereafter cited in text; Antonieta Rivas Mercado, "La campaña de Vasconcelos," in *Obras completas de Antonieta Rivas Mercado,* ed. Luis Mario Schneider (Mexico: Fondo de Cultura Económica, 1987), hereafter cited in text; and Taracena. See also Antonio Castro Leal, introduction to *Páginas escogidas {de José Vasconcelos},* ed. Antonio Castro Leal (Mexico: Botas, 1940), hereafter cited in text; and Genaro Fernández Mac Gregor, prologue to *Vasconcelos,* ed. Genaro Fernández Mac Gregor (Mexico: Secretaría de Educación Pública, 1942), hereafter cited in text.

27. Max Aub, *Guía de narradores de la Revolución Mexicana* (Mexico: Fondo de Cultura Económica, 1969), 45; hereafter cited in text.

28. Alan Knight, "Revolutionary Project, Recalcitrant People: Mexico, 1919–40," in *The Revolutionary Process in Mexico: Essays in Political and Social Change, 1880–1940,* ed. Jaime Rodríguez (Los Angeles: Latin American Center, UCLA, 1990), 229; hereafter cited in text.

29. Also see chapter 1 of Meyer.

30. Emmanuel Carballo, *Protagonistas de la literatura mexicana* (Mexico: Secretaría de Educación Pública, 1986), 25; hereafter cited in text.

31. See for example José Joaquín Blanco, *Se llamaba Vasconcelos. Una evocación crítica* (Mexico: Fondo de Cultura Económica, 1977), 31–32, hereafter cited in text; Carballo, 9; Castro Leal, 6–7; Fernández Mac Gregor, vii-viii; and I. Bar-Lewaw Mulstock, *José Vasconcelos. Vida y obra* (Mexico: Clásica Selecta, 1966), 11–13, hereafter cited in text.

32. Alan Knight, "Weapons and Arches in the Mexican Revolutionary Landscape," in *Everyday Forms of State Formation: Revolution and the Negotiation of Rule in Modern Mexico,* ed. Gilbert M. Joseph and Daniel Nugent (Durham: Duke University Press, 1994), 29, 47–51; hereafter cited in text.

33. Elsie Rockwell, "Schools of the Revolution: Enacting and Contesting State Forms in Tlaxcala, 1910–1930," in *Everyday Forms of State Formation: Revolution and the Negotiation of Rule in Modern Mexico,* ed. Gilbert M. Joseph and Daniel Nugent (Durham: Duke University Press, 1994), 200; hereafter cited in text.

34. See Marjorie Becker, *Setting the Virgin on Fire: Lázaro Cárdenas, Michoacán Peasants, and the Redemption of the Mexican Revolution* (Berkeley: University of California Press, 1995), which studies this multifaceted relationship between Lázaro Cárdenas's deeply anticlerical regime and Michoacán's Catholic peasantry.

35. As a matter of fact, he uses the new preface to condemn Adolf Hitler's Holocaust, tracing its genesis to "Darwinism . . . [which] taken to the social realm by Gobineau, originated the theory of the pure Aryan, defended by the English, [and] taken to an aberrant imposition by nazism." José Vasconcelos, *La raza cósmica. Misión de la raza iberoamericana,* 2d ed. (1948), in *Obras completas* (Mexico: Libreros Mexicanos Unidos, 1958), 2:903; hereafter cited in text as *Raza.*

36. José Vasconcelos, "Conciencia de raza," in *Qué es la revolución* (Mexico: Botas, 1937), 103; hereafter cited in text as "Conciencia." Emphasis in the original.

37. A similarly paradoxical definition of "Hispanic" appears in a document of the University of Massachusetts Amherst titled "Protected Categories of Persons Requiring Equal Opportunity and Affirmative Action Efforts":

> Hispanic. All persons of Mexican, Puerto Rican, Cuban, Central American, South American or other Spanish culture or origin, regardless of race. Persons who may have adopted the spanish [sic] culture but are not otherwise of Spanish origin are to be treated according to their racial identity.

38. Alvaro Matute, "La 'Breve historia de México': una lectura de 1982," *José Vasconcelos de su vida y su obra. Textos selectos de las Jornadas Vasconcelianas de 1982,* ed. Alvaro Matute and Martha Donís (Mexico: UNAM, Textos de Humanidades, 1984), 145; hereafter cited in text.

39. José Vasconcelos, *Breve historia de México* (1937), in *Obras completas* (Mexico: Libreros Mexicanos Unidos, 1961), 4:1305; hereafter cited in text as *Historia.*

40.   José Vasconcelos, "Idolos y rutas," in *Qué es la revolución* (Mexico: Botas, 1937), 154; hereafter cited in text as "Idolos." Emphasis in the original. "Mexicans" appears as *"mejicanos"* in the text, evoking the Spanish spelling with a "j" preferred by nineteenth-century Mexican conservatives, in opposition to the "x" used by nationalist liberals. By 1937, the time of this text's publication, the spelling with "x" was standard practice in Mexico, and, as a rule, Vasconcelos spells *"México"* and *"mexicanos"* with an "x." The spelling with a "j" in this case might just be a significant editorial error.

41.   Cuauhtémoc was the last Aztec emperor who opposed Moctezuma's conciliatory stance toward the Spanish conquerors and uncompromisingly led Tenochtitlan's last stand. The statue Vasconcelos took to Brazil was a reproduction of the one that today stands in Mexico City's Paseo de la Reforma. The history of this monument, from the call for projects in 1877 to its final unveiling in 1887, three years after its designer's death, rests at the center of Porfirian polemics about efforts to develop "an art which could represent the nation in its totality." Daniel Schávelzon, introduction to *La polémica del arte nacional en México, 1850–1910,* ed. Daniel Schávelzon (Mexico: Fondo de Cultura Económica, 1988), 26. The most prominent monument of the Porfirian regime to an Indian leader, the monument is an eclectic combination of styles and traditions, in an attempt to achieve an all-inclusive national whole. Its grandiose base incorporates designs based on those on the ruins of Tula, Uxmal, Mitla, and Palenque, combined with Hellenic classicism. Particularly revealing of the ideology behind such an eclecticism is the figure of Cuauhtémoc himself, who appears in toga and a sort of Greek or Trojan helmet, clothing that does not correspond to the realism of the human figure. Such a poetic license in regard to the subject's clothing is easily justified in an enthusiastic review of the monument by Vicente Reyes, published in the year of its unveiling:

> Aided by all the resources that history and the archaeological science put at the sculptor's disposal, inspired by a praiseworthy eclectic feeling, and eliminating from the composition certain grotesque details of the monarch's martial attire, that, if very exact, would have interrupted the general harmony, the rhythm of the lines and the majesty and severity of the figure, Professor Noreña has created a noble effigy of the heroic Aztec king, partly realist and partly classic. Thus proceeding, he has placed himself in the fair medium, without touching the border of crude realism and without submissively following the footsteps of well known sculptors . . . (Vicente Reyes, "El monumento a Cuauhtémoc" [1887], in *La polémica del arte nacional en México, 1850–1910,* ed. Daniel Schávelzon [Mexico: Fondo de Cultura Económica, 1988], 123–24)

Officially the figure represents Cuauhtémoc, but he must be sanitized for the sensitive eye by dressing him in Greek fashion. While Vasconcelos does not pay attention to the specific aesthetics of the monument, he shares with Reyes a desire to dress up a "crude" Indian reality and heritage with togas.

42. José Vasconcelos, *El desastre* (1938), in *Obras completas* (Mexico: Libreros Mexicanos Unidos, 1957), 1:1336–37; hereafter cited in text as *Desastre*. Emphasis on *Aztec language* in the original. The words Vasconcelos puts in Cuauhtémoc's mouth belong to the Cuban leader Hatuey, who, according to Bartolomé de las Casas, while burning on the stake refused a Franciscan monk's efforts to convert him to Catholicism in the last tragic moments of his life. Bartolomé de las Casas, *Brevísima relación de la destrucción de Las Indias,* ed. André Saint-Lu (1552; reprint, Madrid: Cátedra, 1982), 87–88.

43. Failure for Vasconcelos, as Germán Posada points out, often functions as an inspirational rallying point. Thus the apparently paradoxical statement in his 1910 speech in honor of Gabino Barreda: "success is sterile and mediocre, it accommodates itself to the moment, dies with it, it does not stir desires nor virtues." Defeat, on the other hand, always inspires a desire for a better future; it is rebellious, not compliant. Quoted in Germán Posada, "La idea de América en Vasconcelos," *Historia mexicana* 12 (January-March 1963): 382–83; hereafter cited in text.

44. José Vasconcelos, "Discurso a Cuauhtémoc," in *Discursos, 1920–1950* (Mexico: Botas, 1950), 92; hereafter cited in text as "Cuauhtémoc."

45. Mauricio Tenorio-Trillo, *Mexico at the World's Fairs: Crafting a Modern Nation* (Berkeley: University of California Press, 1996), 205–9.

46. Sylvia Molloy, *At Face Value: Autobiographical Writing in Spanish America* (Cambridge: Cambridge University Press, 1991), 186, emphasis in the original.

47. See Octavio Paz, "Las 'Páginas escogidas' de José Vasconcelos," in *Generaciones y semblanzas. Escritores y letras de México,* vol. 2 of *México en la obra de Octavio Paz,* ed. Octavio Paz and Luis Mario Schneider (Mexico: Fondo de Cultura Económica, 1972), hereafter cited in text; Blanco, 34–35; and Castro Leal, 5–7.

48. Many critics and scholars most often include only the first four volumes as his autobiography, but *La flama,* published posthumously in the year of Vasconcelos's death, also falls into this genre.

49. Ernesto Laclau and Chantal Mouffe, in *Hegemony and Socialist Strategy,* see "the defining characteristic of the symbol [as] the overflowing of the signifier by the signified." In the case of Vasconcelos, his concept of a *raza cósmica*—and its corollary, *Por mi raza hablará el espíritu*—have been deployed by *indigenista* and Chicano movements in struggles foreclosed by Vasconcelos's own theory. While the "signifier" (i.e., the text of *La raza cósmica* itself) refers us to a specifically Hispanocentric worldview, the concept of *la raza* as a political slogan has "signified" a constituency, which overflows that of the text. Beyond the content of the text itself, articulated in alternative political and historical contexts the concept takes on a new political meaning, despite objections from purists who might argue that the concept is being "misread." See

Ernesto Laclau and Chantal Mouffe, *Hegemony and Socialist Strategy: Towards a Radical Democratic Politics* (London: Verso, 1985), 11.

Chapter Three

1. José Vasconcelos, "El nuevo escudo de la Universidad Nacional" (1921), in *José Vasconcelos y la Universidad,* ed. Alvaro Matute (Mexico: UNAM/IPN, Textos de Humanidades, 1987), 127.

2. Gabriella de Beer, *José Vasconcelos and His World* (New York: Las Americas, 1966), 313; hereafter cited in text. One must point out that although Vasconcelos did doubt the validity of his notion of the cosmic race, he did republish his essay in 1948 with a new preface that I mentioned in chapter 2.

3. *"El día de la raza"*—the name given in Mexico to what is known in the United States as Columbus Day. An interesting discussion of the significance of this holiday in Mexico and the transformations in significance that it has suffered in the last century, moving from an originally Hispanophile emphasis to an *indigenista* one, can be found in Miguel Rodríguez, "El 12 de octubre: entre el IV y el V centenario," in *Cultura e identidad nacional,* ed. Roberto Blancarte (Mexico: Fondo de Cultura Económica, 1994).

4. José Vasconcelos, *Discursos, 1920–1950* (Mexico: Botas, 1950), 180–84.

5. America here is conceived as it is understood south of the Rio Grande, as a term representing the whole of the Americas and not just the United States.

6. Leopoldo Zea, *La filosofía como compromiso y otros ensayos* (Mexico: Tezontle, 1952), 155–59; hereafter cited in text.

7. Frederick Hart Langhorst, "Three Latin Americans Look at Us: The United States as Seen in the Essays of José Martí, José Enrique Rodó, and José Vasconcelos" (Ph.D. diss., Emory University, 1975), 132–35.

8. It is interesting to note that this book, which would later become an integral part of the canon of Mexican thought, was not published in Mexico until 1948. In 1925 Vasconcelos's relationships with the Mexican regime were particularly tense and he lived in exile. The book's second edition was produced in Paris in 1927. The Mexican publication in 1948 was the book's third edition.

9. For a discussion taking this perspective about Spanish Catholicism see Tovar. Also Robert Ricard, *The Spiritual Conquest of Mexico* (Berkeley: University of California Press, 1982), hereafter cited in text, provides a good analysis of the missionary efforts in Mexico.

10. A. Basave Fernández del Valle, *La filosofía de José Vasconcelos (El hombre y su sistema)* (Madrid: Ediciones Cultura Hispánica, 1958), 43.

11. Luciano Castillo, "La raza cósmica de José Vasconcelos," *Amauta,* October 1926, 41; hereafter cited in text.

12. Benjamín Carrión, *Los creadores de la nueva América. José Vasconcelos, Manuel Ugarte, F. García Calderón, Alcides Arguedas* (Madrid: Sociedad General Española de Librería, 1928), 45.

13. Margarita Vera, *El pensamiento filosófico de Vasconcelos* (Mexico: Extemporáneos, 1979), 224–28.

14. Nicandro F. Juárez, "José Vasconcelos and La Raza Cósmica," *Aztlán* 3 (1973): 63; hereafter cited in text.

15. Abelardo Villegas, *La filosofía de lo mexicano* (Mexico: Fondo de Cultura Económica, 1960), 93; hereafter cited in text.

16. José Vasconcelos, "El movimiento intelectual contemporáneo de México," in *Obras completas* (Mexico: Libreros Mexicanos Unidos, 1957), 1:74.

17. Enrique Krauze, "El caudillo Vasconcelos" in *José Vasconcelos de su vida y su obra. Textos selectos de las Jornadas Vasconcelianas de 1982,* ed. Alvaro Matute and Martha Donís (Mexico: UNAM, Textos de Humanidades, 1984), 41, emphasis in the original.

18. Didier T. Jaén, introduction to *The Cosmic Race/La raza cósmica,* by José Vasconcelos, trans. Didier T. Jaén (Baltimore: Johns Hopkins University Press, 1997), xix.

19. Quoted in David Brading, *Prophecy and Myth in Mexican History* (Cambridge: Centre of Latin American Studies, [1984?]), 67.

20. Joseph Arthur de Gobineau, *The Moral and Intellectual Diversity of Races, With Particular Reference to Their Respective Influence in the Civil and Political History of Mankind* (Philadelphia, 1856), 149–52; hereafter cited in text.

21. See Ivan Hannaford, *Race: The History of an Idea in the West* (Baltimore: Johns Hopkins University Press, 1996), 264–74; hereafter cited in text.

22. U.S. troops occupied the eastern port of Veracruz between 14 April and 23 November 1914, and sent into Mexican territory a "Punitive Expedition" in pursuit of Pancho Villa. This expedition, under the leadership of General John J. Pershing, remained in Mexico between 15 March 1916 and 5 February 1917, but was unable to capture Villa.

23. Pedro Henríquez Ureña, "La obra de José Enrique Rodó" (1910), in *Conferencias del Ateneo de la Juventud,* ed. Juan Hernández Luna (Mexico: UNAM, Centro de Estudios Filosóficos, 1962).

24. Ashley Montagu, "The Concept of Race in the Human Species in the Light of Genetics," in *The Concept of Race* (London: Collier-Macmillan, 1964); hereafter cited in text.

25. One must point out here that Vasconcelos's theory suffers the effects of those inconsistencies brought about by his movement between a biological and a cultural conception of race. On the one hand, he breaks down race, as Gobineau had done, along the four categories labeled by color—red, yellow, black, and white. Then, however, when talking about miscegenation within similar groups, as in the case of the Greek, Roman, or North American civilizations, he implies a mixture among members of the same broad racial group, but coming from different cultural or national traditions.

26. Emphasis and English in *"a good Indian is a dead Indian"* in the original.

27. José Vasconcelos, "Don Gabino Barreda y las ideas contemporáneas," in *Conferencias del Ateneo de la Juventud,* ed. Juan Hernández Luna (Mexico: UNAM, 1962), 103.

28. It is characteristic of Vasconcelos's skewed perspective that his model only discusses America's tropics and disregards similar regions in Asia or Africa.

29. Note the way in which he states *"even* the black."

30. Most of Vasconcelos's arguments refer to the specific cases of Spain and England, but at times he includes Portuguese and French colonialism as part of the Latin trend, and Dutch colonialism as Saxon.

31. Christopher Domínguez Michael, "Vasconcelos o el hundimiento de la Atlántida," *Vuelta,* July 1995, 34.

32. For a comprehensive discussion of the missionaries' study of Indian knowledge and traditions for the purposes of their conversion, see chapter 2 of Ricard.

33. Emerging from a different time and cultural tradition, the importance of Spanish for communication within the different communities in America today is made evident in the case of Rigoberta Menchú. She has dedicated her life to struggle for Mayan rights and traditions, but was forced to learn Spanish in order to communicate with her fellow Guatemalan Mayans, who speak 22 different languages: "Spanish was a language that linked all of us, because learning twenty two languages in Guatemala is impossible." Elizabeth Burgos, *Me llamo Rigoberta Menchú y así me nació la conciencia* (1985; reprint, Mexico: Siglo Veintiuno, 1996), 188.

34. Nancy Leys Stepan, *"The Hour of Eugenics": Race, Gender, and Nation in Latin America* (Ithaca: Cornell University Press, 1991), 149; hereafter cited in text.

35. David Brading, *Los orígenes del nacionalismo mexicano* (Mexico: ERA, 1991), 15–16.

36. See Fray Servando Teresa de Mier, "Sobre la representación de las Cortes del consulado de México," in *El ensayo político latinoamericano en la formación nacional,* ed. Raymundo Ramos (Mexico: Instituto de Capacitación Política, PRI, 1981).

37. See Lourdes Arizpe, "El 'indio': mito, profecía, prisión," in *América Latina en sus ideas,* ed. Leopoldo Zea (Mexico: Siglo XXI/UNESCO, 1986), 340–42, and Bonfil Batalla, 159.

38. Agustín Basave Benítez, *México mestizo. Análisis del nacionalismo mexicano en torno a la mestizofilia de Andrés Molina Enríquez* (Mexico: Fondo de Cultura Económica, 1993), 14.

Chapter Four

1. The term used in Spanish is *"laica,"* an adjective meaning "lay" or "laical." I have chosen to translate the term as "secular," as this is the standard adjective used in English to refer to an education separated from the church.

The precise definition of a secular education has been a contested issue in Mexico. At the time of the First Congress, Justo Sierra specified that by secular the participants did not have in mind an antireligious education but simply a neutral one in relation to religion. See Josefina Z. Vázquez, *Nacionalismo y educación en México* (Mexico: Colegio de México, 1970), 94; hereafter cited in text. Such a conciliatory understanding of the term came into question during the 1916–1917 Constitutional Congress. Some of the participants, Luis G. Monzón being particularly representative, insisted that the spirit of the term should be understood as scientific and antireligious, proposing the adoption of the more scientifically oriented qualifier *"racional"* (rational) instead of *"laica."* Article 3 of the 1917 Constitution, dedicated to education, maintained the term *"laica"* in its definition of education. It, nevertheless, made the anticlerical shade of the term clear by forbidding the participation of religious corporations and ministries in the educational process. Víctor Gallo M., "La educación preescolar y primaria," in Jaime Torres Bodet and others, *La cultura,* vol. 4 of *México. Cincuenta años de revolución* (Mexico: Fondo de Cultura Económica, 1962), 57–58, hereafter cited in text; and Vázquez, 109–11.

2. José Vasconcelos, *De Robinsón a Odiseo* (1935), in *Obras completas* (Libreros Mexicanos Unidos, 1958), 2:1528; hereafter cited in text as *Robinsón.* Emphasis in the English, *"pioneers"* in the original Spanish.

3. Vasconcelos uses the word *"asco"* in the original. For a discussion of the significance of *"asco"* in Vasconcelos's life and thought see Blanco, chapter 7.

4. Guadalupe Monroy Huitron, *Política Educativa de la Revolución* (Mexico: SEP/Setentas, 1975), 23.

5. Religion certainly did not form part of the curriculum during Vasconcelos's tenure. One must remember that *De Robinsón a Odiseo* was published in 1935.

6. See Víctor Bravo Ahuja, "La educación técnica," in Jaime Torres Bodet and others, *La cultura,* vol. 4 of *México. Cincuenta años de revolución* (Mexico: Fondo de Cultura Económica, 1962), 145.

7. Claude Fell, *José Vasconcelos, los años del águila (1920–1925). Educación, cultura e iberoamericanismo en el México postrevolucionario* (Mexico: UNAM, 1989), 42; hereafter cited in text.

8. This particular type of *Fiesta* took place only once (23 September 1923), yet accurately reflects the spirit of Vasconcelos's ministry.

9. José Vasconcelos, "Creación de los comedores universitarios" (1921), in *José Vasconcelos y la Universidad,* ed. Alvaro Matute (Mexico: UNAM/IPN, Textos de Humanidades, 1987).

10. "La salud del cuerpo—El arte de comer," *El maestro. Revista de cultura nacional* 3 (June 1921): 275 (Mexico: Fondo de Cultura Económica, 1979). See also "La salud del cuerpo—El vegetarianismo," *El maestro. Revista de cultura nacional* 2 (May 1921) (Mexico: Fondo de Cultura Económica, 1979).

11. This neighborhood's poor conditions during the Porfirian era are described in the following terms by Michael Johns:

La Bolsa was described by a popular guidebook as "sort of a native Ghetto, with dirty and microbic streets, repulsive sights and evil smells; where the inhabitants could never be accused of excess in tidiness." The government ignored several petitions for paving, water, and sewers because the settlement, which emerged in the 1900s, was not authorized. La Bolsa was probably the major "crime-spot of the city." Yet frequent petitions for protection brought only sporadic patrols of mounted policemen. (Johns, 39)

12. See Enrique Krauze, *Caudillos culturales en la Revolución Mexicana* (Mexico: Siglo Veintiuno, 1976), 48.

13. Linda Sametz de Walerstein, *Vasconcelos, el hombre del libro. La época de oro de las bibliotecas* (Mexico: UNAM, 1991), 93.

14. In Archivo Histórico de la Secretaría de Educación Pública (AHSEP) 3136–6, 3731–30, 3731–36, and 3731–45.

15. The issue of teachers' celibacy became an important bureaucratic concern within the SEP. The school department had to decide whether or not to accept married female teachers. The argument against married female teachers considered the greater responsibility the teachers would have toward their families, taking attention away from school. It was also argued by one of the ministry's medical experts, Dr. Alberto Román, that pregnancy caused significant changes in a woman's physiology and psychology that could negatively affect her teaching abilities. For his part, Dr. Rafael Santamarina, who supported the work of married females as teachers, argued that their experience as mothers would greatly enhance their role as teachers, and he also warned that unwed women frequently suffered hysteria and psychasthenia. It was also argued that the best teachers were very desirable candidates for marriage and that excluding married women from the ranks of teachers would create a shortage of qualified instructors. After almost a year of discussion, in March 1923 the SEP decided to allow married women to remain as teachers under certain conditions. See "Reglamento para la admisión de las maestras casadas en el servicio escolar," 20 March 1923, AHSEP 3137–22.

16. Gallo dates the decree 1 January 1911, while Vázquez dates it 30 May and Fell 18 June.

17. Gallo, 64–66; Lloyd H. Hughes, *The Mexican Cultural Mission Programme* (Paris: UNESCO, 1950); *Desastre*, 1328–31; Vázquez, 157–58.

18. Roberto Medellín, "Instrucciones acerca del desarrollo del programa de las escuelas rurales," in *Programas generales y detallados para las escuelas rurales, e instrucciones acerca del desarrollo de los mismos* (Secretaría de Educación Pública, Departamento Escolar, Delegación del Estado de Colima. Colima: Tip. del Comercio, 1922), 3–5, emphasis in the original. Available in AHSEP 3126–10.

19. See File of José A. Bazán, Secretaría de Educación Pública, Departamento de Educación y Cultura Indígenas, 1923, AHSEP 783–1; and File of

Margarita Avila, Secretaría de Educación Pública, Departamento de Educación y Cultura Indígenas, 1923, AHSEP 783–3.

20. Salomón Nahmad Sittón and Thomas Weaver, "Manuel Gamio: el primer antropólogo aplicado y su relación con la antropología norteamericana," *América Indígena* 50 (October-December 1990): 291.

21. David Brading, "Manuel Gamio and Official 'Indigenismo' in Mexico" *Bulletin of Latin American Research* 7 (1988): 76–77.

22. John Skirius, "Vasconcelos: de la revolución a la educación," *Revista de la Universidad de México (Nueva época)* 38 (October 1982): 4; hereafter cited in text as 1982a.

23. Antonio Gramsci, *Selections from the Prison Notebooks,* ed. Quintin Hoare and Geoffrey Nowell Smith (New York: International, 1971), 238–39.

24. Here "state" refers to the entity of Tlaxcala, not to the federal nation-state. In my discussion of the relationship between the entities I will use the term "federal" to refer to the larger nation-state.

25. See File of José A. Bazán.

26. See also Knight 1994, 41, for a discussion of "a distinct geography of revolution."

27. Edmundo Bolio, "Los lunes rojos" (1923), in *Los lunes rojos. La educación racionalista en México,* ed. Carlos Martínez Assad (Mexico: SEP/El Caballito, 1986).

28. Carlos Méndez Alcalde, "La escuela racional" (1917), in *Los lunes rojos. La educación racionalista en México,* ed. Carlos Martínez Assad (Mexico: SEP/El Caballito, 1986).

29. J. Jesús Ursua, "El Racionalismo. Estudio dedicado a los señores Profesores del Estado," *El Restaurador* (Colima, Mexico), 5 November 1922.

30. V. V. Ibarra, Informes del Delegado de la Secretaría de Educación Pública en el Estado de Colima, 20 August 1922, 1, AHSEP 3126–10.

31. File of Ciro Esquivel, Secretaría de Educación Pública, Departamento de Educación y Cultura Indígenas, 1923, AHSEP 783–4.

32. File of Margarita Avila.

33. Ibarra, Informes del Delegado de la Secretaría de Educación Pública en el Estado de Colima.

34. Ibarra, Informes del Delegado de la Secretaría de Educación Pública en el Estado de Colima.

35. File of José A. Bazán.

36. File of Ciro Esquivel.

37. File of Martín Jiménez, AHSEP 3126–9.

38. See Archivo General de la Nación, Mexico (AGN) Obregón-Calles 104-A-18.

39. See AGN Obregón-Calles 241-E-E-1.

40. See AGN Obregón-Calles 121-E-C-29.

41. David Alfaro Siqueiros, *Me llamaban el Coronelazo. Memorias* (Mexico: Gandesa, 1977), 183–84; hereafter cited in text.

42. Cuauhtémoc Jerez Jiménez, *Vasconcelos y la educación nacionalista* (Mexico: SEP, 1986), 38; hereafter cited in text.

Chapter Five

1. Vito Alessio Robles, *Desfile sangriento. Mis andanzas con nuestro Ulises. Los Tratados de Bucareli* (1936, 1938, 1937; reprint, Mexico: Porrúa, 1979), 19, 26–28; hereafter cited in text.

2. José Vasconcelos, telegram to Alvaro Obregón, 28(?) January 1924, AGN, Mexico, Obregón-Calles 104-E-29.

3. José Manuel Puig Casauranc, telegram to Alvaro Obregón, 29 January 1924, AGN, Mexico, Obregón-Calles 104-E-29.

4. Alvaro Obregón, letter to José Vasconcelos, 29 January 1924, AGN, Mexico, Obregón-Calles 104-E-29.

5. José Vasconcelos, telegram to Alvaro Obregón, 30(?) January 1924, AGN, Mexico, Obregón-Calles 104-E-29.

6. Alvaro Obregón, letter to José Vasconcelos, 2 July 1924, AGN, Mexico, Obregón-Calles 104-E-29.

7. John Skirius, *José Vasconcelos y la cruzada de 1929* (Mexico: Siglo Veintiuno, 1982), 52; hereafter cited in text as 1982b.

8. John Skirius, "Vasconcelos and México de Afuera (1928)," *Aztlán* 7 (Fall 1976): 486–88, hereafter cited in text; Juan Gómez-Quiñones, "Notes on an Interpretation of the Relations Between the Mexican Community in the United States and Mexico," in *Mexican-U.S. Relations: Conflict and Convergence,* ed. Carlos Vásquez and Manuel García y Griego (Los Angeles: UCLA Chicano Studies Research Center and UCLA Latin American Center, 1983), 428.

9. José Vasconcelos, "El México de Afuera," *El universal,* 11 June 1928, Primera Sección, 3; hereafter cited in text as "Afuera."

10. Rodolfo Uranga, "El pueblo debe imponerse ya, dice José Vasconcelos," *La opinión,* 2 October 1928, 1+. Ironically, as the candidate celebrated the opportunities open to Mexicans in the United States the same issue of *La opinión,* on the same page where his remarks were printed, reports that the previous day 200 Mexican property owners had been summarily deported in what appeared to be a process of collusion between police forces and certain businesspeople who would then profit by selling the properties forfeited by the deported Mexicans. Among the deportees were people who had lived in the United States for more than 10 years. Vasconcelos did not seem to be concerned about such abuses at this moment. Luis F. Bustamante, "Maniobras en Texas contra los mexicanos propietarios," *La opinión,* 2 October 1928, 1+.

11. According to official figures, between 1925 and 1929 an average of 52,000 persons left Mexico each year. Yet other official figures give larger numbers. According to the ministry of interior *(Secretaría de Gobernación),* between 1927 and 1928 476,000 people left the country. Just in the states of Jalisco and Michoacán, important fronts in the *Cristero* War, 35,000 and 23,000 people, respectively, left between January 1926 and December 1928. Meyer, 192.

12. José Vasconcelos, "El retorno," *La opinión*, 17 September 1928, 3; "Vasconcelos lanza en Sonora un Manifiesto a la Nación," *La opinión*, 11 November 1928, 1+.

13. See also *Tormenta*, 1182. Vasconcelos is not alone in perceiving this phenomenon. One can see a similar perspective, written six decades later, in Luis Rafael Sánchez, "El cuarteto nuevayorkés," in *La guagua aérea* (Puerto Rico: Editorial Cultural, 1994).

14. José Vasconcelos, "Noche californiana," *La opinión*, 30 July 1928, 3; *Desastre*, 1787–88; *Tormenta*, 1125–26, 1133–35.

15. "No busquemos genios, sino un hombre honrado," *La opinión*, 6 August 1928, 1+.

16. A copy of Vasconcelos's electoral platform is available in Skirius 1982b, 207–20.

17. Skirius 1982b, 76, 79; Salvador Azuela, *La aventura vasconcelista—1929* (Mexico: Diana, 1980), 130, hereafter cited in text; Hugo Pineda, *José Vasconcelos. Político mexicano, 1928–1929* (Mexico: Edutex, 1975), hereafter cited in text.

18. "La salvación de México es la democracia: J. Vasconcelos," *La opinión*, 14 August 1928, 1+; Skirius 1982b, 26–27, 45. At the time of Vasconcelos's campaign, Augusto César Sandino led a guerrilla army in opposition to the U.S. Marines. Vasconcelos and many of his followers declared their admiration for Sandino.

19. "Del sur de la América avanza una civilización triunfadora, sólido valladar de la sajona," *La opinión*, 15 August 1928, 1+.

20. José Vasconcelos, *El proconsulado* (1939), in *Obras completas* (Mexico: Libreros Mexicanos Unidos, 1958), 2:172–73; hereafter cited in text as *El proconsulado*.

21. "Campaña electoral en pro de Vasconcelos," *La opinión*, 8 August 1928, 1.

22. A reproduction of the pamphlet distributed by the "Non Partisan Mexican Election Committee" is available in Pineda, 158–62.

23. Kathryn S. Blair, *A la sombra del Angel* (Mexico: Alianza Editorial, 1995), 459–63; hereafter cited in text.

24. Fabienne Bradu, *Antonieta (1900–1931)* (Mexico: Fondo de Cultura Económica, 1991), 150.

25. Magdaleno, 171–78; José Vasconcelos, *La flama. Los de arriba en la Revolución* (Mexico: Compañía Editorial Continental, 1959), 176–79, hereafter cited in text as *Flama*.

26. Meyer, *La guerra de los cristeros*, vol. 1 of *La cristiada* (Mexico: Siglo Veintiuno, 1994), 315; Meyer, 368; Rivas Mercado, 69; *El proconsulado*, 103–4.

27. Meyer, 238, 346, 371; Meyer, *Los cristeros*, vol. 3 of *La cristiada* (Mexico: Siglo Veintiuno, 1994), 271.

28. Manuel Gómez Morín did stay in Mexico and later formed the *Partido Acción Nacional*, or PAN (national action party), for many years Mexico's principal opposition party.

29. *El proconsulado* includes only the "resolutions" of the *"Plan de Guaymas."* A complete version appears in José Vasconcelos, *Cartas políticas de José Vasconcelos. (Primera serie) 1924–1936,* ed. Alfonso Taracena (Mexico: Clásica Selecta, 1959), 180–83; hereafter cited in text as *Cartas.*

30. Magdaleno, 207–11; Skirius 1982b, 188; José Vasconcelos, "Topilejo (relato)" in *La sonata mágica* (1933; reprint, Mexico: Consejo Nacional Para la Cultura y las Artes, 1990).

31. Quetzalcóatl, one must add, is the figure that tradition tells us the Aztecs expected to return from the east at the time of Hernán Cortés's arrival on Mexican shores. It was for this reason that Moctezuma welcomed the Spanish conquerors to Tenochtitlan, thinking that Cortés, their leader, was the returning Quetzalcóatl.

Chapter Six

1. This text appears in *En el ocaso de mi vida*'s introductory section and is also reproduced in the last section, titled "Testament," of Alvaro Matute's edition of texts by Vasconcelos related to the National University, *José Vasconcelos y la Universidad.*

2. José Vasconcelos, *En el ocaso de mi vida* (Mexico: La Prensa, 1957), xiv–xvi, xix; hereafter cited in text as *Vida.*

3. G. Nicotra Di Leopoldo, *Pensamientos inéditos de José Vasconcelos* (Mexico: Botas, 1970), 23.

4. Joaquín Cárdenas Noriega, *Vasconcelos visto por la Casa Blanca, según los archivos de Washington, D.C.* (Mexico: Joaquín Cárdenas N., 1978) 240–41; Alejandro Rosas Robles, "Calles y Vasconcelos: histórica reconciliación," *Reforma,* 24 October 1995, 9D; Taracena, 133; *Flama,* 465–69.

5. Joaquín Cárdenas Noriega, *José Vasconcelos 1882–1982. Educador, político y profeta* (Mexico: Océano, 1982), 245–46, hereafter cited in text; Taracena, 122–26.

6. José Vasconcelos, *Letanías del atardecer* (Mexico: Clásica Selecta, 1959).

Selected Bibliography

Primary Sources

Spanish Editions

La sonata mágica. 1933. Reprint, Mexico: Consejo Nacional para la Cultura y las Artes, 1990. Reprint of the 1933 anthology of short stories and essays.

Qué es la revolución. Mexico: Botas, 1937. Collection of mainly political essays. They provide an example of some of the most far right political positions of the author.

Hernán Cortés. Creador de la nacionalidad. 2d ed. Mexico: Jus, 1985. Biography of Hernán Cortés. It is a good example of Vasconcelos's understanding of the role of the conqueror in Mexican history.

La raza cósmica. Misión de la raza iberoamericana, 2d ed. Mexico: Espasa-Calpe, 1948. This is the most popular edition of Vasconcelos's classic racial theory and travel narrative. It includes the 1948 prologue, prepared for this edition (by 1992 it was in its 15th printing).

Discursos, 1920–1950. Mexico: Botas, 1950. Speeches of Vasconcelos.

Obras completas. 4 vols. Mexico: Libreros Mexicanos Unidos, 1957–1961. Although this collection does not contain all of the written works of Vasconcelos, it is the most complete collection of them. The first volume includes a three-page biography of the author and a chronological bibliography. What is missing in this collection are most of his journalistic writings, the fifth volume of his memoirs, *La flama,* and the collection of poetry, *Letanías del atardecer* (both published posthumously in 1959). The four volumes are divided into the following sections:

Vol. 1: "Early Works," including his law thesis. "Literary Works," including his short stories, his play *Prometeo vencedor* (1916), and the first three volumes of his memoirs—*Ulises criollo* (1936), *La tormenta* (1937), and *El desastre* (1938), dedicated to his youth and participation in the *Maderista* revolution, his participation in the "war of factions," and his tenure as minister of education, respectively.

Vol. 2: Continues the "Literary Works" selection, including the fourth volume of his memoirs, *El proconsulado* (1939), dedicated to his presidential campaign and his exile after the electoral defeat. The section also includes more short stories and travel narratives. A second section is dedicated to "Letters and Documents." A third section is titled "Social Works." This section includes *La raza cósmica* (1925) and *Indología*

205

(1926), which present his racial theories; *Bolivarismo y monroísmo* (1934), an interpretation of Latin American history; *De Robinsón a Odiseo* (1935), presenting his pedagogical ideas; and an interpretation of the legacy of Simón Bolívar.
    Vol. 3: Dedicated in its entirety to "Philosophical Works."
    Vol. 4: Continues his "Philosophical Works" and includes a section titled "Historical Works," consisting exclusively of his controversial *Breve historia de México* (1936).
Cartas políticas de José Vasconcelos. (Primera serie) 1924–1936. Edited by Alfonso Taracena. Mexico: Clásica Selecta, 1959. Political letters of Vasconcelos.
La flama. Los de arriba en la Revolución. Mexico: Compañía Editorial Continental, 1959. Posthumously published fifth volume of his memoirs dedicated to the *Cristero* War, Vasconcelos's presidential campaign, and events thereafter.
Letanías del atardecer. Mexico: Clásica Selecta, 1959. Posthumously published collection of verse reflecting Vasconcelos's deep religious beliefs and negation of the human condition.
Memorias. Mexico: Fondo de Cultura Económica, 1982. This two-volume collection includes in its first volume *Ulises criollo* and *La tormenta* and in its second volume *El desastre* and *El proconsulado*. In 1982 the Fondo de Cultura Económica also published a two-volume paperback edition of *Ulises criollo*.
José Vasconcelos y la Universidad. Edited by Alvaro Matute. Mexico: UNAM/IPN, Textos de Humanidades, 1987. Anthology of texts related to education and the National University, introduced by the editor. These include speeches, memoranda, and essays.
Obra selecta. Edited by Christopher Domínguez Michael. Caracas: Biblioteca Ayacucho, 1992. Includes a prologue by the editor and a useful chronology and bibliography. Divided into four sections: (1) "Formative Texts," (2) "National Education," (3) "The American Teacher," and (4) "Memoirs: Literature and Politics."

English Editions

With Manuel Gamio. *Aspects of Mexican Civilization {Lectures on the Harris Foundation 1926}.* Chicago: University of Chicago Press, 1926. Series of lectures given by Vasconcelos and Manuel Gamio at the University of Chicago in 1926. Provides the reader with an interesting comparison of Vasconcelos's Hispanocentric understanding of Mexican culture and civilization and Gamio's *indigenista* approach.
A Mexican Ulysses: An Autobiography. Translated and abridged by W. Rex Crawford. Bloomington: Indiana University Press, 1963. A 260-page rendition of the four volumes of Vasconcelos's memoirs. Includes a list of names at the end.

The Cosmic Race/La raza cósmica. Translated by Didier T. Jaén. Baltimore: Johns Hopkins University Press, 1997. Reprint of the 1979 bilingual edition published by the Department of Chicano Studies of California State University. As with the 1979 edition, the text includes an introduction and copious footnotes by the translator. This new edition adds an afterword by Joseba Gabilondo. It also includes a bibliography.

Secondary Sources

Alessio Robles, Vito. *Desfile sangriento. Mis andanzas con nuestro Ulises. Los Tratados de Bucareli.* 1936, 1938, 1937. Reprint, México: Porrúa, 1979. Particularly interesting for the student of Vasconcelos is the second title of this collection. Here, Alessio Robles, head of the National Anti-re-electionist Party, gives his very critical assessment of his personal relationship with Vasconcelos.

Ardao, Arturo. "Panamericanismo y latinoamericanismo." In *América Latina en sus ideas,* edited by Leopoldo Zea, 157–71. Mexico: Siglo XXI/UNESCO, 1986. Discusses the genealogy of the concepts of "Latin Americanism" and "Panamericanism" from the mid nineteenth century to the second half of the twentieth century.

Azuela, Salvador. *La aventura vasconcelista—1929.* Mexico: Diana, 1980. First-hand account of Vasconcelos's presidential campaign by one of his supporters.

Bar-Lewaw Mulstock, I. *José Vasconcelos. Vida y obra.* Mexico: Clásica Selecta, 1966. Presents Vasconcelos's life and work, very much based on his own works. It presents a very positive image of the Mexican writer. Pays attention to his philosophy and social thought.

Basave Benítez, Agustín. *México mestizo. Análisis del nacionalismo mexicano en torno a la mestizofilia de Andrés Molina Enríquez.* Mexico: Fondo de Cultura Económica, 1993. Although the bulk of this book is dedicated to the work of Andrés Molina Enríquez, its first and last chapters provide a very good brief overview of Mexican thought about *mestizaje.*

Basave Fernández del Valle, A. *La filosofía de José Vasconcelos (El hombre y su sistema).* Madrid: Ediciones Cultura Hispánica, 1958. Study of Vasconcelos's philosophy.

Blair, Kathryn S. *A la sombra del Angel.* Mexico: Alianza Editorial, 1995. Novelized biography of Antonieta Rivas Mercado by her son's wife. Provides an interesting context of Mexico City's intellectual life in the 1920s. Its entire third part is dedicated to Vasconcelos's presidential campaign and Rivas Mercado's love affair with the candidate.

Blanco, José Joaquín. *Se llamaba Vasconcelos. Una evocación crítica.* Mexico: Fondo de Cultura Económica, 1977. As the subtitle indicates, this is an essayistic critical evocation of the contradictory life and times of Vasconcelos.

Bonfil Batalla, Guillermo. *México profundo. Una civilización negada.* Mexico: Grijalbo, 1994. Study of the status of the Indian in Mexico. Argues that beneath the veneer of a westernized nation lays a deep Indian tradition that has been denied for centuries. It is an impassioned call for official recognition, encouragement, and incorporation of this civilization into contemporary Mexico's public life.

Carballo, Emmanuel. *Protagonistas de la literatura mexicana.* Mexico: Secretaría de Educación Pública, 1986. Includes a chapter of interviews conducted by Carballo with Vasconcelos at different moments of his life.

Cárdenas Noriega, Joaquín. *Vasconcelos visto por la Casa Blanca, según los archivos de Washington, D.C.* Mexico: Joaquín Cárdenas N., 1978. Study of the U.S. role in Vasconcelos's presidential campaign based on the State Department's archives.

———. *José Vasconcelos 1882–1982. Educador, político y profeta.* Mexico: Océano, 1982. Detailed biography of Vasconcelos by one of his principal admirers.

de Beer, Gabriella. *José Vasconcelos and His World.* New York: Las Americas, 1966. To my knowledge, the most complete intellectual biography and study of Vasconcelos's work available in English. Includes a very complete bibliography.

Domínguez Michael, Christopher. "Vasconcelos o el hundimiento de la Atlántida." *Vuelta,* July 1995, 33–39. Discusses the mystic streak behind Vasconcelos's *La raza cósmica.* Very interesting discussion of his relationship to the grandeur of the Amazons.

Fell, Claude. *José Vasconcelos, los años del águila (1920–1925). Educación, cultura e iberoamericanismo en el México postrevolucionario.* Mexico: UNAM, 1989. In my opinion the most comprehensive study of Vasconcelos's work at the *Universidad Nacional* and *Secretaría de Educación Pública.* Discusses not only the man but also the institutions and their various branches.

Gamio, Manuel. *Forjando patria.* 1916. Reprint, Mexico: Porrúa, 1982. Gamio's seminal defense of ethnology as an instrument to understand the Indian and forge a coherent nation in Mexico.

Gómez-Quiñones, Juan. "Notes on an Interpretation of the Relations Between the Mexican Community in the United States and Mexico." In *Mexican-U.S. Relations: Conflict and Convergence,* edited by Carlos Vásquez and Manuel García y Griego, 417–39. Los Angeles: UCLA Chicano Studies Research Center and UCLA Latin American Center, 1983. As the title indicates, studies the relationship between the Mexican community in the United States and Mexico. A section of the article is dedicated to Vasconcelos's stay in California and the role of Mexicans in the United States during his presidential campaign.

Haddox, John H. *Vasconcelos of Mexico: Philosopher and Prophet.* Austin: University of Texas Press, 1967. Study of Vasconcelos's philosophy.

Hannaford, Ivan. *Race: The History of an Idea in the West*. Baltimore: Johns Hopkins University Press, 1996. Traces the creation and the development of the understanding of the category of "race" in the western tradition.

Hernández Luna, Juan, ed. *Conferencias del Ateneo de la Juventud*. Mexico: UNAM, Centro de Estudios Filosóficos, 1962. Includes the six conferences given at the Ateneo de la Juventud on the occasion of the centennial celebrations of Mexico's independence. Includes a very informative introduction about the Ateneo by the editor and a series of remembrances of the organization by some of its most prominent members, including Vasconcelos.

Juárez, Nicandro F. "José Vasconcelos and La Raza Cósmica." *Aztlán* 3 (1973): 51–82. Discusses some of the contradictions in Vasconcelos's racial theory.

Knight, Alan. "Revolutionary Project, Recalcitrant People: Mexico, 1919–40." In *The Revolutionary Process in Mexico: Essays in Political and Social Change, 1880–1940*, edited by Jaime Rodríguez, 227–64. Los Angeles: Latin American Center, UCLA, 1990.

——. "Weapons and Arches in the Mexican Revolutionary Landscape." In *Everyday Forms of State Formation: Revolution and the Negotiation of Rule in Modern Mexico*, edited by Gilbert M. Joseph and Daniel Nugent, 24–66. Durham: Duke University Press, 1994. Written by one of today's most prominent scholars of the Mexican Revolution, both of these articles present the contradictions between official revolutionary policy and the people upon whom the policies had to be implemented.

Krauze, Enrique. *Caudillos culturales en la Revolución Mexicana*. Mexico: Siglo Veintiuno, 1976. A now classic study of the young intellectuals of the postrevolutionary period, by another of today's most prominent historians of the Mexican Revolution.

——. *Mexicanos eminentes*. Mexico: Tusquets, 1999. This book provides brief biographical sketches of prominent Mexicans. It includes a chapter called "Pasión y contemplación en Vasconcelos."

Lecturas clásicas para niños. 1924. Reprint, Mexico: Secretaría de Educación Pública, 1971. Facsimile of a two-volume anthology of children's literature published by the *Secretaría de Educación Pública*.

Leys Stepan, Nancy. *"The Hour of Eugenics": Race, Gender, and Nation in Latin America*. Ithaca: Cornell University Press, 1991. Study of the use of eugenics in the projects of national formation in twentieth-century Latin America.

El maestro. Revista de cultura nacional. 1921–1923. Revistas Literarias Mexicanas Modernas. Mexico: Fondo de Cultura Económica, 1979. Facsimile of the journal of the *Secretaría de Educación Pública*.

Magdaleno, Mauricio. *Las palabras perdidas*. 1956. Reprint, México: Porrúa, 1976. Recollections of Vasconcelos's presidential campaign by one of his collaborators.

Martínez Assad, Carlos, ed. *Los lunes rojos. La educación racionalista en México.* Mexico: SEP/El Caballito, 1986. Interesting anthology of primary texts about the experiments with rationalist education in Mexico. Includes essays, speeches, and other documents about this anarchist pedagogy particularly popular in the Mexican southeast during the first quarter of the century.

Matute, Alvaro, and Martha Donís, eds. *José Vasconcelos de su vida y su obra. Textos selectos de las Jornadas Vasconcelianas de 1982.* Mexico: UNAM, Textos de Humanidades, 1984. Selected texts of a cycle of conferences commemorating the centenary of Vasconcelos's birth.

Meyer, Jean. *La cristiada.* 3 vols. Mexico: Siglo Veintiuno, 1994. Seminal three-volume history of the *Cristero* War.

Mistral, Gabriela, ed. *Lecturas para mujeres.* 1923. Reprint, Mexico: Porrúa, 1967. Edited by the Nobel Prize winner and close collaborator of Vasconcelos, this is an anthology of texts intended for women originally published by the *Secretaría de Educación Pública.*

Molloy, Sylvia. *At Face Value: Autobiographical Writing in Spanish America.* Cambridge: Cambridge University Press, 1991. Molloy's influential study of Spanish-American autobiographical writing dedicates chapter 10, "First memories, first myths: Vasconcelos' *Ulises criollo,*" to the former minister of education.

Phelan, John L. "El origen de la idea de Latinoamérica." In *Fuentes de la cultura latinoamericana,* edited by Leopoldo Zea. Vol. 1. Mexico: Fondo de Cultura Económica, 1993. Discusses the origins of the notion of a Latin America among Saintsimonian circles in mid-nineteenth-century France.

Pineda, Hugo. *José Vasconcelos. Político mexicano, 1928–1929.* Mexico: Edutex, 1975. History of Vasconcelos's presidential campaign. Pays particular attention to Vasconcelos's platform. Also provides in an appendix reproductions of six original documents related to the campaign and its aftermath.

Posada, Germán. "La idea de América en Vasconcelos." *Historia mexicana* 12 (January–March 1963): 379–403. Discusses Vasconcelos's Americanist ideology.

Rivas Mercado, Antonieta. "La campaña de Vasconcelos." In *Obras completas de Antonieta Rivas Mercado,* edited by Luis Mario Schneider, 33–179. Mexico: Fondo de Cultura Económica, 1987. Rivas Mercado's personal narrative of Vasconcelos's presidential campaign. Much of it is reproduced in Vasconcelos's own memoirs.

Robles, Martha. *Entre el poder y las letras. Vasconcelos en sus memorias.* Mexico: Fondo de Cultura Económica, 1989. Biographical study of Vasconcelos through his memoirs.

Rockwell, Elsie. "Schools of the Revolution: Enacting and Contesting State Forms in Tlaxcala, 1910–1930." In *Everyday Forms of State Formation:*

Revolution and the Negotiation of Rule in Modern Mexico, edited by Gilbert M. Joseph and Daniel Nugent, 170–208. Durham: Duke University Press, 1994. Study of the multiple interest groups that struggled with and against each other in the formation of a new school system in the Mexican state of Tlaxcala.

Skirius, John. "Vasconcelos and México de Afuera (1928)." *Aztlán* 7 (Fall 1976): 479–97. Studies the relationship between Vasconcelos and the Mexican community of the United States in 1928.

———. *José Vasconcelos y la cruzada de 1929.* Mexico: Siglo Veintiuno, 1982. Probably the best documented and comprehensive history of Vasconcelos's presidential campaign.

Taracena, Alfonso. *José Vasconcelos.* Mexico: Porrúa, 1982. Intellectual and political biography of Vasconcelos by one of his close associates.

Vázquez, Josefina Z. *Nacionalismo y educación en México.* Mexico: Colegio de México, 1970. Very informative study of the development of Mexican education with a particular emphasis on its nationalist tendencies.

Villegas, Abelardo. *La filosofía de lo mexicano.* Mexico: Fondo de Cultura Económica, 1960. Study of the way in which Mexican philosophers have attempted to understand the category of Mexicanness.

———. *El pensamiento mexicano en el siglo XX.* Mexico: Fondo de Cultura Económica, 1993. A good introduction to Mexican intellectual history in the twentieth century.

Villoro, Luis. *Los grandes momentos del indigenismo en México.* 1950. Reprint, Mexico: La Casa Chata, 1979. Classic study from an existentialist perspective of the way in which the Indian has been seen by hegemonic Mexican culture from the Conquest to the first half of the twentieth century.

Index

The Author

Luis Antonio Marentes was born and raised in Mexico City. He studied at the University of Texas at Austin, where he obtained a Ph.D. in comparative literature, with an emphasis on Latin American and Russian literature, in 1994. He is an assistant professor in the department of Spanish and Portuguese of the University of Massachusetts Amherst. He has published articles on José Vasconcelos and José Revueltas.

3691089

NOV 0 5 2002

FEB 2 5 2003

MAY 0 8 2001

DEC 2 7 2002